California Polyphony

MUSIC IN AMERICAN LIFE

*A list of books in the series appears
at the end of this book.*

California
Polyphony

Ethnic Voices,
Musical Crossroads

MINA YANG

University of Illinois Press

URBANA AND CHICAGO

Library of Congress Cataloging-in-Publication Data
Yang, Mina.
California polyphony : ethnic voices, musical crossroads /
Mina Yang.
p.   cm. — (Music in American life)
Includes bibliographical references and index.
ISBN-13 978-0-252-03243-1 (cloth : alk. paper)
ISBN-10 0-252-03243-8 (cloth : alk. paper)
1. Music—California—History and criticism.
2. Ethnicity in music.
3. Popular music—Social aspects—California.
I. Title.
ML200.7.C2Y36   2008
780.9794—dc22   2007030766

for my parents,
for their constant support

Contents

Acknowledgments

The author gratefully acknowledges permission granted from the following copyright holders:

The David and Sylvia Teitelbaum Fund, as successors to Henry and Sidney Cowell.

Regents of the University of California and the UCLA Oral History Program, Department of Special Collections, Charles E. Young Research Library.

Hal Leonard Corporation for permission to reprint lyrics from "Tangerine" from the Paramount Picture *The Fleet's In*. Words by Johnny Mercer; Music by Victor Schertzinger. Copyright © 1942 (Renewed 1969) by Famous Music LLC. International Copyright Secured. All Rights Reserved.

C. F. Peters Corporation for permission to reprint Lou Harrison's *First Concerto for Flute and Percussion*.

Guillermo E. Hernández for permission to reprint "Radios y Chicanos" from the forthcoming Arhoolie CD 7046/47: *The Chicano Experience*. No publisher or composer known.

Special thanks also to the staffs of the University of California music libraries at Berkeley, Los Angeles, and San Diego; the Bancroft Library at UC Berkeley; UCLA and UCSD Special Collections; the San Francisco Public Library; and the Los Angeles Public Library for their invaluable knowledge and assistance.

Chapter 3 was originally published as "A Thin Blue Line down Central Avenue: The LAPD and the Demise of a Musical Hub" in *Black Music Research Journal* 22, no. 2 (2002): 217–39. Reprinted by permission.

California Polyphony

Introduction

The importance of California on the international economic and political stage is undeniable. In the last few years, California and France have vied for and alternatively occupied fifth place in the world economic order. The wealthiest and most populous state in the Union, California enjoys political leverage that surpasses that of many first world nations. As the home of Hollywood and Silicon Valley, it plays just as significant a role in the international cultural marketplace, and in myriad small and big ways, its denizens influence how people in distant lands dress, talk, and think.

California is also at the forefront of major demographic and cultural shifts. The 2000 census quantified the demographic trend toward pluralism apparent in the United States population as a whole but even more conspicuous in that of the western state. According to the latest census figures, California's population, currently at 33.9 million, changed dramatically in the preceding decade. The white population dropped by nearly half a million and became outnumbered by the nonwhite population. Latinos, whose population grew by 35 percent statewide, replaced whites as the largest ethnic group in both the city and county of Los Angeles and in the cities of Inglewood and Compton. The Asian population rose 35.5 percent and became the third largest racial group in the state, increasing its margin over the African American population by more than half a million. Asians made up at least 20 percent of the population in four counties of the San Francisco Bay Area and Silicon Valley. Although the population of black Californians remained the same, their percentage of the whole dropped slightly as the general population continued to grow. Some 7 percent of San Franciscans designated themselves as multiracial, as did 5.2 percent of Angelenos.[1]

Such significant demographic changes have only recently begun to challenge in any serious way the dominant black and white racial paradigm pervasive in American political discourses.[2] Even within California, the implications of the state's rapidly changing racial makeup are met with deep ambivalence, as evidenced by the 1996 passage of Proposition 209, banning affirmative action, and the 2003 defeat of Proposition 54, which would have prohibited state and local governments from collecting data on race, ethnicity, or national origin for purposes of classification, employment, and access to housing, health care, and education. Michael Omi and Howard Winant contend that these efforts to "erase" race are propelled by neoconservative strategies designed to reverse the sociopolitical reforms of the civil rights era. In their view, race, understood as neither a biological essence (fixed, concrete, and objective) nor an illusion (a purely ideological construct), *does* matter. They stress that racial projects—ideological work that is "simultaneously an interpretation, representation, or explanation of racial dynamics, and an effort to reorganize and redistribute resources along particular racial lines"—pervade every aspect of American life, from the social and political to the cultural.[3]

Since the first days of European settlement in what was to become California, race relations have had a major impact in shaping the power dynamics among its various constituents, its emerging economic structures of resource allocation and divisions of labor, and its cultural and intellectual life. My study of California music is an attempt to identify and make transparent the ways in which musical development and racial projects have been and continue to be closely entwined. Even though California has produced many important composers, musicians, record producers, and independent labels, its musical culture is still relegated to the margins in larger studies of American music.[4] In a recent article about California music, *New York Times* music critic John Rockwell identified some of its fundamental differences from East Coast music—soft versus hard, sweet and pretty versus angular and dissonant, sensual versus cerebral, optimistic pioneer (looking forward to Asia) versus fearful refugee (looking back to Europe) —and protested (perhaps too loudly) that "one needn't be defensive about California music; one can be proud."[5]

Negligence or underestimation of California music stems in part from its refusal to conform neatly within the narrative structure laid out in conventional, Atlantic-centric American music surveys. It comprises too many different subcultural groups jostling to have their voices heard, too many hybrid and crossover experiments that cannot be contained within the usual dichotomies of European/American, black/white, or cultivated/vernacular categories that structure most histories of American music. Although recent studies have done much to rehabilitate the reputations of individual Californian musicians and to bring attention to the region's ethnic musical enclaves, there is yet no study that attempts to view California musical culture through a wider lens or grapples with the sheer diversity of musical expression and the enormous range of creativity found there.[6] This book foregrounds the very quality missing in the more specialized studies about California music—its multifaceted relationship with a racially and ethnically diverse population. It does so by taking Omi and Winant's cue and acknowledging the centrality of race in California's musical history.

This book also constitutes a critique of the ideology of multiculturalism that permeates much of the discussion on contemporary American and, even more markedly, California culture. Even as interracial conflicts have marred California's history and continue to threaten its present-day prosperity and delicate balance of power, discourses surrounding race have been subsumed by California boosters unequivocally delighting in the region's legacy of multiculturalism. With its origin in cosmopolitanism and its foreseeable future in an increasingly evident pluralism, California celebrates its diversity as a source of strength and pride. The 7th Annual L.A. Arts Open House, to name one fairly typical event, which was held in October 2001, "showed off a stunning spectrum of cultural diversity . . . in a burst of color, song and crafts." In 150 locations throughout Los Angeles County, 75,000 people watched and listened to Filipino dancers, a Persian dance troupe, a Sufi music ensemble, Native American storytellers and singers, an African American theater company, and so on. The potential of the cultural fair for engagement with current political issues was not lost on the organizers, participants, or audience members. The *Los Angeles Times* reported: "Though the events were designed to carry celebratory themes, the terrorist attacks of Sept. 11 heightened awareness of the need for cultural understanding, especially of the Middle East."[7]

But such cultural understanding is not always forthcoming, and the show of cultural diversity can mask deeper divisions and inequalities. Cultural critic Lisa Lowe cautions against simple readings of multiculturalism in her provocative essay "Imagining Los Angeles in the Production of Multiculturalism." She describes two contrasting representations of Los Angeles—the dystopic picture of a future Los Angeles, a pastiche of the third world, which Ridley Scott conjured up in the 1982 film *Blade Runner,* and the more utopic vision of the city as a site of multicultural spectacle as orchestrated by the 1990 Los Angeles Festival of the Arts, not unlike the more recent L.A. Arts Open House. According to Lowe, the images and narratives of pluralism promulgated by the festival, as well as by the L.A. Arts Open House, depoliticize multiculturalism by commodifying and containing difference, erasing actual geographical separations and historical disruptions, creating the illusion of inclusion, and obscuring real economic and social disparities. In effect, the performance of multiculturalism, enacted regularly in the name of interethnic harmony, reinforces the status quo by functioning as an "exotic, colorful advertisement of Los Angeles."[8]

Rather than stage yet another self-congratulatory celebration of California's cultural diversity, the case studies presented in this book closely examine the ideological assumptions and subtext embedded in a variety of social and musical praxes contained within the state. Scholarly work on the relationship between music and race has increased dramatically and grown in sophistication in the last ten years. Musicologists, ethnographers, and cultural historians are revisiting Western canonical works and popular and vernacular musics to explore issues of appropriation, representation, exoticism, identity construction, and cultural syncretism from postcolonial, poststructural, and a host of other points of view.[9] In a landmark study on music and race, Ronald Radano and Philip V. Bohlman pose a forceful challenge to traditional scholarly views that claim music's autonomy from social and political concerns: "Discourses about music fundamentally derive from the construction and deployment of racial categories, just as these same categories grow even more complicated and confused as a result of their sonic-discursive projection within the metaphysics of music."[10] In the United States in particular, the understanding of music is often predicated on the construction and performance of racial categories and hierarchies, given how both music and race are so deeply enmeshed with our social interactions and identity formations. As Radano and Bohlman suggest, however, music can be a means of resisting, as well as reinforcing, dominant racial categories. Through music, individuals and communities cross cultural boundaries, upend socially mandated protocols, and communicate with one another in a language of immediacy and visceral power. Because of the polyvalent and fluid nature of musical meaning, music can often be found at the vortex of cultural battles that break out during times of instability and change, intimately embedded in the ongoing process of racial formation.

I build on the recent work of cultural theorists and musicologists in considering how contemporary racial categories shaped the production and reception of California musical discourses and in turn were challenged by new contexts of understanding race, ethnicity, gender, class, sexuality, and other axes of identity created by the music. As the locus of fierce debates about immigration and miscegenation, the construction of romantic myths about the exotic other, the efflorescence of the civil rights movement and identity politics, outbreaks of race riots, and the emergence of new world cities encompassing transnational, polyglot communities, California in every phase of its growth has had to confront the race question in deliberate and overt ways. Music, as one of the fundamental activities with which human beings articulate belonging and identity, has been and continues to be implicated in the region's untidy history of race and culture. The following chapters demonstrate that music was made in California against the backdrop of power struggles and antagonistic confrontations between its many constituents—the gritty reality that belies the rosy, one-dimensional portrait of interethnic harmony purveyed at multicultural fairs.

This book is not intended to be a survey of California music. Rather, it presents a series of case studies in roughly chronological order. I chose the topics of each chapter for their relevance to the outstanding concerns of nonwhite populations in general and to California culture specifically: immigration, boosterism, police and the technologies of spatial control, film and media representation, orientalism, the civil rights movement, and interracial encounters that transpire outside the reductive strictures of the black/white paradigm. I also felt it was imperative to include each of the four largest racial groups of California (white, black, Latin, and Asian) and to address the different types of music (classical, experimental, jazz, rhythm and blues, rock, and hip-hop) that factor significantly into the larger history of American music. The book starts with a brief early history of California, then focuses on the most tumultuous and fertile eras in California cultural history: the turn of the nineteenth into the twentieth century, a time of ambitious building projects and grandiose visions; the interwar years, when the California counterculture began to emerge in earnest; the postwar period of progress and setbacks in race relations; Hollywood's Golden Age and the decline that followed; the civil rights era of the 1960s; and the cataclysmic decade of the 1990s, when manmade and natural disaster lurked around every corner. During these same years, American racial discourses moved between opposing poles: at the turn of the century, between eugenics and melting-pot assimilation; in the interwar years, between isolationist exclusion and cultural pluralism; during the civil rights era, between integration and cultural nationalism; and more recently, between race-blindness and multiculturalism. The debates surrounding race left their imprint on California music, which functioned variously as a means of representing or erasing racial difference, defining and contesting ethnic identities, facilitating intercultural dialogue, and dismantling binary categories. The six chapters together read like a parallel or alternative history of American music, incomplete and spotty as it may be, that foregrounds interactions between social, political, and cultural agents and untangles the web of connections between the different racial groups and musical expressions encompassed within California.

With each chapter, I explore a different facet of the relationship between music and race in California, beginning with the establishment of the Anglo elite, then turning to subsequent attempts to resist or maintain the power structure by the state's diverse constituents. The first chapter provides the historical context from which later musical and social currents emerged. It outlines the growth of the region, starting with the influx of fortune seekers from around the world during the gold rush, and chronicles the various stages of growth as wave after wave of immigration helped shape a unique and highly volatile culture. The end of the nineteenth and the beginning of the twentieth century was an especially turbulent time in America, with various groups vying for dominance in the cultural sphere. In California, this time period gave birth to an urban elite made up of business, political, social, and cultural leaders who garnered immense power through the control of the state's capital, transportation systems, manufacturing and agricultural industries, media, educational and cultural institutions, oil production, and film studios. As in the rest of the United States, culture in California underwent segmentation and the resultant sacralization of highbrow arts. The European classical music tradition, newly established in this remote western outpost, became the standard practice against which other musics were measured. Even as the powerbrokers of San Francisco and Los Angeles sought to replicate European high culture, however, other Californians were increasingly touting their own sense of exceptionalism—attributed to the region's lack of a single common tradition, diverse population, and the "pioneering spirit" of its denizens. The first chapter surveys both the building of brick-and-mortar cultural institutions of the establishment and the imaginings of a new California by its boosters and critics.

Although the elite tried to shape and manipulate California's image to its best advantage, it could control neither the influx of peoples from other parts of the world nor the growing tide of countercultural attacks against establishment mores. Whereas the elite clung to a Eurocentric worldview, those of the counterculture often invoked the racially exotic in their search for alternative lifestyles and creative inspiration. Chapter 2 examines how a group of maverick composers—Henry Cowell, John Cage, Lou Harrison, and Harry Partch—working in relative isolation as Californians, homosexual artists, and ultramodern experimentalists, turned to Asia as a common reference point in a strategic move that distanced California from European and East Coast musical traditions. Through musical and theoretical works that give expression to the desires and projections of the exotic other, they fashioned alternatives to the San Francisco establishment's pale imitation of Atlantic-centric musical culture as well as to the heteronormative brands of modernist music then current in New York. This chapter unpacks the meanings and motivations encompassed within the wide range of orientalist practices adopted by the Californian experimentalists that helped secure for the West Coast a distinctive presence within the international new music community.

The composers discussed in chapter 2 were compelled, for the most part, to hide their sexuality or to suffer the consequence of losing some of the privileges accorded to Euro-American men in the early twentieth century. The subsequent chapters investigate the ways in which minorities of color have musically negotiated their precarious position in California's complex and ever-changing social order during the rest of the century. At key moments in the history of modern California, tensions arising from black and white confrontations have erupted into turf battles, fought on the street and in the media. Such volatile racial dynamics underlie the relationship of the African Angeleno community to two of the most scrutinized institutions in Southern California, the police and the film industry, which have both played a part in the containment and marginalization of black creativity. Chapter 3 revisits the peak of Central Avenue's nightclub scene in South Central during a boom decade for black Los Angeles. In the 1940s—during the war and for a few years thereafter—the clubs in L.A.'s premier black neighborhood enjoyed unprecedented financial prosperity and moved a step closer toward racial integration as blacks and whites attended the performances of popular jazz, blues, and R&B artists. During William Parker's years atop the Los Angeles Police Department's power structure, the police increased its presence on Central Avenue and hastened the neighborhood's demise. Chapter 3 traces the impact of the LAPD's actions and policies in the decline of Central Avenue as a vital center of black music and the effect of this cultural suppression on jazz historiography.

Chapter 4 focuses on a cultural institution, simultaneously emblematic and transcendent of Los Angeles, that broadcasts California's normative values and hegemonic representations to the rest of the world: Hollywood. The presence of the film industry in California in effect renders the local global as the particularities of California's political, social, and cultural life are regularly translated into filmic images for the consumption of national and international audiences. During World War II, California confronted significant challenges to its prewar sociopolitical order, as women and minorities entered the workforce in unprecedented numbers and the region continued to be flooded with immigrants from the rest of the country. The noir genre responded to the social anxieties of the time with storylines and archetypal characters that captured and resolved the tensions introduced by wartime changes. This chapter examines how film noir deployed black music to connote femininity and moral turpitude and to function as a potent subtext affirming the reactionary ethos of the postwar period.

As central as the black/white racial dynamics have been in California's modern history, other racial groups, especially Latin and Asian American, have contributed enormously to the region's sociopolitical and cultural life. Their relationship to the white mainstream is further complicated by their relationships with one another, marked on the one hand by respect and a sense of common purpose and on the other by antagonism born out of competition and difference. Chapter 5 surveys the musical culture of East Los Angeles barrios, home to the largest population of Mexican Americans. Music provided the Mexican American community with a means of resisting and opposing the Anglo establishment's efforts to simultaneously mythologize California's Spanish past and render invisible its Mexican American present. This immigrant population's "assimilation" into the American mainstream often entailed bypassing white culture altogether. For the Mexican American youths coming of age in the postwar era, black music and nationalist ideology proved to be instrumental in the imagination and construction of a Chicano identity. During the civil rights movement in particular, rock and roll resounded in dance halls across the Southland and blared out of low-riding cars cruising down Whittier Boulevard. Rock became an integral building block of the Chicano youth subculture, which in turn spawned the political activism of the burgeoning Chicano movement. This chapter situates eastside rock within a larger system of signs that make up the Chicano subcultural style.

Chapter 6 looks at how Korean and black Angelenos have imagined and negotiated their differences through hip-hop during the last fifteen years. Many African Americans saw the trial and the subsequent acquittal of the police officers charged with the brutal beating of Rodney King as a parable of racial justice gone wrong, yet at its conclusion, Korean store owners, not white police officers, suffered the brunt of black anger and violence. In this chapter, I question how young Korean Angelenos, who are mostly 1.5– and second-generation Americans, have negotiated the complex racial terrain of post-1992 Los Angeles in their construction of a viable Korean American identity; how black music, hip-hop in particular, inflects their understanding of and identification with African American culture even in light of the conflicts that were characterized reductively by mainstream media as black versus Korean; and how their cultural practices, specifically the production and consumption of music, have changed as a result of the riots. This final chapter also moves the discussion of California music outward, as younger generations of Korean

Americans signal their affinity with the larger Korean diasporic community through their engagement with transnational hip-hop.

The studies presented here range from historical overviews of music and culture in California to more specific intersections of musical and racial matters. Because of the kaleidoscopic nature of California culture, I am convinced that a series of snapshots of different communities during significant historical moments better represents its musical development than a linear narrative or a monograph driven by a single grand thesis. The politics of race and music in California is much too complex to be contained within a conventional chronological narrative of musical evolution or to be reduced to a collection of sociological data and analyses. I hope to have highlighted some of the more interesting and illuminating aspects of the intersection between race and culture in order to provide a general picture of this complex region as well as to add color and texture to the stories of musical performances, encounters, actors, compositions, and discourses cited here. To the extent that I have succeeded in achieving my goals, what emerges is a richer, if more complicated and less sanguine, account of musical life than that offered in the footnotes of American music history books or at the multicultural fairs that dot the California landscape on a typical sunny weekend.

1. The Early History of California Cultural and Musical Life

California's population exploded during each of its boom periods, as immigrants from all over the world converged there in pursuit of the California dream, based half on truth and half on myth, of a land abundant in wealth and possibilities. The histories of the various groups who migrated to California from the mid-nineteenth to the early twentieth century were marred by conflicts between the old and new arrivals. The construction of culture involved the demarcation, reinforcement, and transgression of boundaries between the various constituencies, as Californians defined themselves as much by their differentiation from the other occupants of the increasingly crowded cultural space as by their affirmative claim on particular value systems. From the very beginning, prevailing aesthetic and ideological currents showed signs of polarization: between those of the northern and southern parts of the state, the Anglo majority and ethnic minorities, and the establishment and the counterculture that began to emerge at the turn of the century.

By the 1920s, California was already outdistancing most of the country in population growth and cultural endowments. Cultural foundations in Los Angeles and San Francisco were laid piecemeal throughout the second half of the nineteenth century; in the twentieth century, public and private expenditures in the cultural arena surged, overtaking those of older American cities in a few giant strides. During the many boom and bust economic cycles of the region, capital accumulated in the hands of a few who determined the allocation of funding for the arts. In order to solidify their social positions and improve their cities' images, the newly minted elite lavished large sums of money and energy into the construction of institutions for the propagation of highbrow culture, such as universities and concert halls. These institutions were not impervious, however, to the intellectual and aesthetic trends shaped by the various subcultures and countercultures that thronged in the western frontier lands. By the mid-twentieth century, Californians could hear symphonies and operas performed at the highest caliber alongside a fare of avant-garde music that worked to subvert elitist ideals of bourgeois gentility. Gleaming new concert halls—designed to be the exclusive and hallowed domains of high art for the white upper crust—showed fissures from the start, letting in snatches of the colorful and chaotic urban life outside their walls.

Immigration and Growth, 1848–1945

From the beginning of European settlement, racially motivated violence and rivalries made their impact felt in the political and cultural life of the region. Since Juan Rodríguez Cabrillo's sighting of Los Angeles, the Spanish had established twenty-one missions, four presidios, and two pueblos along the entire Californian coastline between 1769 and 1823. Although the missions were fairly prosperous, given the productivity of native labor, the Spanish did not settle in California in significant numbers. After winning independence from Spain in 1821, Mexico gained control of California and the southwestern states but in 1848 lost the war against the United States and ceded its territories in North America. Against the overwhelming migration of Anglo Americans, the Californios—as the Hispanics and mestizos living in California in the pre-American era were called—eventually lost their sizable fortunes. The region catapulted into the American era, with different rules and a new power structure.[1]

   The gold rush unleashed a massive wave of immigration into California from all corners of the world. Following President James Polk's State of the Union message of December 1848 confirming the discovery of gold, California was deluged by 90,000 Americans and foreigners from Latin America, Europe, and Asia. The population exploded from 15,000 in the beginning of 1848 to 224,435 only three years later.[2] Lawlessness soon ran rampant in the mines. The presence of foreigners increased and intensified the conflicts that naturally arose within a society founded on greed. The early Californians successfully mounted a campaign to make life in the mines miserable for nonwhites. The California legislature enacted the foreign miners' license tax, which levied heavy monthly fines on noncitizens. With nonwhites barred from testifying in the court of law, white miners could and did victimize and loot nonwhite miners with impunity. Native Americans, suffering from disease, malnutrition, overwork, and violence inflicted upon them by American bullies and frightened homesteaders, were virtually wiped out by 1880. Already by the time of California's admission into statehood on September 9, 1850, the region was marked by both cosmopolitanism and a strong streak of reactionary nativism.

The subsequent decades saw a general economic expansion, with boom and bust cycles resulting from the discovery of the Comstock mine in nearby Nevada and the establishment of industrial bases and agriculture, followed by runaway inflation, real estate and stock market speculations, and severe droughts. While San Francisco continued to grow steadily after its initial period of settlement in the mid-nineteenth century, Los Angeles exploded from the 1880s on, attracting wave after wave of immigrants from the late nineteenth into the twentieth century. Los Angeles grew at a staggering rate of 351 percent in the 1880s and sustained triple-digit growth for the next several decades; San Francisco, by contrast, maintained a steady rate of growth in the 15–28 percent range during the same period.[3] Los Angeles overtook the northern city in population figures by 1920 and reached a population of 2.6 million by the end of that decade. The pull toward Los Angeles took on a magnetic force with the discovery of oil, the birth of the modern film industry, the establishment of a manufacturing base, which included the aviation and automotive industries, and the expansion of agricultural production made possible by the diversion of water from Owens Valley.

Above and beyond these economic incentives was the vision of a land of sunshine and Mediterranean-inspired idyll promoted by the Chamber of Commerce and boosted untiringly by land speculators, which succeeded in turning Los Angeles into a highly desirable destination for tourists and immigrants in search of a new life. In the Midwest, the chamber launched a massive promotional campaign, disseminating brochures and flyers that touted Los Angeles as an arcadian garden of citrus fruits and Anglo brotherhood, a haven from the decaying and darkening cities back east.[4] During its first decades of growth, Los Angeles attracted migrants who were predominantly American-born and white; in 1920, only 17 percent of Angelenos had been born abroad, as opposed to 35 percent of New Yorkers.[5]

California as a whole continued to experience growth and change into the 1930s. After the boom of the preceding decade and the 1929 crash, Californians were faced with massive labor disputes, epitomized by the 1934 Waterfront Strike in San Francisco, political seesawing between the Far Right and Left, and the incessant flow of displaced migrant workers from the Dust Bowl. The relatively new and untested infrastructure of California was ill-equipped to handle the huge influx of immigrants. More than three hundred thousand arrived between 1930 and 1934 alone, overwhelming the already struggling economy with staggering rates of unemployment. By June 1934, 1,225,000 Californians, out of a total population of 6,000,000, were dependent on public assistance.[6]

Immigrants of color were especially vulnerable to the economic and political vicissitudes of the region. California was home to a sizable population of foreign immigrants by the beginning of the twentieth century, with growing numbers of Asians and Mexicans in particular. By 1924, when the passage of the National Origins Act curtailed immigration from Asia, approximately one million Asians from China, Japan, Korea, the Philippines, and India had entered the United States, and a majority of them had settled in California (see table 1.1).[7] The large Asian presence in the West fomented the growth of a virulent strain of anti-Asian prejudice during the latter half of the nineteenth century, leading to race riots and massacres. In order to mitigate the anti-Chinese furor in San Francisco, the U.S. Senate passed the Chinese Exclusion Act of 1882, the first American legislation designed to exclude immigrants on the account of race and ethnicity. Following the bombing of Pearl Harbor, anti-Asian agitators finally succeeded in quelling the "yellow peril" in their midst with the wholesale removal and relocation of Japanese Americans into concentration camps in the interior of the country. Increasing numbers of African Americans and Mexican sojourners immigrated to California to alleviate the problem of labor shortage that plagued the economy throughout its boom periods, further exacerbated by the departure of Japanese Americans. As the state's population of African Americans and Mexicans reached the hundreds of thousands, racial hatred was transferred to these new arrivals, and racial hostilities erupted into violence with alarming frequency.

The 1929 crash and the ensuing years of the Great Depression augmented Anglo-Americans' sense of victimization and strengthened their resolve to protect their interests against the infringement of outsiders. World War II

Table 1.1. Population of San Francisco and Los Angeles, broken down by race, 1880–1960

		White	Negro	Indian	Chinese	Japanese	Filipino	Other	Total
1880	SF city	210,496		45	21,745	45		1,898	233,959
	LA city	10,379		97	605			102	11,183
1920	SF county	490,022	2,414					14,240	506,676
	LA county	894,507	18,738					23,210	936,455
1940	SF city	602,701	4,846	224	17,782	5,280	3,483	220	634,536
	LA city	1,406,430	63,774	862	4,736	23,321	4,498	652	1,504,277
1960	SF city	2,436,665	238,754	3,883	52,984	24,462	21,451	5,160	2,783,359
	LA city	6,148,220	464,717	8,839	19,730	81,204	12,869	7,117	6,742,696

Source: United States Department of Commerce, Bureau of the Census, *Tenth, Fourteenth, Sixteenth, Eighteenth Census of the United States* (Washington, D.C.: U.S. Government Printing Office, 1887, 1922, 1943, 1963).

tapped into the rising tide of patriotism sweeping the country, furnishing Americans with enemies to fight and moral issues to defend. Struggling to define Americanism in the face of calamitous sociopolitical turbulences, white Californians pilloried the new arrivals in the region. Their constant confrontation with the nonwhite other influenced the ongoing project of cultural construction, providing antitheses against which to gauge their cultural differences.[8]

The Building of the Cultural Infrastructure

Because the gold rush attracted primarily young men of some means who could afford their fare to this distant land, San Francisco had at its inception a population that was roughly 80 percent male, young and single, relatively well-educated, and drawn from all over the world. The dearth of family life gave rise to an urban setting that encouraged public gathering and outdoor living. Even after the peak years of mining, San Francisco residents continued to live in hotels and eat at restaurants, spending their evenings in theaters, opera houses, and saloons.

From the early gold rush days, San Francisco was a town of letters, boasting successful bookstores, two literary journals, and more daily newspapers than contemporary London.[9] Because of its isolation from other metropolitan centers before the completion of the Central Pacific Railroad in 1869, San Francisco had to rely on its own writers to provide recreation and edification and eventually produced such well-known authors as Jack London, Frank Norris, and Ambrose Bierce. Along with their compatriots in the other arts, they convened as the Bohemian Club, founded in the early 1870s, to exchange ideas and socialize over a good meal. San Francisco, under the leadership of Bohemian Club members, reached a peak of artistic activity during the 1890s, when the city enjoyed the commerce of goods and men flowing through its port on their northward trek to the mines of Klondike following the discovery of gold in 1896 or to the Philippines during the Spanish-American War of 1898. The thriving economy nourished the arts during the brilliant fin de siècle, its momentum interrupted only with the destructive earthquake and fire of 1906.

As in the older cities in the East, the patronage of the arts fell on the shoulders of the wealthy elite in San Francisco, whose numbers were growing by the end of the nineteenth century. Affluent businessmen, whose fortunes were made in the gold and silver mines, railroads, banks, and other newly installed institutions in the West, controlled every aspect of society, from the political to the mundane. Although the general population was diverse, with half its denizens having been born overseas, the social structure of San Francisco resembled that of New York, Boston, Philadelphia, or Brooklyn: less than 5 percent of the male labor force of the city owned between 75 and 80 percent of property, and four out of five affluent men were born in the United States.[10] Prompted by the threat of being overtaken by its rapidly growing neighbors Los Angeles, Portland, and Seattle during the last decade of the nineteenth century, the moneyed set, predominantly Anglo American, invested heavily in the arts and the beautification of San Francisco. Cultural philanthropy was a means through which the elite achieved and maintained visible social prestige both within and outside of their community. As San Francisco grew in cultural stature, its glory was reflected back upon its generous benefactors.

The relationships formed by private associations, the municipal government, and the arts community and supported by individual philanthropists contributed significantly in the establishment of museums, libraries, and concert halls. When the San Francisco Museum of Art and the San Francisco Art Association had differences, for example, the mayor, the board of supervisors, and the city attorney all pitched in to reach a resolution.[11] These far-reaching relationships were formalized in the institution of the Arts Commission in 1931, which was given the power to distribute municipal money to art and music organizations.

Wealthy philanthropists also provided funds for educational institutions. Leland Stanford, one of the "Big Four" original investors of the Southern Pacific Railroad, founded a university in Palo Alto in 1891 in memory of his son who had died as a young boy. He endowed $20 million in the construction of an educational center that would rival the best universities in the East. In the meantime, the University of California at Berkeley was expanding, growing from its minuscule faculty of seventeen full professors, five associates, six assistants, and nine instructors in 1891 to become a world-class institution.[12] In 1896, Phoebe Apperson Hearst, the widow of Senator George Hearst and the mother of newspaper tycoon William Randolph Hearst, sponsored an architectural competition for a design of an expanded Berkeley campus, and in 1903, the university began construction to enlarge the dimensions of the campus to its present size.

Small arts organizations also cropped up with increasing frequency in the early decades of the twentieth century. In 1902, the same year that an art department was established at UC Berkeley, the California Society of Artists was founded and the First Secessional Art Exhibition opened in San Francisco. In 1903, Carmel, a small town south of the Bay Area along the Pacific Coast, began its incarnation as an artist colony. In 1907, the California School of Arts and Crafts, which was renamed the California College of Arts and Crafts in 1936, opened its doors in Oakland, and in 1916, the California

School of Fine Arts was established in San Francisco. Throughout the 1920s, many exhibitions of local art and avant-garde works from Europe were held in the newly built museums and galleries in the area.[13]

Unlike San Francisco, Los Angeles grew as a result of the immigration of families, not of single men. Furthermore, the majority of the immigrants came from the Midwest, bringing to the Southland Anglo-Protestant values of conservatism and a lifestyle revolving around church and family. The rapid and horizontal nature of the city's growth impeded the consolidation of civic life, as each suburb upheld its own autonomous sovereignty. The fortunes of the city's oligarchs, led by publisher of the *Los Angeles Times* Harrison Gray Otis and his heir Harry Chandler, were based on the constant demand for new land parcels, subdivided for ever more strips of tract housing. There was, therefore, little incentive to slow the decentralizing, centrifugal direction of the city's expansion. Moreover, the wealthy was factionalized, with the Jewish business elite controlling the westside and the gentile old guard of Otis and Chandler monopolizing downtown interests.[14]

Despite these fundamental differences between Los Angeles and the eastern cities and San Francisco, Southern California experienced phenomenal growth in its cultural and intellectual life during the turn of the century. The first boom of the 1880s brought many from the East Coast who sought to recreate the sophistication of New England in the Mediterranean climate of Pasadena. Educational institutions emulating their models in New England were established: the University of Southern California in 1880; the State Normal School, now the University of California at Los Angeles, in 1882; Occidental College in 1887; Pomona College in 1888; and La Verne College, Whittier College, and Throop University, now the California Institute of Technology, in 1891. The easier access provided by the railroad and the opening of the Panama Canal enabled performing artists, art and music teachers, and multitudes of students to visit and sometimes stay on in the land of sunshine. The Los Angeles Chamber of Commerce engaged the services of professional troubadours to sing the praises of the newly mythologized Eden, and the railroad interests sunk money into the construction of tourist hotels. Charles Fletcher Lummis, for one, was hired by the *Los Angeles Times* to write about the region in celebratory prose. Along with Helen Hunt Jackson's *Ramona*, Lummis's *Land of Sunshine* widely propagated the romantic myths of California's mission past (see chapter 5).

In 1906, Los Angeles was able to boast of the founding of the Los Angeles Art Institute, the Painters' Club of Los Angeles, and the Fine Arts League and the establishment of a weekly art review in the *Times*. Another event that transpired that same year had even greater repercussions in the cultural life of the Southland: George Van Guysling and Otis M. Grove founded a motion picture studio in Los Angeles. Filmmakers had first come to the West Coast to get as far as possible from the East Coast film industry in order to bypass patent laws. Once they settled into their new surroundings, they found the varied landscapes, the mild climate, and the limitless flow of cheap labor ideal for their purposes. And thus Hollywood was born, wielding a strong influence on the cultural life of the entire country and, even more emphatically, of Southern California during the course of the twentieth century. During its golden years, Hollywood created a vision of the good life that exerted a powerful influence on the popular imagination as Americans struggled to survive the Depression and World War II.[15]

Other institutionalized forms of creative life outside of Hollywood thrived as the population in the Southland exploded in the twentieth century. Many associations for artists were founded in the second and third decades in Los Angeles, Santa Barbara, and San Diego. The Los Angeles Museum of History, Science and Art held its first art exhibition in 1913, although the establishment of an entirely art-oriented museum had to wait until 1965 with the founding of the Los Angeles County Museum.[16] Henry E. Huntington spent $10.5 million in the installment of his library and art gallery in San Marino in 1919, where he housed his tremendous collection of books and treasures. In 1925, Jacob Zeitlin moved to Los Angeles, opening up a bookstore, At the Sign of the Grasshopper, which attracted a bohemian following of intellectuals and artists. From 1929 to 1930, the circle around Zeitlin, including historian Carey McWilliams, impresario Merle Armitage, architect Lloyd Wright (son of the more famous architect Frank Lloyd Wright), and radio personality José Rodríguez, published a progressive journal called *Opinion*.

The speed with which the cultural and intellectual infrastructure of California was built hints at the urgency felt by San Francisco's and Los Angeles's Anglo powerbrokers to stake a claim on a cultural identity that would maintain exclusivity and dominance in the rapidly changing region. Even before the metaphorical inaugural ribbon was cut asunder, however, the clamor of dissenting voices, challenging establishment avowals of cultural superiority, was rising in volume and intensity. Out of a space co-occupied by a number of competing discourses, a distinctly Californian ethos began to emerge and flourish.

Ideological and Aesthetic Currents

The vast empty spaces of California, devoid of a single dominant history or tradition, proved to be fertile ground for the imagination to take off in a profusion of directions. Because of its geographical isolation, particularly in the days before railroads, California fostered the development of highly individual and idiosyncratic sensibilities, unhampered by consideration for larger national or global trends. On the other hand, its constant influx of immigrants from Europe, Asia, Latin America, and elsewhere in the United States kept Californians apprised of European modernism, new American art, and nonwestern cultural practices. In addition, the lifestyle of modern-day America, invented in large part in California—or, more specifically, in Hollywood—of fast cars, conspicuous consumption, and the fusion of reality and fantasy, was indelibly shaping West Coast culture. With no tradition to call their own, Californians invented, appropriated, and assembled myriad aesthetic systems that then engendered fantastical creations.

The cityscapes of San Francisco, Los Angeles, and smaller surrounding cities underwent dramatic transformation in the early decades of the twentieth century, spawning architecture that gave concrete expression to the diversity of aesthetic visions vying for prominence in the developing region. The physical transformation wrought on the region during this era was staggeringly massive. To accommodate the tremendous population growth, whole towns were conjured up out of nowhere.[17] In addition to the necessity of building in order to accommodate the new arrivals, construction in the state was spurred by the catastrophic earthquake and fire of 1906 in San Francisco. The new buildings in San Francisco reflected the civic pride of its citizens who self-consciously erected monuments in the reconstruction of their beloved city, whereas housing tracts and retail strips in Los Angeles satisfied the immediate needs of an increasingly automotive and suburban population.

In both cities, the underlying aesthetic dictating architectural design was one of eclecticism and individualism. The heterogeneous populations, sharing no common tradition, created environments punctuated by eccentricity as well as by drab conventionality. Exotic themes were often deployed for their kitschy effect. Reyner Banham points to the famous Grauman's Chinese Theatre (see figure 1.1) as an example of an architectural monument that acts as a signifier of cultural values and status in the absence of history, "when traditional cultural and social restraints have been overthrown and replaced by the preferences of a mobile, affluent, consumer-oriented society, in which 'cultural values' and ancient symbols are handled primarily as methods of claiming or establishing status."[18] In architecture of this sort, as well as in the Hispanic mission style that borrows from an imagined, mythologized past, histories and their attendant value systems were fabricated and claimed by assembling together disparate cultural symbols.

Similar images of exoticism took center stage in the world fairs held in California between 1894 and 1940. The business, political, and cultural lead-

Figure 1.1. Grauman's Chinese Theatre. (Author's collection)

ers of the state, with the help of federal subsidies, paid for the construction of these fairs, designed to promote California as a land of abundance and an entrepôt of strategic importance to the national economy and world affairs.[19] The early fairs touted the natural endowments of the region and its agricultural production. Following the 1898 acquisition of Guam and the Philippines, indicative of the expansion of U.S. colonial interests in the Pacific, the Panama Pacific International Expositions (in San Francisco in 1915 and in San Diego from 1915 to 1917) and the Golden Gate International Exposition (on San Francisco's Treasure Island from 1939 to 1940) began to identify the state as an industrial and cultural hub of the Pacific Basin, an emergent transnational space, and to celebrate the diversity of its people.

The promotion of pluralism as a uniquely Californian attribute belied the white supremacist agenda behind the design and program of the fairs. The San Diego fair featured an anthropological exhibit classifying different racial types and the progress of man along racial lines, very much in keeping with contemporary social Darwinist ideology. Before the opening of the Panama Pacific exposition in San Francisco, Herbert Hoover, future U.S. president and the exposition representative in England, explained how the San Francisco pageant would dramatize the "racial progress" evident in the white westward expansion: "Eventually California formed the last great conflict of these races [the Northern Aryan and the Latin] for the actual possession of the land. There the meekly religious Southerner vanished like a mist before the more virile Northerner."[20] David Starr Jordan, the former president of Stanford University and a leader of the eugenics movement, organized the fair's National Conference on Race Betterment. Exhibits established by the Race Betterment Foundation and the United States Department of Labor promulgated the eugenicist message, displaying frightening images and "scientific" evidence of the dangers of racial contamination that could result from unchecked immigration. The fair's "Zone" exhibited caricatures of Native American, African, and Samoan villages, Turkish and Arabic bazaars, a Japanese junkshop, and an underground Chinese chamber of horrors for the amusement of the Californian public. California's early forays into multicultural representation and exhibition were tainted by the racist ideologies of the day.

A vocal minority did bring attention to the actual plight of nonwhite residents in California. For example, Carey McWilliams, one of the most influential writers of the period, portrayed Southern California as a region marred by greed, prejudice, and hypocrisy in a series of landmark studies: *California: The Great Exception, Southern California: An Island on the Land,* and *North from Mexico.* In Los Angeles, in particular, the image of California as a new Eden was fiercely contested between the establishment boosters and their critics. Despite, or perhaps even because of, the strong hold of corporate consciousness in culture as represented by Hollywood and in the social and political arenas by the pro-business, pro-expansion boosters of the *Los Angeles Times,* a vigorous subculture of dissidents had emerged and gained foothold. Their opposition to the oligarchy's conservative, pro-growth agenda achieved the greatest publicity in Upton Sinclair's run for governor of the state in 1933. Although the author of *The Jungle* lost the race, his competitiveness as a candidate in this traditional stronghold of conservatism suggests the extent to which popular opinion was receptive to the influence of politically radical artists and intellectuals during this time.

In direct opposition to the establishment's rhetoric of boosterism, the counterculture evoked imageries of dystopia, of a land of crime and repression, which was popularized in film and literature in the noir genre. The imagined California of noir filmmakers and writers challenged the very foundation of the California mythology. Noir disseminated an alternative image that debunked and invalidated California's romantic myths by unveiling the darker side of its mission past, the uneasy détente of its pluralistic population, and the dashed hopes of its pioneers, ultimately revealing the empty spaces behind the colorful facades (see chapter 4).

The Emergence of Musical Culture: Musical Life in the Early 1900s

Contemporary accounts of musical life in newspapers and periodicals from the first half of the twentieth century document the rapid growth of musical institutions, performance and educational, and the professionalization of musical scholarship and criticism in California. At the turn of the century, during a time of tremendous expansion, the first modern music reviews chronicled the self-conscious aspirations of Californians to "achieve" according to the cultural standards set by Europe and the East Coast. Members of California's elite, like their counterparts elsewhere in America, described vividly by Lawrence Levine, spent enormous sums of money on conserving and consuming "sacralized" highbrow musical culture—specifically, the symphonic and operatic repertoire—in order to maintain social distinctions advantageous to themselves.[21] Simulations of European culture, however, failed to resonate with popular Californian mythologies of pioneerism and individualism. The growth of alternative musics and discourses kept apace with the development of musical institutions. By midcentury, Californians were displaying distinctive musical sensibilities and aesthetic ideals that moved them beyond the wholesale importation of European musical culture to the creation of a diverse, if fractured, regional culture.

In San Francisco, music was presented from the early pioneer days and peaked in volume of activity and level of quality during the golden era of the 1890s and into the new century. Improvised entertainment in saloons turned into amateur gatherings of choirs and orchestras, eventually necessitating the construction of concerts halls that accommodated performances of renowned international stars and ultimately led to the cultivation of native talent. Opera was especially popular, with the Tivoli Opera House presenting local artists as well as members of the Metropolitan Opera touring company. The first staged opera, Vincenzo Bellini's *Sonnambula,* was presented as early as 1851, followed shortly thereafter by performances of Chinese opera by the visiting Hong Took Tong Opera troupe.[22] As the city prospered and the railroad tracks connected California to the rest of the country, crowd-drawing names flashed with increasing frequency across the marquees of new theaters and concert halls.

Following the temporary abeyance of cultural growth after the 1906 earthquake, the San Francisco community showed an active and renewed interest in organizing and funding civic musical institutions. According to critic J. C. Freund, San Franciscans sought to acquire cultural status through the founding of a symphony orchestra but faced a few obstacles in achieving this end:

> San Francisco wants a symphony orchestra. The absence of one is unquestionably a sore spot in the artistic conscience of the city. San Francisco is a very peculiar city, entirely different in some respects from any other city in America. . . . There is something about the very atmosphere of San Francisco which seems to defy every musty tradition which incrusts and hampers most other cities of America . . . and of the world. It is essentially a city of promise—the city of the Golden Gate. But if San Francisco is going to lift itself up to the sense of the times, it will have to give over this battle of giants and establish co-operation among its citizens for artistic ends.[23]

As early as 1910, the critic was noting the countervailing forces within Californian culture that pulled its development in two opposing directions, tradition and innovation.

San Franciscans did finally muster the cooperation necessary to establish musical organizations worthy of international recognition. The San Francisco Symphony was founded in 1911; the San Francisco Opera Company followed twelve years later. Semiprofessional and amateur orchestras and choruses in Oakland, Sacramento, and other nearby cities were organized soon thereafter. In 1932, the War Memorial Opera House was built to house both the symphony and the opera (see figure 1.2). The Beaux-Arts design of the building signaled the desire of San Franciscans to evoke and to match the splendor and sumptuousness of European concert halls. The musical works played in such grand halls reflected the aspirations of the city's elite to emulate the European bourgeoisie. The San Francisco concert calendar of 1920 presented more soloists of European than American origin and a repertoire more foreign than American.[24]

Figure 1.2. War Memorial Opera House. (Author's collection)

The establishment of a major orchestra and an opera company gave San Franciscans a sense of validation and the confidence to broadcast to the rest of the world that their city had arrived as a major player on the international cultural stage. The self-consciousness that spurred these cultural projects is conveyed in a 1912 article by critic Alfred Metzger in the *Pacific Coast Musical Review:*

> When a community has shaken off the yoke of mediocrity and is ready to appreciate art in its highest phase, presented in the most efficient manner, in fact, when a community has graduated into the metropolitan class, then it would be unwise and indeed injurious and dangerous when anyone, sufficiently influential to make an impression, would encourage or support movements destined to keep such community back in its progress and retain it in the provincialism rampant during the infancy of its advancement in culture.
>
> It is for these reasons that the *Pacific Coast Musical Review* is gradually changing its lenient and easy going attitude toward musical enterprises in this city, and is more and more demanding the highest efficiency in musical endeavors. We ask our professional musicians today to exhibit their talents in a manner equivalent to the test that is offered in any metropolis.

Performing the self-imposed task of instilling in San Francisco's listening public the values of a musical culture with a long tradition and history, Metzger chastised the San Francisco audience: "There is altogether too little interest shown in public concerts and consequently there is a certain lack of familiarity with the proper performance of great works of art which often is surprising."[25]

The level of appreciation for the symphony's offerings rose significantly in the next twenty years. When conductor Alfred Hertz retired after fifteen years of service in 1930, the *San Francisco Examiner* commended his legacy: "When he came to San Francisco the orchestra was painfully striving to emerge from mediocrity and barely succeeding. Today . . . it is one of the great orchestras of America. . . . For no man ever worked harder than Alfred Hertz. . . . Under his baton folk grew urbane. He filled their lives with beauty."[26] From 1934 to 1935, the San Francisco Symphony was not able to offer any concerts due to fiscal problems, but in 1935, the community voted to subsidize the symphony with $100,000 annually through the Arts Commission. With a world-class orchestra within city boundaries, San Franciscans saw themselves as equals to their urbane peers back east, even allocating their own tax money to fund institutions that bolstered their image.[27]

In Los Angeles, following the boom of the 1880s, many musical organizations were assembled, including the Los Angeles Symphony, started under the direction of Harley Hamilton in 1898.[28] In the early part of the twentieth century, energetic entrepreneur and musical impresario Len Behymer laid the foundation of professional music management that enabled Los Angeles to enjoy a vital concert scene, with international stars gracing its stages. In 1919, William A. Clark offered to subsidize the Los Angeles Philharmonic Orchestra, supporting its efforts to attract the best professional musicians and to grow into a world-class institution with an endowment of $3 million between 1919 and 1934.

The official establishment of the Philharmonic stirred much excitement in the community, giving Angelenos the sense of having at last arrived as a metropolitan city worthy of notice. Caroline Estes Smith described the Philharmonic's opening night in rapturous terms: "The elite of the Los Angeles musical and social world was there to witness the birth of the most prodigious infant in symphonic history. . . . In the moments when fine bits flowed out with masterly precision and beauty, members of the audience looked at each other and gasped or nodded in approval. Sighs of content came from many parts of the house. At other moments the silence itself was breathless when the woodwinds floated through space giving their delicate vibrations like whispering zephyrs." Reviews in the local press matched Smith's enthusiasm with flowery language of their own.[29]

Elite Angelenos, not unlike their northern neighbors, looked to the new orchestra to project to the rest of the world an image of sophistication and invested its founding with exaggerated significance. The "sacralization" process in Los Angeles was uneven, however, because of the city's strong current of populism, as evidenced by the successful enterprise of Behymer's rival Frederick Blanchard, who sold alternative and inexpensive musical entertainment with the slogan "Popular prices will prevail."[30] In 1921, the Theatre Arts Alliance tapped into the populist leaning of the Los Angeles community and transformed the Hollywood Bowl into an outdoor musical amphitheater for light classics and picnics under the stars, often featuring the new Philharmonic.[31]

An even stronger indicator of the region's populism was the expansion of the entertainment industry in the 1920s, which shaped the musical life of the region in several significant ways. As Los Angeles assumed the position of the entertainment capital of the world, it became the home of countless musicians working in studios and composing scores for popular consumption, employed in unprecedented numbers to fill the demand for motion pictures, recordings, and radio broadcasts. At the same time that Hollywood served as a magnet for musical talent, it encouraged artistic production that almost always prioritized commercial success over aesthetic concerns. The sheer quantity of musical activities subsequent to the birth of Hollywood was astounding; according to a contemporary account, the level of quality of the music was open to debate:

> For if activity is the important factor in the cultural growth of a people, the southwest lives up to the claims advanced on her behalf by the representatives of the chambers of commerce and the czars of entertainment in Hollywood. With the possible exception of New York there is probably no other comparable district in the world where dwell so many people who make their livelihood by musical means—where there are so many musical performances, organizations, films, radio programs, and recording establishments. But if quality, good taste, originality and imagination are to decide musical stature, the lines are sharply drawn between those who are outraged by what they term commercialism in music and those who are inclined to point with satisfaction to the amount of music-making and listening that goes on incessantly in the region.[32]

The following decades saw an increased polarization between commercial music written for mass consumption, excoriated famously by émigré social critic Theodor Adorno, and concert music.[33] Professional organizations and small associations of music connoisseurs began to emerge from the interstices of the growing, profit-driven culture industry and the civically sanctioned institutions of symphony orchestras and opera companies.

Concert Life from the 1930s

Having fashioned a musical culture after an imagined European model, many Californians were content to attend reruns of the same programs, consisting mostly of late-eighteenth- to nineteenth-century concert warhorses. However, with the social instability brought about by the constant arrival of new peoples, such complacency was under threat from the beginning. Musicians working in Hollywood studios and in Central Avenue clubs, European émigrés, Works Progress Administration–employed teachers and performers, immigrant and visiting foreign musicians, and native-born composers enlivened the music scene and challenged the hegemonic position of establishment institutions in the next decades.

Thanks to Hollywood, the number of musicians in Los Angeles reached a critical mass within the span of a generation, creating a community of musicians with highly developed skills and abilities. Hollywood offered employment to many of the refugee musicians from the Old World, which had been overtaken by Fascist forces. The increased European presence in Los Angeles before and during World War II had an enormous impact on the concert life of this area. Some of the earliest musicians in Los Angeles were German-born Americans who had settled in California at the end of the nineteenth century. The wave of immigration in the 1930s and 1940s left an even greater legacy, transforming the fledgling musical scene into one of sophistication, populated by musicians and composers of international stature. The highly skilled performers from the Old World joined the Los Angeles Philharmonic, the Hollywood studio orchestras, and the faculties of UCLA, USC, and Occidental College and formed new ensembles or regrouped as string quartets and piano trios in their new surroundings.

American entrepreneurial spirit was inspired and sustained in large part by the European émigré community in Peter Yates's Evenings on the Roof concert series, a forward-looking chamber music series that provided Angelenos with an alternative to the commercially motivated concerts of the larger musical venues. Yates, along with his pianist wife, Frances Mullen, began the series in 1938 with performances by Mullen and a few friends. The first printed program stated the principal aim of the series: "Programs are for the pleasure of the performers and will be played regardless of the audience."[34] Through the years, Yates and Mullen associated with Igor Stravinsky, Henry

Cowell, and Arnold Schoenberg and his pupils, corresponded with Charles Ives, and counted Otto Klemperer and Artur Schnabel as regular attendees of their concerts.

From the outset, Yates delved enthusiastically into the music of contemporary European composers, many of whom were now exiled in the United States. A third of the music programmed was devoted to twentieth-century music, and in addition, several composers, such as Schoenberg, Béla Bartók, and Ferruccio Busoni, were featured in concerts that presented their music exclusively. Stravinsky, who also attended the series regularly, heard his music performed often in this venue.[35] Experienced European professionals, like pianists Ingolf Dahl and Richard Buhlig, violinist Adolph Rebner, and harpsichordist Alice Ehlers, mixed with local musicians, such as Mullen and Wesley Kuhnle. Visiting virtuosos and composers, including Ernst Krenek, John Cage, Aaron Copland, and Joseph Szigeti, also attended or participated in the concerts when they were in town. The high level of playing achieved by these performers served to expose American new music in the best possible light as well. Ives's music was featured prominently from the beginning, with Mullen performing his Concord Sonata and songs in the first year of the enterprise. Walter Piston, Roy Harris, and Lou Harrison had their works premiered, and the compositions published in Cowell's New Music Quarterly were programmed regularly.[36]

In addition to Yates's series, the Los Angeles Chapter of Pro-Musica, the Elizabeth Sprague Coolidge Organization, the Coleman Chamber Music Association, and the UCLA Music Department offered concerts of new music.[37] Elizabeth Sprague Coolidge, a Chicago native, spent many winter months in California and contributed generously to the musical culture in the West Coast, with commissions for compositions by émigré composers and the sponsorship of concerts at the Los Angeles Public Library, UCLA, USC, Claremont College, Mills College, Occidental College, Santa Barbara, and Ojai. In 1937, she underwrote the performance of Schoenberg's four string quartets, two of which were commissioned by her, at UCLA's Royce Hall. In addition, she assisted Darius Milhaud, Tedesco Castelnuovo, Ernst Toch, and the Pro Arte Quartet in their relocation to the United States through commissioning new works and/or securing performances and engagements for them in their exile.[38]

The universities in the Bay Area were gaining respect nationally as they grew in physical size and financial endowments. In the mid-1930s, Coolidge began to divert some of her funds to help expand the music programs at Stanford and Berkeley, universities that up until this point had offered significantly less in their musical programs even compared to the much smaller Mills

College in Oakland. By midcentury, Berkeley's semiprofessional orchestra was functioning as a stepping stone for many members of the San Francisco Symphony, and its music department included nationally recognized composers like Ernest Bloch and Roger Sessions. The San Francisco Conservatory of Music instituted the Pioneer Workshop on American Opera and elected to continue the Composers' Forum, started under the Federal Music Project (FMP) during the Great Depression, as a department in 1941. By the beginning of the 1930s, Redfern Mason could write about San Francisco:

> If Californians, Inc., and the Chamber of Commerce appreciated the advertising value of artists and composers they would play up the element in the life of our community more than they do. Who, for example, is advertising San Francisco more than any other living individual today? It is Yehudi Menuhin. That young imp of Jove has carried the fame of California far and wide. So is Ruggiero Ricci, and people are asking what kind of place is this San Francisco. May be that it has the knack of producing phenomenal people.[39]

The improvements in music education, for young students as well as at the university level, fostered the development of local talent throughout the state.[40]

Several venues provided performance opportunities for new music written by Bay Area composers. Cowell's New Music Society moved to San Francisco following the lukewarm reception of its 1925 opening concert in Los Angeles. The Society presented concerts featuring works written by local and international ultramodern composers and introduced Bay Area audiences to the music of ethnic communities residing among them.[41] Cowell invited Chinese, Japanese, and Latin American musicians to perform in his popular ethnomusicology classes in San Francisco as well as in the New Music Society concerts. Young iconoclasts associated with Cowell, such as Cage and Harrison, organized their own concerts, engaging their friends to perform their unconventional works (see chapter 2).

The FMP also played an important role in the transformation of San Francisco and Los Angeles from fledgling music scenes into major cultural centers. During the worst years of the Great Depression, the government, at both federal and state levels, instituted agencies to provide employment for artists, including writers, painters, designers, actors, and musicians. The initiatives undertaken by these agencies, designed to get artists off relief doles and working once again in their trained professions, ushered in a new era of government arts funding, unprecedented in U.S. history. In California, the FMP alleviated the dire situation facing many musicians as the dawning of new recording technologies coincided with a general economic downturn. FMP-sponsored ensembles performed for more diverse audiences than the privately run orchestras, and the music teachers on the FMP payroll availed their services to students of all economic classes. During the run of the program, Californians heard much greater quantities of much more eclectic music than they had previously. The Glendale Units in Southern California, for example, consisted of a concert orchestra, a Mexican tipica orchestra, a military band, a banjo ensemble, a Hawaiian or native South Sea group, several modern dance bands, and a chorus.[42]

The heightened activity in the musical arena in all venues and the gradual acclimation to the sounds of modern and ethnic musics helped raise the audiences' appreciation for new music dramatically. The *Argonaut* reported on Cowell's upcoming concert, predicting the acceptance of his once radical techniques by the audience:

> As is well known, Cowell, in his search for new resonances and tonal qualities in the piano, occasionally plays the instrument with his fists and forearms and plucks its strings from inside the core. . . . As often happens, the radical has drifted by slow degrees into an accepted position, without being aware of it.
>
> And so the concert Cowell will give at the Veteran's Auditorium Friday night will not be an occasion for catcalls, ribaldry and pontifical excommunications in the presses, as it might have been had he played exactly the same program 15 years ago.[43]

A concert featuring Stravinsky conducting his own *Suite Italienne, Divertimento,* and *Duo Concertante* was likewise received warmly by an appreciative audience: "The audience was surprised—but it was not shocked as were audiences of a decade ago. Instead of hooting and jeering, last night's audience applauded with interest and pleasure, and kept applauding until an encore was forthcoming."[44] A concert of Schoenberg's music, including the Chamber Symphony op. 9 and *Pierrot Lunaire,* brought the composer a measure of respect and admiration: "No commotion greeted the appearance of Arnold Schoenberg, Viennese modernist, in a concert of his own works with the New Music Society last night at the Veteran's Auditorium. In three decades of controversy he has won a strong position. Many people have decided that his music is beautiful. Others who do not understand him are convinced that he deserves respect."[45] In a 1941 issue of *Modern Music,* Alfred Frankenstein reported that the new music scene in San Francisco was reaching maturity: "San Francisco, which has for years been a citadel of modern music, though a comparatively small one, is seeing more activity on the contemporary front this season than for many past."[46]

In Los Angeles, however, critic José Rodríguez complained as late as 1940 about the inadequacy of the musical organizations that were then serving the new listening public: "The rub came when the people were confronted with arbitrary definitions, were denied their appetite for novelty and inclusiveness, were not cunningly and wisely led to true standards of appreciation."[47] Rodriguez found the Los Angeles music scene dominated by the Philharmonic and Hollywood Bowl wanting, its music failing to capture the pioneering spirit he attributed to Californians. But even here, in the heart of the commercial culture industry, new music that was novel and adventurous was being performed and winning advocates. In 1942, when rising demand prompted the Evenings on the Roof concert series to move to a larger performance space in Hollywood's Assistance League Playhouse, the *Los Angeles Times* took notice and declared, "'Evenings on the Roof' programs, one of which took place last night in the Assistance League Playhouse, are becoming events of importance in community music life."[48] As in politics, the corporate dominance of the culture industry in Los Angeles provoked and sustained a countercultural movement of intellectuals and artists in music, eventually producing a rich array of alternatives to the more predictable fare purveyed by Hollywood and the Philharmonic. Further, the shift in the Los Angeles demographics from a primarily WASP to an ethnically diverse population and the emergence of independent recording labels and popular music venues during the course of the twentieth century led to the formation of numerous subcultures that came to play increasingly prominent roles in the larger musical arena.

California Musical Culture at Midcentury

Taking stock of their musical accomplishments, Californians oscillated between feelings of pride and inadequacy. In 1939, Frankenstein, music editor of the *San Francisco Chronicle* and faculty member in the Berkeley Music Department, assessed both the positive signs of growth and the shortcomings in his city's musical culture, citing first the credit items on the ledger:

> San Francisco possesses an Opera Company second to none in the country.
> . . . It is one of the only three cities in the country with permanent opera companies, the other two boasting populations five to ten times larger than ours.
> San Francisco is the only city in the country to grant its symphony any sort of support from the public purse. It possesses one of the major symphony orchestras of the country led by one of the foremost conductors of the world. . . .
> San Francisco and the Bay Region boast an annual summer festival of chamber music unequalled in the world, with as many as 35 concerts given in a space of six weeks by many of the world's leading string quartets and assisting artists.

But on the debit side, he voiced several concerns. Frankenstein wondered whether people attended the opera for the music or for social prestige alone: "Is the big push for the opera or for the social parade of the subscription nights?" Further, Californians' inferiority complex as arrivistes led them to depend unduly on the star system in their concert programming, banking on internationally recognized names at the expense of neglecting their own talents. Frankenstein worried that local musicians were being deprived of the opportunities necessary to prosper in their own native city: "It is time we begin to think about the ultimate significance of what we are doing to our tastes, our talents, and our musical growth. If there is ever going to be any permanence and solidity, and native cultural value to our American music, on which we annually spend a very respectable sum of millions, it will have to be anchored here and now, where we are and in our own life, and not forever fed us from elsewhere in return for our shekels."[49] Frankenstein's assessment signaled a shift in perspective by establishment critics, who now questioned the validity of a musical culture that was largely imported and therefore divorced from the sensibilities and ideals of its denizens. His criticism typifies the frequent self-evaluations found in music writings at the time, as Californians set out to build a culture that conformed to their self-identification as a community of pioneers.

By mid-twentieth century, countercultural and subcultural musical movements were developing a vital presence outside of established institutions, chipping away at the elite's definition of California culture. Although they received little or none of the public money spent on symphony orchestras and opera companies and only rare public notices in the mainstream media, small independent organizations were better able to provide audiences with alternative types of music—music "anchored here and now." The attempts of those making up the Anglo elite to cloister themselves from those lower on the socioeconomic scale within the exclusive bastion of European classical music succeeded only intermittently. Their dominance over California's cultural life was tenuous, partial at best, with their treasured domains of high art vulnerable to challenges from within and without. As California's demographic constitution changed dramatically throughout the twentieth century, music became yet another site of contestation between the various racial and ethnic groups that vied for their share of California's promised riches. Early California musical historiography is comprised mainly of documents, institutions, and personalities positioned within the dominant class of Euro-Americans; later musical developments, discussed in the following chapters, are characterized by the meeting of the sounds and peoples of diverse origins that, amid the din of sociopolitical clashes, gave birth both to sweet harmonies and grinding dissonances.

2. The Transpacific Gaze

*Orientalism, Queerness,
and Californian Experimentalism*

While the Anglo elite exerted considerable energy and allocated valuable resources to recreate European-styled bourgeois concert culture in the new state, other Californians were finding inspiration in the bounty of nonwestern musics transplanted into the American soil. In the first decades of the twentieth century, California experienced tremendous changes, with immigrants in the hundreds of thousands arriving from the rest of the United States and the world. Even as the power structure struggled to maintain the status quo by disenfranchising minority populations, state officials and the Chamber of Commerce constructed and projected the image of California as a multiethnic haven, of a region that could claim a special relationship with the Orient unavailable to the East Coast. Californian composers likewise looked to Asia to forge an experimental ideology that was distinct from the musical culture of the Atlantic, thereby defining the Pacific Rim as a space for the propagation of alternative musical discourses. Henry Cowell, John Cage, Lou Harrison, and Harry Partch adopted orientalism as a subversive strategy, circumventing many of the fundamental precepts governing Western music through the deployment of Asian-inspired concepts and sounds. In the first half of the twentieth century, experimental orientalism became the very basis and the common point of reference within the wide range of music produced by the Californian avant-garde. Racial difference underscored the real and metaphorical distance between California and the Atlantic coast and hinted at the possibility of defining the self in other non-normative ways.

Orientalist elements in Western music started to appear as early as the eighteenth century and became increasingly common at the turn of the twentieth century.[1] From the exotic locales that dressed up Giacomo Puccini's operas to the emulation of gamelan sounds in Claude Debussy's *L'Isle joyeuse,* mystical fables, pentatonic themes, unusual instruments, and other fantastical wonders captivated Western composers and audiences in search of new sources of titillation. In California, such orientalist tropes permeated operas and symphonic works of the fin-de-siècle. Joseph Redding, lawyer and one-time president of the Bohemian Club, wrote a critically acclaimed opera, *Fay-Yen-Fah,* based on a Chinese legend, that evoked an imaginary landscape populated by mythical creatures. The composer, who most likely had little direct contact with Chinese culture, peppered the opera score liberally with pentatonic passages and other musical markers of orientalism. Henry Eichheim, another Californian composer, traveled extensively in Asia, experiencing the indigenous musics of various East, Southeast, and South Asian cultures directly, and later wrote "adaptations" of these exotic musics to conform to Western harmonic and metrical frameworks.[2]

Beginning with Cowell, there was a notable shift in the usage of Asian sources. The composers associated with Cowell invoked Asia in their experimental rhetoric to a degree hitherto unknown, frequently inverting the relationship between the two spheres by privileging the East, imagined as a site of ancient wisdom, over the West, weighed down by the burden of outworn traditions.[3] The change in attitude toward Asia from earlier musical orientalists to Cowell's circle is not just one of degree, however, but of kind, actuated by stylistic, regional, socioeconomic, and perhaps even sexual rebellions against established practices and mores. Triply marginalized by the musical establishment—as ultramodern, Californian, and gay—Cowell, Cage, Harrison, and Partch pitted Asia against Europe, California against New York, and orientalist ellipsis against heteronormative assertions.

In his groundbreaking book *Orientalism,* Edward Said contends that the fascination Western intellectuals bring to the exploration of Eastern cultures is coextensive with Western imperialistic designs and that the knowledge of the Oriental other is constructed within a network of colonialist discourse that reflects and maintains the unequal power relations between the East and West.[4] In response to Said's unequivocal indictment against orientalism, J. J. Clarke, in *Oriental Enlightenment,* calls for more nuanced analyses of individual orientalist projects, pointing out that while orientalist discourse is grounded in historically and politically specific contexts, it is by no means uniform in its support or agreement with imperialistic ideologies. The Californian experimentalists imbibed the imageries and rhetoric of California boosterism but promulgated their own iconoclastic version of Californian exceptionalism in the promotion of West Coast music. They were in effect following a long tradition that, according to Clarke, had accompanied the

ascendancy of European modernism, in which orientalism assumes a countercultural, counter-hegemonic role, undermining rather than reinforcing
Europe's established position.[5]

Although the Californian composers' subversive stance seems at first
glance to lend support to Clarke's argument, their orientalist strategies ultimately bear out Said's objections. As important as they claimed Asia was as a
source of inspiration, the Californian composers' knowledge of Asian cultures
and music was relatively superficial in their formative years, and they did
not, in the end, transcend their origins in the West. Even as they carved out
alternative spaces in contradistinction to the New York modernist school,
the San Francisco musical establishment, and the dominant heterosexist
culture on both coasts, they evoked imaginary soundscapes that often had
little correlation to actual musics being made in Asia during that time. Their
early works further contributed to the mystification of the Orient begun by
California's official boosters and manifest, in varying degrees, the tensions
between Western ideologies and Eastern essences, binary oppositions that
refuse to break down completely.

Rather than holding up their orientalist works and ideas to some illusory
test of Asian authenticity, this chapter will examine and critique their engagement with the Orient as a means of negotiating their positionality and
minoritized identities in the new music community in particular and in
American society more generally. Because, as Said reminds us, Westerners
filter knowledge of the other through their Occidental consciousness and
represent the Orient from a vantage point of power, these Californian composers revealed, in their orientalist works, more about their own individual
sensibilities than any specific Asian cultures.

Sexuality, Race, and Music in
Post-Prohibition San Francisco

In the 1920s and 1930s, a collective of gay composers interested in experimental orientalism emerged in a city with a unique configuration of race,
sex, commercial entertainment, and politics. As discussed in chapter 1, San
Francisco was cosmopolitan from the days of the gold rush, and by the end
of the nineteenth century, it contained the largest Chinatown in the United
States. Reflecting on their early formative years, the four Californian composers all emphasized their proximity and receptiveness to the music of
California's immigrant and indigenous communities in their youth. Cowell,
for instance, recalled that, living near Chinatown as a child, "I hummed
Japanese and Chinese and Tahitian tunes, just as normally as I hummed the

British tunes carried through the Tennessee mountains from my mother; and more directly, Irish tunes from my father; and also fairly directly, classical melodies of Haydn and Mozart from my old Royal College teacher." Likewise, Partch grew up listening to "Christian hymns, Chinese lullabies, Yaqui Indian ritual, Congo puberty ritual, Cantonese music hall, and Okies in California vineyards." Harrison attended the Chinese opera in San Francisco regularly: "I actually had heard a great deal more Chinese opera than European opera by the time I was adult, very much more, and well, you see it wasn't so *stuffy*, nor so expensive." Cage recalled organizing a classical shakuhachi concert in Los Angeles in the early 1930s.[6]

Nonwestern cultures provided not only musical counterpoints to Europeanist concert repertoires but also, and of special significance for these gay composers, specific associations of non-normative lifestyles and alternative sexualities. Beginning with the influx of single men during the gold rush, San Francisco had acquired the reputation of a "wide-open town," boasting a remarkably high density of entertainment and pleasure venues within its urban core. Even with the sporadic efforts of vigilantes and high society women to police and contain vice and prostitution in the city, businesses catering to various nighttime activities continued to prosper in the first decades of the twentieth century. Following the repeal of Prohibition in 1933, new nightclubs and gay bars in North Beach presenting transgender and multiracial stage shows flourished, thanks in no small part to their promotion in official tourist publications. Nearby Chinatown was another popular tourist destination, offering, in addition to its exotic sights, tastes, and sounds, the illicit pleasures of its thriving sex commerce and gambling and opium dens.[7]

The official promotion of race and sex tourism reached its apogee with the Golden Gate International Exposition of 1939. Themed "A Pageant of the Pacific," the expo featured art and ethnological exhibits of Asian and Latin American cultures and even offered weekly flights to Hong Kong. In keeping with the theme, the fair planners envisioned a design based on "eclectic exoticism." Entering the main gate between two tall elephant towers, modeled after those of Cambodia's Angkor Wat, visitors were greeted by the eighty-foot-tall *Pacifica*, the sculptural centerpiece of the Court of the Seven Seas and the fair.[8] More lighthearted but just as keen on selling exoticism, along with generous helpings of sexual and bizarre spectacles, was the section of the fair called the Gayway, featuring the Chinese Village, Ripley's Odditorium, Virgins in Cellophane, and Sally Rand's Nude Ranch. A sense of competition with New York, which held a world fair the same year, spawned at least some of the more distinctively Californian blend of sexual and racial difference purveyed at the Golden Gate expo.[9] Thus, when Harrison heard his first live Balinese gamelan orchestra at the 1939 expo, fifty years after Debussy's famous introduction to the gamelan at the Paris world fair, the Asian music was encoded with associations that resonated in particularly loaded ways for a young gay Californian composer.[10]

As Nadine Hubbs eloquently argues in *The Queer Composition of America's Sound,* pre-Stonewall gay composers constructed their musical selves against dominant discursive categories and forged musicosexual codes that both signaled and obscured their minoritized status. Although Hubbs includes Cowell, Cage, Harrison, and Partch in her list of significant gay composers, she proffers them not as exemplars but as exceptions to the widely recognized stylistic identification of American-styled neoclassicism with queerness. According to Hubbs, the New York gay modernist circle around Aaron Copland and Virgil Thomson, the focus of her study, clustered musically around attributes of tonality, simplicity, and Frenchness, while the Californians clustered around non-tonality and experimentalism, which in her scheme occupies the "masculine and heteronormative" end of the sexual spectrum.[11] Rather than situate the Californians' brand of experimentalism as oppositional to the neoclassical style on sexual grounds (which Hubbs does more convincingly for postwar serialism), I see the contrasts of the California to the New York school as arising from different regional affinities. Both the New York and California groups of gay composers expressed, sublimated, or hid their sexuality with their particular musical choices: in the case of Copland and his circle, with neoclassicism, and in the case of Cowell and his circle, with orientalism. Whereas the New Yorkers traced their musical lineage back to the French and pro-Stravinsky Nadia Boulanger, the Californians began their careers absorbing the transgressive sexual and racial sights and sounds surrounding them in San Francisco. Just as Copland turned his gaze transatlantically in his effort to forge a national style that could compete on the international stage, these Californian composers turned their gaze transpacifically to carve out a space for themselves among their musical peers, hetero- and homosexual, American and European.[12]

Although these composers make the connection between Asia and California in their music explicit, they are less forthcoming about the connection between their music and sexuality, not surprising given the homophobic and repressive conditions of pre-Stonewall American culture. But their silence does not refute the possibility, as Hubbs and Philip Brett assert, that composers' sexual identity—in the form of their membership in gay subcultures, reaction to their minoritized status in relation to the mainstream, and inculcation in the codes of the closet—influences and shapes their creative outlook in fundamental ways.[13] Further, the Californians' common recourse to orientalism in their otherwise very different experimentalist systems suggests that perhaps their interest in Asia, like their homosexuality and West Coast origins, provided a bond with one another that gave them the requisite fortitude to break so dramatically from accepted conventions and traditions. In an environment that tolerated and even commodified sexual and racial difference (albeit within strict limits that were constantly under negotiation), the Californian experimentalists found in their imagined Orient a rich trove of alternative and subversive ideas, hidden codes potentially meaningful to other queer sensibilities, and a colorful banner to flag their exceptionalism vis-à-vis Atlantic culture.

Henry Cowell, Champion of Californian Music

Born in 1897 in Menlo Park, Henry Cowell was the first of the Californian experimentalists to make a mark on the international new music scene. As chronicled in Michael Hicks's meticulous biography, Cowell's adventurous approach to music was rooted and cultivated in California's bohemian community.[14] Cowell, more than anyone else, established California as an important site of ultramodern experimentation, energetically promoting Californian and American music in his diverse roles as composer, theorist, writer, teacher, and administrator.

Early on in his career, Cowell experienced New York as the antithesis to California when he set off to the East Coast to study at the Institute of Musical Art (later renamed the Juilliard School) in 1916. Confronted with his difference from his peers in New York, Cowell expressed in his letters home his feelings of being completely at odds musically and socially with the conservatory community. During this time, Cowell met and befriended Leo Ornstein, who had achieved fame and notoriety in New York in the second decade of the twentieth century with his radically new piano style. Ornstein's use of tone clusters suggested to Cowell new ways of exploring his own tone clusters, and Ornstein's oft-performed piano piece, A la Chinoise, may have helped Cowell cement the association of Asian themes with musical radicalism.[15] It is notable that Cowell did not write any significant works that reference Asian music before his forays into New York's new music scene and his encounters with other ultramodern composers.[16] While Ornstein soon after abandoned his experimental style and New York modernism took off in other directions, Cowell continued to explore the possible permutations of musical orientalism.

Cowell found in the theosophical community the Temple of the People, in Halcyon near Pismo Beach, a Californian context for further nurturing his nascent orientalist ideas. The Theosophical Society, founded by Madame Blavatsky in 1875, espouses a religious belief that combines Asian philosophies with elements of paganism, Western science, and socialism. In Halcyon in the summer of 1920, Cowell met the French American composer Dane Rudhyar, who shared with the younger musician his thoughts linking music with the theosophical notions of Eastern mysticism. In articles penned in the 1920s, Rudhyar prescribed Asian music as an antidote for the metaphysical aimlessness of contemporary Western music: "Oriental music is there, *if properly understood,* to tell us its secret, and to illumine our darkness."[17] In "Oriental Influence in American Music," an essay included in Cowell's 1933 *American Composers on American Music,* Rudhyar proclaimed: "The gateway to the Orient is through Occidental America."[18] Theosophical poet and Cowell's spiritual mentor John Varian echoed the French American composer, presaging, "There is a new race birthing here in the West. In the ages coming, it will be a large factor in a new civilization now starting around the Pacific—of a quite different nature from that of the Atlantic. Oriental races will be in it. China, gigantic and enduring, will have its age-old mind and soul in its making."[19]

Guided by other composers, such as Rudhyar and his former teacher Charles Seeger, who were likewise finding inspiration in nonwestern musics, Cowell increasingly sought alternative musical ideas in Asian cultures. He underscored the differences between Eastern and Western music in a 1929 article recording a dialogue between himself and an "erudite, cultivated and skeptical scholar from Pekin [*sic*]":

> Most of your rules have to do with the combination of tones to achieve what you call harmony. Your Occidental counterpoint, presumably a study of how to combine melodies, is mainly concerned with relating them by such smooth intervals that they run together and confuse the ear as to their individual existence.
>
> Our rules, on the contrary, are devised to keep these melodies as distinct as possible so that the ear does not lose their individual progress but is enabled to follow any one singly to its destination.[20]

The Chinese expert emphasizes the reverse prioritization of harmony and counterpoint in Chinese music, finding Western rhythmic development wanting and even dismissing Stravinsky's metrical manipulations as uninteresting, since all of the lines move together and lack any real independence.

It was as late as 1931 that Cowell, granted a Guggenheim Fellowship, undertook his first serious study of nonwestern musics. For two years, he worked in Berlin under the guidance of the comparative musicologist Erich von Hornbostel, who was then the preeminent scholar of Asian and folk musics.

Cowell immersed himself in the collection of twenty-two thousand phono-graphs of exotic musics in the Phonogramm-Archiv of the Psychological Institute of the University of Berlin and practiced Indonesian music with the prince of Java for two hours every morning for three months.[21]

In the meanwhile, Cowell was working tirelessly to bring new music to California and, conversely, California to new music. In 1925, Cowell founded the New Music Society, an organization dedicated to the presentation of chal-lenging, ultramodern music written by American and European composers. By the 1930s, the New Music Society was presenting performances of tradi-tional Japanese and Latin American musics alongside the works of radical Euro-American composers, first in Los Angeles, then in San Francisco.[22] In his prodigious efforts on behalf of the Society, Cowell corresponded with and promoted East Coast modernists, most notably Carl Ruggles and Charles Ives, but more important, he championed West Coast experimentalism and placed nonwestern music at the very center of this new experimental aesthetic. By focusing such attention on the Orient, Cowell bypassed altogether the burn-ing question of the day in new music circles: Schoenberg or Stravinsky?[23] Cowell's New Music Society provided a forum in which Californian com-posers could keep abreast of ultramodern currents in the rest of the United States yet maintain their difference from the Atlantic modernists by their frequent invocation of the Pacific.

Following his immersion in Asian musics in Berlin, Cowell became in-creasingly interested in percussion music and wrote one of his most sig-nificant scores for a percussion ensemble. His experiences with nonwestern musics inform the instrumentation and structure of *Ostinato Pianissimo* (1934). Its percussion band—in addition to traditional Western instruments played unconventionally, such as the piano, xylophone, and tambourine—calls for rice bowls from India, a bongo and güiro from Cuba, woodblocks and gongs like the ones he heard growing up in Chinese neighborhoods, and a miscellany of drums. Each player repeats an ostinato figure, differing in pitch pattern and duration, and each repetition is distinguished by varying accent patterns.

Ostinato Pianissimo was one of the first major works written for an all-percussion ensemble in the West. As such, it bears a passing resemblance to Edgard Varèse's *Ionisation,* with which Cowell was certainly familiar; he had performed the piano part in its premiere the previous year and had published the score in the New Music Society Music Editions series.[24] The earlier work includes many of the same instruments Cowell eventually chose, in addition to a few others: sirens, gong, tam-tam, bongos, drums, güiro, Chinese blocks, cloches, cymbals, glockenspiel, and piano. The similarities end there, however, and the differences between the two works highlight the fundamentally different aesthetic orientations of Atlantic modernism and the newly emerging Pacific Rim experimentalism. *Ostinato Pianissimo* unfolds with the accumulation of layers of different rhythmic patterns, played entirely pianissimo until the very end. The result is static and nondevelopmental, reminiscent of Indonesian gamelan music. *Ionisation,* on the other hand, deploys its revolutionary ensemble to articulate a traditional dramatic structure, and the complex rhythms, dynamic changes, and the sliding tones of the sirens work in concert to develop a musical idea.

Varèse toppled the primacy of harmony and melody traditional in Western music but retained the structure, with hierarchical relationships between the work's constituent parts. Cowell, in addition to essentially negating pitch and harmony, also undermined the overarching metric grid of the work, giving each voice its own meter with no relation to the bar lines. In measures 64 to 67, two-thirds of the way into *Ionisation,* one section ends and another begins, the break demarcated by a long fermata followed by a rest and a dying away of the siren (see example 2.1).

When the meter shifts, as it does in the first few measures of the new section, it does so for all the instruments sounding at that moment, and the various rhythmic cells remain tied to the metrical framework of the entire ensemble. The ostinato figures and the accent patterns in Cowell's work, by contrast, are generated individually using numerical ratios, and once the layers are combined, the piece proceeds in *moto perpetuo,* in a mechanistic and nondramatic fashion.[25] In measures 50 to 55 in *Ostinato Pianissimo,* the final instruments, the woodblocks, enter, adding another layer, yet another different rhythmic profile, which is absorbed into the overall texture of the continuously spinning ostinati (see example 2.2).

Unlike in *Ionisation,* none of the instruments of *Ostinato Pianissimo* exerts dominance at any point of the work, and the composer's role is significantly reduced, limited to generating the ostinato figures and indicating the start and end points of each line. As a result, the two works sound vastly different. *Ionisation* reflects Varèse's affinity for urban life and futuristic machines, with its shrieking sirens and resonant use of percussions. *Ostinato Pianissimo* is, by contrast, a study in quietude and nonaction, which exploits the variegated timbres of the instruments to weave a tapestry of delicate sounds.

Although the instrumentation in Varèse's work was borrowed from other cultures and signaled a major departure from Western convention, his compositional design—based on contrast, development, and climax and release—hearkens back to the structural framework of traditional Western art music. Cowell breaks even more radically with Western tradition, focusing his

Example 2.1. Varèse, *Ionisation*, mm. 64–67

Example 2.2. Cowell, *Ostinato Pianissimo*, mm. 50–53

innovations on those musical elements his Chinese scholar deemed integral to Asian music: counterpoint and rhythm. It is possible to see in Cowell's greater affinity to Asian musical techniques not just a rejection of Atlantic culture but also his discomfort, as a gay man, with the kind of masculinist gestures that characterize much of Varèse's music. As Susan McClary argues, the sonata form, which Varèse continues to employ in his most revolutionary scores, can be read in sexualized terms, as a metonym of male heterosexual aggression.[26] Even while abandoning the harmonic structure of conventional sonata form, Varèse exaggerates the aggressive qualities inferred in earlier tonal sonatas. With the composer doing little to discourage masculinist readings of his music, the reception of his music was often couched in language brimming with phallic imageries.[27] In his own percussion piece, Cowell chose to replace those aspects of *Ionisation* that carried hetero-masculine associations with procedures derived from Asian models. As in his work for the New Music Society, Cowell acknowledged and participated in Atlantic modernism even while he signaled his difference from the New York modernists via orientalism.

By the 1930s, Cowell had successfully established an experimental music scene in California and was mentoring younger Californian composers. Cowell helped situate his students' experimentation within what he saw as a larger cultural shift toward the Pacific Rim. In articles such as "Drums along the Pacific" in the 1940 issue of *Modern Music*, Cowell announced the arrival of a new kind of music emergent in the West Coast:

During the last two years an extraordinary interest in percussion music has developed on the Pacific coast. In Seattle, San Francisco, Oakland and Los Angeles, orchestras have been formed to play music for percussion instruments alone. They are directed chiefly by two young Western composers, John Cage and Lou Harrison, who have concocted innumerable creations for these instruments, and have induced others like Ray Green of San Francisco, Gerald Strang of Long Beach, and J. M. Beyer, formerly of New York, to write for them. . . . Music by all these men has been rehearsed regularly in the various percussion orchestral groups, who thus acquire an ability to render intricate rhythms far beyond the capacity of professional symphony men, and to control countless gradations of tone-quality, many hitherto unsuspected.[28]

Contemporary critics were susceptible to the suggestion that Cage and Harrison's novel techniques hailed from the Orient. A *San Francisco Chronicle* review of one of their percussion concerts noted, "We are still very far from the subtlety of rhythmic speech the Arabs and Indians get out of their little hand drums or the symphonic grandeur of the Balinese percussion orchestras, but such experiments as that of last night point toward interesting developments."[29]

Even as he publicized and promoted California's exceptional musical culture, built on the edifice of orientalism, Cowell was serving time in San Quentin for sexual misconduct with a seventeen-year-old boy.[30] Unwittingly, Cowell brought into the open issues of sexuality that had previously been cloaked in secrecy in the music world. His public humiliation cleaved the new music community into opposing camps of allies and foes along the lines of those who supported or were themselves homosexuals and those, like Ives, who railed against effeminacy in music and cut off ties with the Californian.[31] Cowell's Californian protégés, Cage and Harrison, also gay, would have to grapple with not just their regional but also their sexual differences in a world made much more conscious of such identity markers.

Cage and Harrison's Double Music, Double Lives

Belonging to the same generation and sharing common musical genealogical roots, John Cage and Lou Harrison began their careers as friends and collaborators but then later struck out in divergent directions. Although a deep engagement with Asian cultures shaped both of their lives, the impact of Asia on their music and personal belief system was registered in completely different ways, lending support to Said's contention that orientalist practices ultimately reveal more about the Western individual than any essential truths about the Orient.

Cage was born in Los Angeles in 1912 and came to music relatively late. He studied composition spottily, first with local pianist Richard Buhlig, then with Cowell and Adolph Weiss in New York, and eventually with Arnold Schoenberg in the mid-1930s.[32] Harrison was born in Portland, Oregon, in 1917 and grew up mostly in the San Francisco Bay Area. From the mid-1930s to 1942, when he moved to Los Angeles to study with Schoenberg, Harrison took private lessons with Cowell, attended Cowell's Music of the Peoples of the World class, and listened to vast quantities of music, including Chinese opera and Japanese shakuhachi compositions.[33]

Introduced by Cowell, the two young Californians together explored the richness of Asian and percussion musics and organized annual percussion concerts in San Francisco from 1939 to 1941. *Double Music* (1941), for a percussion quartet, was composed collaboratively for a joint concert, with Cage and Harrison each contributing two halves of the score. The piece follows the principle of micro-/macrocosmic rhythmic structure, in which the large parts of a composition employ the same proportion as the phrases of a single unit. After determining the length of the work—two hundred measures—the composers went their separate ways and wrote their respective halves independent of one another.[34] About the final product, Cage remarked, "The result required no change, and indicates to me that there is a deeply rewarding world of musical experience to be found in this way. The peculiarities of a single personality disappear almost entirely and there comes into perception through the music a natural friendliness, which has the aspect of a festival."[35] Harrison later remembered, "Of course I sort of knew what John was going to do and he knew what I was going to do because we were so close together artistically at that time."[36]

In *Double Music,* Cage and Harrison used collage technique to create a composition organized on principles very different from those in the works of their contemporaries. They deployed instruments found in their immediate surroundings, which provided a wealth of percussion instruments foreign to a traditional European orchestra: buffalo bells, brake drums, sistra (Ethiopian metal rattles), sleigh bells, thunder sheets, Japanese temple gongs, tam tams, cowbells, Chinese gongs, and water gongs. Because the four layers of *Double Music* were not conceived of in toto, the melodic lines retain their independence (see example 2.3). In the opening, for example, both Cage and Harrison introduce motivic cells that are made up of quarter notes and eighth notes and use a limited range of pitches moving in stepwise motion. Cage (soprano line), after repeating his two-measure motif, deconstructs the theme into smaller segments. Harrison (alto line) repeats the eight-note motif as an ostinato. Since the beginning of Harrison's motif does not align

Example 2.3. Cage and Harrison, *Double Music*, mm. 1–8

metrically within the 4/4 framework and Cage's theme contains syncopation, the combination of the two parts results in an ever-shifting fabric of rhythmic counterpoint. The Japanese temple gong adds another wash of color to the overall timbre.

Cage and Harrison took away different lessons from this collaboration. Although both composers situated their subsequent musical innovations within orientalist frameworks, their resulting works sound fundamentally dissimilar. In a 1946 article, Cage laid out the following as the key attributes of Oriental music: "In general, then, there may be pointed out certain large musical conditions which are characteristically Oriental. They are: that the music be non-thematic, non-harmonic, non-motival; that it have (a) an integral step-wise use of scale, (b) structural rhythm, (c) an integral use of percussive sound and (d) pitch distances less than a semi-tone."[37] Even earlier, Cage was exploiting these very characteristics in his own works, such as *Amores* (1943), the first prepared piano piece written independent of dance.[38] For the third movement, the "Trio for Seven Woodblocks" (originally the last movement of his 1936 *Trio*), Cage again constructed a micro-/macrocosmic structure, using the number three to generate the overall form, as well as the small details (see example 2.4). The movement is made up of thirty-three measures, it has only three pitches sounded throughout, and there are three rhythmic motives that recur in various combinations. Cage downplayed the importance of harmony and simplified other musical components in order to concentrate almost exclusively on rhythmic manipulation. Instead of a formal design based on harmonic tension and resolution, on climax and denouement, Cage employed a formal framework based on the division of

Example 2.4. Cage, *Amores,* "Trio for Seven Woodblocks," mm. 1–4

time into specified units of duration. The contrasting rhythmic patterns of the various layers, interwoven in cross-rhythmic relationships with each other, become foregrounded in the absence of harmonic or melodic development. The changes brought about by the subtle shifts in rhythmic alignment make up the "development" of the musical idea.

In contrast, Harrison focuses more on the melodic and contrapuntal, rather than on the rhythmic and structural, elements of music. *First Concerto for Flute and Percussion* (1939), dedicated to Cowell, is scored for one flute soloist and two percussionists, who play a variety of instruments (see example 2.5). The percussion parts clearly show Harrison's indebtedness to Asian musics, with the ostinato structure recalling Indonesian gamelan music and the timbres the Chinese opera. The juxtaposition of the flute, a European melodic instrument, with Asian percussion instruments results in an unusual combination of timbres, a hybrid assemblage of unlike sounds. In the first movement, their difference is underscored rhythmically: the percussions repeat a three-bar ostinato in 4/8 meter forty-five times as the flute plays its melody in 6/8 meter. The unmatched meters between the parts create two independent layers, relating to each other only on the level of the basic eighth-note beat. Around this time, Harrison was experimenting with what he calls "rhythmicles," or rhythmic cells that accumulate to form a mosaic-like surface. The tuneful pentatonic flute melody is pieced together by linking the three principal rhythmicles a, b, and c. Already, in these early pieces, Harrison is emulating elements from different musical idioms, to be combined at will in his hybrid, East-meets-West collages. Cage's orientalism, in comparison, is apparent more as an abstract framework than as an actual sonic model.

When Harrison and Cage moved to New York in the 1940s, their musical and personal paths diverged even more dramatically. The young composers began to better understand their place in the larger new music world and their identities as homosexual artists, as had Cowell, once they were submerged

FIRST CONCERTO
for Flute and Percussion

Percussion I and II

LOU HARRISON

First Player
tortoise shell or large
  temple-block
tin can rattle
  or tambourines, rattles only
3 graduated gongs
rasp or guiro

Second Player
3 graduated drums
large bell
inverted large brass bowl
  (hemispherical Chinese brass
  bowl, upside down, giving
  a melodious "ping")

I

play 45 times, starting before the flute enters, then add the final beat

Edition Peters 6541

Example 2.5. Harrison, *First Concerto for Flute and Percussion,* First Movement.
(Copyright © 1964 by C. F. Peters Corporation). (Used by permission)

Flute

to Henry Cowell

FIRST CONCERTO
for Flute and Percussion

LOU HARRISON

I

*) Earnest, fresh, and fastish in ♪

Play groups 2-9 again without repetitions; Coda follows.

* 1 accidentals are valid only for the immediately following note
  2 the numbers on top of the bars correspond with the recurring pattern of the percussion instruments and may serve as rehearsal numbers
  3 notes preceded by a ♭ should tend to be played flat; those preceded by a ♯, sharp

Edition Peters 6541

Example 2.5. Continued

in New York, in many ways the polar opposite of California. Cage began his life partnership with dancer Merce Cunningham and associated with prominent artists of the New York avant-garde, including Jackson Pollock, Robert Rauschenberg, and Jasper Johns. Harrison wrote reviews for *Modern Music* and Virgil Thomson's *New York Herald Tribune,* championing the music of Ives, Ruggles, Varèse, and the Second Viennese School. During his first decade in New York, Cage consolidated his ideas about indeterminacy, which eventually earned him fame as one of the most important artists of the twentieth century. Harrison, on the other hand, was too busy to write much music during his New York years, and what music he did write grew overly dense and complicated. His feeling of being trapped in a compositional cul-de-sac, compounded by the stress of living in a noisy, frenetic city, led to a nervous breakdown in 1947. Whereas Cage remained in New York until the end of his life, winning more and more accolades, Harrison returned to California, eventually settling down in Aptos, a small seaside town near Santa Cruz.

Their different experiences of California and distinctively individual interpretations of Asian culture framed their reactions to New York and guided the subsequent course of their careers. For Harrison, the less tolerant conditions he perceived in the East Coast made the transition from San Francisco to New York especially difficult. He later recalled: "At that time [late 1930s to early 1940s], San Francisco was really fairly relaxed already about being gay. I never had any trouble with it at all. None of my friends did either. The first time I encountered that feeling of tightness and constraint, or uptightness, was in New York."[39] Just as important for Harrison was California's special relationship with Asia, which he missed in the East Coast: "On the West Coast my experience had been that the nearest relation we had as Americans was Asia. You know, San Francisco is close to Asia, whereas in New York, you are just a stone's throw from Europe. It's a completely different civilization. So that took some difficulty, made some difficulty for me. When I got back I immediately refelt the connections with Asia."[40] Upon his return to California, Harrison dedicated himself more fully to navigating musical orientalism, learning to speak in the musical languages of various nonwestern cultures. Following his first visit to Asia, Harrison wrote *Moogunkwha, Se Tang Ak* (1961) for a Korean court orchestra, *Concerto in Slendro* (1961), *Prelude* (1962) for piri (Korean double-reed instrument) and harmonium, and the large-scale *Pacifika Rondo* (1963), written for the University of Hawaii's Festival of Music and Art of This Century, scored for sheng (Chinese free-reed mouth organ), jalataranga (Indonesian tuned bowls), psalteries, fang hsiang (tuned iron slabs hung in a decorated rack), piri, and pak (six slabs of heavy hardwood), along with a standard string orchestra.

Although Harrison himself finds speculative the idea that "Orientalisms" characterize the music of gay composers,[41] his use of orientalist elements in his larger works suggests that his interest in Asia and his identification with queerness were inextricably interlinked. One of his most ambitious projects, *Young Caesar: An Opera for Puppets ("X-Rated")*, which received its premiere at the California Institute of Technology in 1971, revolves around the homosexual affair of young Caesar and Nicomedes, the king of Bithynia in Asia Minor. Their union provided Harrison with the opportunity to fully maximize what he described in the program notes as the basic theme of the opera: the meeting of East and West. To musically represent the affair between these powerful men—the physical mingling of the Roman with the Greek, Mesopotamian and Byzantine—Harrison combined various Western and Eastern instruments: the classical aulos with the gamelan, violins and violas with a predominantly Asian instrumental ensemble.[42] With *Young Caesar*, Harrison synthesized his attraction to the alterity of nonwestern cultures with his social and political commitments as a member of California's gay community. The composer, who once acknowledged that "the homosexual, as one of society's 'others'— defined, and sometimes alienated, by the mainstream—may be attracted to other outsiders, to exotic cultures," remarked of the opera: "I shouldn't be a bit surprised that that brewing underneath also helped lead to my opera, *Young Caesar*, because of that feeling of support from a minority group".[43]

For Cage, who had grown up in a much more conservative Los Angeles in a family with Protestant evangelical leanings, New York offered an opportunity to start his life with Cunningham with a clean slate after leaving his wife, Xenia, on the other coast. Jonathan Katz traces Cage's conversion to Zen Buddhism back to the psychic and creative crisis the composer suffered in ending his marriage and embarking upon a committed homosexual relationship, noting that Cage turned to Eastern religions only after he had failed to reap any real benefits from the Western remedy of psychoanalysis.[44] Cage's musical works from this time mirror his personal decision, made under the guidance of Asian spiritual teachings, to detach himself from his inner emotional turmoil and engage more actively with the outer world. His most famous work, *4'33"*, in effect removed the intrusive presence of the creator's ego from the music, thus creating the conditions necessary, as a visiting Indian musician coached him, "to quiet the mind thus making it susceptible to divine influences."[45]

By pointing out that Cage only extracted ideas from Asian philosophies that reinforced modernist tenets apparent in his works from the start, David W. Patterson interrogates the conventional belief that the composer's encounter with Buddhism engendered his most significant ideas.[46] Even while

betraying the influence of Buddhist master Daisetz Suzuki's teaching, *4′33″*
extends Cage's major musical concerns from earlier times and represents in
many ways a culmination of ideas already implicit in *Double Music:* time
durations structure the work, and chance determines the ways in which different sounds combine during the musical performance. Nevertheless, the
importance of Asia to Cage's developing personal and aesthetic philosophies
during his first years in New York should be understood not simply as a means
of dressing old ideas with orientalist spirituality but rather as instrumental
in bringing about a convergence of his most private struggles and earlier
musical tendencies.

Contrary to John Corbett's assertion that the "political blank slate of ex-
perimentality" gave composers such as Harrison and Cage license to imitate
and domesticate exotic cultures within Western frameworks, both composers,
approaching the Orient as gay artists, acted in fully political, albeit disparate,
ways.[47] Harrison was openly gay from a young age and took an active part in
the gay rights and anti-war movements of the 1960s, writing, for example,
a set of *Peace Pieces* in protest against American involvement in Vietnam.
In discussing the fourth piece of the set, based on the Buddhist text the
Heart Sutra, Harrison concurs with his interviewer that the main lesson to
be learned about homosexuality from Buddhism is the importance of communication.[48] Cage reached quite the opposite conclusion in his study of Buddhism. In his silence and retreat into the closet, Cage resisted the binarism
of the hetero/homo oppositional discourse on his own terms, working, as
Katz puts it, "not to challenge power but to escape it."[49] What Corbett argues,
in line with Said's thesis, is that an inequality of power always underlies the
encounter between East and West. But in discussing these composers' orientalist practices without considering their minority status as homosexuals,
Corbett misses an important complicating factor in the web of power between
these composers, the heterosexual majority, and their imagined Orient.

Harry Partch, the Hobo Orientalist

Born in Oakland in 1901 to parents who had lived in China as missionaries, Harry Partch grew up in various frontier towns of the Southwest, then
returned to California as a young adult to commence a lifelong journey as
a peripatetic artist.[50] In many ways, Partch stood outside of the circle of
Californian composers associated with Cowell. Even while living in the San
Francisco Bay Area in the 1920s, he seemed to have had no contact with
Cowell or his New Music Society, and although he enjoyed a long friend-
ship with Harrison, his relationships with Cage and Cowell were strained at

best.[51] However, because he shared a similar set of creative preoccupations with Cowell and his protégés, he is often grouped with them as a representative of the Californian maverick tradition. As an experimental composer interested in exotic musics, Partch's career offers yet another illuminating example of the intersection of Californian exceptionalism, orientalism, and queer identification.

Partch, perhaps more than anyone else, forged an independent path, eyeing with suspicion and even paranoia all those belonging to the establishment. He indicted the European concert tradition on socioeconomic, regional, sexual, and aesthetic grounds. As a one-time hobo and an always struggling artist, he found the bourgeois pretensions of concert culture unbearable: "If you mean that Beethoven should become our one musical standard, I think it's . . . a pity. This sort of music has only the feeblest roots in our culture, and those among a class of people that thinks of concerts as social occasions."[52] Partch accounted for his belated recognition as a major American artist by pointing to the disadvantage of his geographic positioning: "But I was in the Paris scene never, the New York scene seldom, and California was among the bushes."[53] Philip Blackburn, entrusted with the compilation of Partch's documents, suggests that the artist's sexuality also left its mark on his creative outlook: "Homosexual by birth, musical revolutionary by choice, Partch was an outsider. . . . His public rage at the musical and cultural injustices of the Twentieth Century must have been fueled by the knowledge that his private life also removed him from the mainstream and could not be discussed in public."[54]

The outsider position Partch insisted upon throughout his life influenced his music in several significant ways. Partch once explained: "There is the ancient tradition of probing, of a lonely, lonely searching—looking for contemporary answers to ancient questions; I like to think the same kind of searching that illuminated the Renaissance, and ancient Greece and the T'ang Dynasty of China."[55] Railing against the overcivilized and overspecialized state of the modern West, Partch sought to resurrect and capture the spirit of antiquity of the ancient Greeks that, in his view, still animated Asian cultures. From their actual and imagined music, Partch generated iconoclastic musical systems and instruments. From their dramatic traditions, he concocted theories of corporeality and the integrated drama. Like the other Californian experimentalists, Partch repudiated traditional Western conventions and forged his new musical system with the aid of orientalism.

In 1930, Partch commemorated his new beginning as a lonely pioneering artist by burning his early music and started to compose with a clearer vision of his subsequent musical direction. That same year, Partch set to music verses penned by eighth-century Chinese poet Li Po, composing with the new scales and techniques generated by his theories of just intonation. Inspired by Hermann Helmholtz's *On the Sensations of Tone* and the music theories of ancient Greece and nonwestern cultures, Partch had devised a compositional system that used unfamiliar ratios from higher up in the overtone series, based on the division of the octave into forty-three tones, and a new ratio-based notation to score such microtones. With the composition of the Li Po songs, the first major work based on his acoustical theories, Partch chose a Chinese subject to signal his rift from the European musical tradition.

Partch described his compositional objectives in the liner notes of an acetate recording made in 1942: "The six lyrics of Li Po are set to music in the manner of the most ancient of cultured musical forms. In this art the vitality of spoken inflections is retained in the music, every syllable and inflection of the spoken expression being harmonized by the accompanying instrument. The musical accompaniment, or, more properly, complement, in addition to being a harmonization, is an enhancement of the text-mood and frequently a musical elaboration of ideas expressed."[56] The voice alternates between intoning and singing, and the Adapted Viola, one of Partch's inventions, switches from accompanying the voice with dense chords made up of double and triple stops to spinning lyric melodies. The inflection of the voice follows the rhythm and substance of the words sensitively, rising and falling in pitch, accelerating and slowing down, bringing into relief the dramatic contour of each poem. Just intonation allows the instruments to more closely mimic the inflections of the voice, not unlike the instrumental accompaniment of the Chinese opera, which Partch attended regularly in San Francisco.

A reference to Chinese music is made explicitly in the third song, "On Hearing the Flute at Lo-Cheng One Spring Night":

> Whence comes this voice of sweet bamboo.
> Flying in the dark?
> It flies with the spring wind.
> Hovering over the city of Lo.
> How memories of home come back tonight!
> Hark! The plaintive tune of "Willow-breaking."

The voice quotes a Chinese folk melody in vocalise (wordless singing), in an imitation of a bamboo flute. The mellifluous tune is rendered tenderly, giving no hint of the agitation about to be unleashed by the viola. As the tune fades out, the viola enters with a tremolo that grows increasingly hurried and anxious. The recitation of the poem begins, the voice reflecting the agitated mood of the viola. The dramatization of the poem reaches its climax with the line "How memories of home come back tonight!" After the enunciation of "Hark!" the folk melody fades in and the viola fades out. Again, the tune is reassuringly calm, if remote and plaintive. The reciter makes one last statement accompanied by a quieter viola tremolo, naming the tune as "Willow-breaking." The song ends with a last hearing of the Chinese tune, fading away into nothingness.

This song comprises two layers of music—first, the Chinese melody of the past, recalled with nostalgia, and second, the intense tremolo of the viola that complements the anxious declamation of the speaker, suggestive of flight. The two layers overlap but are not made to relate in any way, except perhaps as antitheses of one another. The duality set up in the song represents the duality of time and place: the present (the West), in which the composer/reciter is pursued by something troubling, and the past (ancient China), of which only the vestige of a beautiful haunting tune remains as a reminder of all that has been lost. Parch later explained his attraction to this subject, revealing his strong feeling of allegiance to the East and a correspondingly negative attitude toward the West: "I find that a Chinese poem giving names of characters, and exact place names, that describes some trivial incident in a narrative way, is more moving than a European poem portraying a grand and abstract state of mind and incapable of being located in *any* sense." He added, "I am patently not a Westerner."[57]

To find archaic analogues of his musical system, Partch spent 1934 to 1935 in Europe on a Carnegie grant meeting with experts on ancient Greece and nonwestern music. Following his first taste of professional success with the positive reviews of the Li Po songs and the Carnegie-funded European tour, Partch dropped out of concert culture—indeed, out of all society—assuming the role of an outlaw for the rest of the decade. His hobo existence came about as a result of the difficult economic conditions that prevailed in the United States during the 1930s, but perhaps it lasted longer because of his resistance to reentering society and playing by its rules.

Although Partch chose to distance himself from mainstream society, his ideas can be traced directly back to contemporary issues. In recent years, queer and feminist theorists have examined the intricate relationship between emerging discourses of race and sex at the turn of the twentieth century that clustered around binary constructs of homo- and heterosexuality, such as inverted/normal, black/white, primitive/modern, nature/civilization, and body/mind.[58] In his call for a return to a holistic conception of the dramatic and musical arts, Partch stressed his preference for the queer side of each schema, elevating the natural and bodily aspects of primitive and nonwestern cultures over the abstract and cerebral aspects of modern Western civilization.

Partch "distrusted all types of avant-gardism on the ground that they were contrivances of over-civilized cliques" but found beauty in the natural life: "On the one side we have the real music you make by cutting up a piece of wood and hitting it and on the other, the kind of music you get by calling in a piano tuner to tune a totally false scale."[59] Starting with the musical/dramatic works that grew out of his hobo experiences, Partch created a visionary realm with its own musical and dramatic logic and with a special emphasis on the ritualistic aspects of theater. His "corporeal theater" is large-scale in design, bringing together dramatic scenarios, dances, chants, songs, and aural and visual interplays of his sculptural instruments, and is framed within primitivist and orientalist fantasies inspired by ancient Greek, African, and Asian theatrical traditions.

His final and most ambitious musical drama, *Delusion of the Fury* (1966), is made up of two acts: the first act, "On a Japanese Theme," is an adaptation of two Noh dramas, *Atsumori* by Zeami and *Ikuta* by Zembo Motoyasu, and the second act is a retelling of the Ethiopian story "Justice." W. Anthony Sheppard speculates that Partch pieced together a mental image of Japanese drama, of which he most likely did not have any direct experience, through the study of recordings and books about the Noh and Kabuki theatrical traditions and by extrapolating from his knowledge of Chinese opera.[60] For *Delusion,* it was his wish that "the singers would be skilled also in the arts of dancing, acting, miming, as they are in Noh and Kabuki."[61] It is notable that Partch sought inspiration in Noh just two years after Benjamin Britten, the British composer who also used orientalist techniques to suggest the homoerotic, premiered his adaptation of a Noh play, *Curlew River.*[62] Finding no evidence of Partch's knowledge of Britten's work, I am compelled to see both of these gay artists' turn to a traditional Japanese art as a means of escaping the homophobic tenor of modern times for a ritualistic and exotic world of an idealized Orient. Noh, in particular, can be especially attractive for gay artists, with its all-male casts performing gender in a highly stylized and elegant fashion. Partch further emphasized the primitive and corporeal by pairing the Japanese-based drama with a traditional African tale—the clear binary opposite of white and civilized in twentieth-century Western discourses.

The mix of instrumental exotica and the freedom Partch took with the borrowed narratives resulted in a work uniquely his, with little resemblance to actual Asian and African dramas. Considering that his sources encompassed traditions as disparate as ancient Greek drama and the Noh, experienced indirectly at that, it is not surprising that Partch's theatrical works depart significantly from their putative models. What these other traditions provided for the experimental composer were alternatives, egresses from the modern Western culture that he felt to be so stifling. By elevating other cultures above contemporary Western culture, Partch reinforced the binary opposition between the West and the East, positing on the one characteristics of mechanism and modernity, specialization and abstractness, and on the other, of naturalism and primitivism, wholeness and corporeality.

Denied the opportunity to study in Asia, he could only imagine the music and dramatic works that so inspired him. Acknowledging that his music would sound just as foreign to Asian listeners as to Western ones, Partch noted, "The bewilderment of many Orientals [in my audience] is easily equal to the bewilderment of many Caucasians."[63] Still, he persisted in thinking of his music as more Eastern than Western, writing in a proposal for a grant to study Noh and Kabuki in Japan, "I should like to demonstrate to Orientals . . . that at least one Occidental has been thinking and producing in their musical and dramatic terms throughout the better part of his life."[64] Out of place in twentieth-century America, Partch imagined into being an Orient in which the natural, dramatic, and queer could coexist in perfect (just-intoned) harmony.

California, Central Node of Transnational Pacific Culture

In the early decades of the twentieth century, there emerged in California a Pacific consciousness, a sense of affinity with the Pacific Rim, a newly defined region that would bestow upon the western United States cultural diversity and richness absent in the East Coast. The powerful vision of a transnational region extending across the Pacific Rim—an economic and cultural network with California at the very center—spurred the construction of grandiose projects like the 1939 world fair. Likewise, in an attempt to open new paths independent of European traditions, California's experimental composers looked to Asia for inspiration and in effect created a transpacific network of musicians.

In his travels through Thailand, India, Pakistan, Turkey, Lebanon, and Japan, Cowell promoted American and Californian music and was a staunch advocate for the creation of "global" music, "music in which the Orient and the Occident were not separated, but all fused into one and the same thing."[65] Harrison visited Asia and Latin America for extended periods and apprenticed with masters in various musical traditions. In response to Cowell's 1961 speech at the East-West Music Encounter Conference in Tokyo entreating the audience to embrace hybrid music, Harrison reflected:

It is as though the world is a round continuum of music. Perhaps here a particular kind of expression is at its most intense & perfect. Then by gradual &
geographic degrees we move to some other center with a special expression.
Anywhere on the planet we may do this—always by insensible degrees the music
changes, & always the music is a compound, a hybrid of collected virtues. This
whole round living world of music—the Human Music—rouses & delights me,
it stirs me to "trans-ethnic," a planetary music.[66]

Harrison helped spawn "trans-ethnic" musics through his teaching at local
universities and through the construction of gamelans. In an interview in
1989, Harrison pointed out with pride the expanding interest in gamelans
in this region: "In 1958 the ethno-musicologist Mantle Hood brought the
first Javanese Gamelan to this country at UCLA and now there are about
a hundred and twenty-five. You are now in the county of Santa Cruz, the
smallest in California, but you will find sixteen gamelans here and all tuned
differently."[67] Cage's visits to Japan resulted in renewed interest among native
Japanese composers, who had been playing catch-up with Western modern
musical developments, in the traditional music of their own culture. Japan's
best-known modern composer, Tōru Takemitsu, claimed that he had at first
"struggled to avoid being 'Japanese,' to avoid 'Japanese' qualities," but through
his "contact with John Cage . . . [came] to recognise the value of my own
tradition."[68] Japanese music was exported and then reimported into Japan,
stamped with Western validation, before native composers could adopt it as
a legitimate musical source.

By situating California as the central node within the Pacific Rim cultural
network, Californian artists constructed a stage on which they were the main
actors rather than marginal characters occupying the periphery of Atlantic
metropoles. With this strategic move, the Californian composers were able
to achieve international renown perhaps unattainable had they competed
with Atlantic composers on their own terms. Further, by invoking Asia,
they created a new category that provided a compelling alternative to the
categories of French-styled neoclassicism and academic serialism and to the
heteronormative values that dominated American culture in the early- to
mid-twentieth century.

Regardless of their marginalized status vis-à-vis the musical establishment
and their sexual orientation, one must keep in mind that as white men, they
enjoyed privileges unavailable to racial minorities and women, and that any
orientalist project, undergirded by unequal power relations and shaped by
exoticizing and distanciating tendencies, cannot shake itself entirely free
of its Western ideological trappings. Even while recognizing the contribu-

tions of these composers in awakening interest in Asian musics, we should be wary of mistaking friendly cultural exchanges for real engagement with social and political inequities. As mainstream media, statesmen, world fair planners, and ethnographers represented the multiplicity of ethnic voices contained within the state from Western perspectives, so the Californian composers diluted, distilled, and processed the music and the philosophies of the East for the appraisal and consumption of a primarily Euro-American new music community. These Californians were accepted into the fraternity of the international music community (especially Cage and Cowell, to a lesser degree Harrison and Partch) by invoking the East, yet for a long time, actual Asian composers could be invited to join only under their patronage and in token numbers. The Californian experimentalists ultimately did not escape the larger contradiction of a society that stood to gain enormously from propagating the myth of cultural pluralism but came up short in actually empowering minority communities or integrating nonwhites into the mainstream cultural life of California.

As Asians moved to California in ever-growing numbers and became increasingly westernized in their musical endeavors, Californian composers continued to tap into some exotic Asian essence to give their works spiritual depth and distinctiveness felt to be lacking in Western contemporary music. Various Buddhist and Hindustani precepts have inspired composers ranging from Terry Riley to Pauline Oliveros in the development of new syncretic compositional processes. Such compositional methods generate music that lies at a great distance from the actual lived experience of Asian Californians yet is identified as a product uniquely Californian, as fruit of the Pacific Rim. The first generation of experimental composers contributed to the creation of the Pacific Rim as a musical meta-region, giving birth to an ideological construction of enduring value in a state that has experienced tremendous changes in race relations and demographics over the past 150 years.

3. A Thin Blue Line down Central Avenue

The LAPD and the Demise of a Musical Hub

While the Anglo elite turned toward Europe and the avant-garde toward Asia, California's nonwhite peoples produced music that demonstrated the vitality of their communities and the rich rewards of intercultural collaboration. Such cultural exuberance was not always welcomed by the power structure, however, and music became another locus wherein minority communities were policed, regulated, and disenfranchised. In the 1940s, the expansion of black California, particularly apparent in the musical nightlife on Central Avenue, provoked strong reactions on the part of the white establishment. Even as some Anglo Californians, like Henry Cowell and his circle of experimental composers, celebrated nonwestern cultures in distant lands, the musics of their nonwhite neighbors were being suppressed or silenced altogether.

Between 1890 and 1920, the Los Angeles Chamber of Commerce blanketed the country with publicity about the new arcadian city growing out west. Its boosters made sure that the agricultural products of the region found nationwide distribution and sent the city's newspapers to all the large markets back east and in the Midwest. Pamphlets and newspaper ads touted the weather, the natural bounties, and many other real and imagined attributes of the Southland. Thanks in large measure to the industriousness of the chamber boosters, Los Angeles was the best-publicized region of the United States during this period.[1]

Their campaign worked almost too well. Legions of new migrants arrived in the city in the next few decades, but the teeming tide of humanity brought with it many who lay well outside of the chamber's target population: impoverished farm workers from the Dust Bowl, foreigners from south of the border, and African Americans from the Deep South. The decade of the 1940s, in particular, was a time of agonizing growing pains for the city as migrants of color poured into the region to partake in the flush wartime economy of the Southland. The population as a whole increased more than 30 percent, and the nonwhite population grew by a staggering 116 percent. The young city had experienced dramatic population growth spurts in the past, but the boom of this decade transformed the demographics of the city irrevocably, helping to sprout pockets of black, brown, and yellow in the erstwhile lily-white field.

From the days of Spanish colonization, black men and women had played an integral role in California's history. Among the Californios and mestizos in the pre-American era were descendants of the African and mulatto men who had accompanied the first Spanish missionaries and conquistadores to the region. The gold rush triggered another wave of black immigration, as slaves from the South and freedmen from the North made the westward trek in search of a better life. With European immigration, especially from southern and eastern Europe, trickling down to almost zero following the passage of the 1924 Immigration Restriction Act, African Americans were actively recruited to California to help stem the labor shortage. The growth of the black population in California was never as dramatic, however, as in the decade of World War II, particularly in Los Angeles. In 1920, there were approximately 15,000 African Americans in Los Angeles; by 1930, 39,000; and following the massive wartime migration, more than 170,000, making up 9 percent of the city's population.[2]

Blacks were tolerated to different degrees during the course of California's modern history. Even while many blacks moved to California to escape Jim Crow laws in the South, they encountered in the West segregation and racism in new guises. In the years before and after statehood, the state legislature considered several bills that would have limited or eliminated black immigration altogether. After statehood, not only were black Californians denied the right to own property, but Californios of African descent were forced to relinquish to the United States government the sizable acreage their families had owned for generations. As their numbers grew, black Californians faced heightened racial tension, which increasingly erupted into violence. With competition intensifying for housing and jobs, white labor unions and the Ku Klux Klan stepped up their maneuvers of intimidation and terror against the black population. The 1940s in particular brought to the surface the deep-seated anxiety of the Los Angeles establishment in the face of the rapid expansion of minority communities. In 1942, the Mexican community was targeted in the Sleepy Lagoon case, and with the passage of President Franklin D. Roosevelt's Executive Order 9066, Japanese Americans were rounded up for deportation to internment camps. The following year, white servicemen, abetted by the police, instigated a large-scale attack on Mexican American and African American youths, setting off the Zoot Suit riots.[3]

Against this backdrop of racial violence and fear, black music thrived. Denied access to most of the city's residential neighborhoods by racist housing covenants and crowded into the few tracts of leftover land, Los Angeles's black community grew dense with people and activity in the war years. Here a vital musical culture, ranging from youth performances in school orchestras to late-night jam sessions of some of the most exciting jazz and blues musicians of the time, grew and prospered.[4] Black Angeleno musicians created communal spaces that minimized, if not entirely erased, geographic and racial boundaries, as not only African Americans from outside of California but also European, Mexican, and Japanese Americans living in nearby neighborhoods convened to make music together on a regular basis.[5]

With its magnetic appeal, black music attracted white audiences from all over the Southland. The Los Angeles establishment objected more to the regular and visible attendance of white patrons in South Central clubs than to the participation of a few nonblack musicians. Threatened by a cultural force that refused to stay contained in the ghettos, the L.A. oligarchy pulled out its guns. Central Avenue, the main hub of black music, became the site of fierce, even violent, contestation between the new progressive social practices of integration and the reactionary countermeasures of the city's power structure. Contrary to the boosters' propaganda touting cultural pluralism, official tolerance, much less embrace, of nonwhite cultures—especially one that, like black music, crossed racial boundaries and refused to play by establishment rules—was decidedly not forthcoming.

Central Avenue, South Central

Before Los Angeles's South Central had become indelibly linked in the public mind with gang wars and riots, its main strip, Central Avenue, boasted glamorous nightclubs and swinging dance halls that rivaled the better-known African American music centers back east. White saxophonist Art Pepper paints an idyllic picture of "the Stem" as he remembers it from the 1940s:

> It was a beautiful time. It was a festive time. The women dressed up in frills and feathers and long earrings and hats with things hanging off them, fancy dresses with slits in the skirts, and they wore black silk stockings that were rolled and wedgie shoes. Most of the men wore big, wide-brimmed hats and zoot suits with wide collars, small cuffs, and large knees, and their coats were real long

with padded shoulders. They wore flashy ties with diamond stickpins; they wore lots of jewelry; and you could smell powder and perfume everywhere. And as you walked down the street you heard music coming out of everyplace. And everybody was happy. . . .

[T]here were all kinds of places to go, and if you walked in with a horn everyone would shout, "Yeah! Great! Get it out of the case and blow some!" They didn't care if you played better than somebody else. Nobody was trying to cut anybody or take their job, so we'd get together and blow.[6]

Less than a decade after reaching its dizzying height during the war years, however, the Central Avenue club scene was on its way to extinction, and fifty years later, little remains of its former glory.

What caused the precipitous decline of this vital and vigorous musical culture? Clearly a number of factors—social, economic, and political—propelled Central Avenue on its downward trajectory. The downsized postwar economy threw many out of work, and unemployment hit the African American community particularly hard, leaving little money for cultural or recreational activities. After the U.S. Supreme Court ruled in 1948 that housing covenants were illegal, upwardly mobile black families moved out of South Central in droves, seeking more commodious living conditions in the west side of the city. The 1953 merger of the black Musicians' Union 767 with the white Musicians' Union 47 opened up opportunities for black musicians to play in other venues throughout the city and diffused the musical talent on Central Avenue. Nightclubs in general suffered as the rapid adoption of television kept their clientele at home.

While acknowledging the deleterious effects of these factors on the clubs, many musicians from the era point to the Los Angeles Police Department as the real culprit behind the demise of Central Avenue. As singer Ernie Andrews remembers, the police "harassed the people—tear up their joints and put them in jail, you know, just keep harassing them, harassing them, harassing them, and putting them in jail and whatnots."[7] Trumpeter Art Farmer concurs: "The police started really becoming a problem. I remember, you would walk down the street, and every time they'd see you they would stop you and search you."[8] Jazz trumpeter Clora Bryant maintains, "They'd catch you over there, and you'd better not have a ticket out or something, you know, the least little thing and you were going down."[9] In his autobiography *Raise Up off Me,* pianist Hampton Hawes conjures up a dystopic snapshot of Central Avenue after the invasion of the police: "On any weekend night on Central Avenue [along] the forties [numbered blocks] you could probably see more blinking red lights than on any other thoroughfare in the country. Seen from a distance you'd think it was some kind of far-out holocaust, a fifty-car smashup, Watts '65. But it was only the cops jamming brothers."[10] Increased police presence on the avenue transformed street life from a festive to a nightmarish scene in only a few short years.

In the 1940s, the LAPD was beginning to fashion itself in a new image. William H. Parker was appointed chief in 1950, and during his fifteen-year stewardship, the LAPD turned itself around completely, from a department under the thumb of city hall and corrupted by its associations with mobsters to one of the best-paid, most emulated police forces in the world. That the time period in which the LAPD's status rose also saw the decline of Central Avenue is hardly coincidental; I would posit that the two events had a direct impact on one another. The modern LAPD, which came of age in the 1940s and was shaped by the reactionary forces that governed the Los Angeles civic arena, was (and, some would argue, continues to be) instrumental in the suppression of progressive social, political, and cultural movements and in the preservation of the power structure. Its combative and despotic rule over street life in South Central and elsewhere in Los Angeles incurred costs and benefits that went far beyond the fate of a dozen nightclubs. I examine here why the LAPD at this pivotal moment in its history targeted Central Avenue, how it used generally accepted perceptions of the South Central music scene to win support for its often unconstitutional actions from the Los Angeles establishment and white populace, and how its "success" in destroying the Central Avenue economy both bolstered its position in the short run and undermined its standing in the long run.

The LAPD before and during the Parker Era

The LAPD in the mid-twentieth century looked back on a short but heavily checkered past. Not infrequently, underpaid police officers gave in to the temptation of lining their pockets with payoffs from vice operators in the Los Angeles underworld of gambling, prostitution, and liquor and narcotics trafficking. To appease both the reform-minded Protestant voting population and the politicians whose elections were financed by mobsters, the police department played a duplicitous double role, selling protection to select vice operators and raising arrest numbers by apprehending their competition.

Highly respected criminologist August Vollmer was hired as police chief in 1923 and raised the professional standards of the department considerably, but his position lasted only a year, and his reforms proved to be almost as short-lived. James Davis, LAPD chief from 1926 to 1929 and then again from 1933 to 1938, left a deeper imprint. He encouraged his men to carry out dragnets (sweeps of entire streets of people, innocent or guilty) and bum blockades (illegal police bulwarks that turned away "vagrants" and migrants at various points along the state border during the Depression). His Intelligence Squad spied on, collected dossiers of, and intimidated critics and foes of the department; his Red Squad raided meetings of labor unions, Socialists, the American Civil Liberties Union, and any other groups suspected of subversion. With the mayoral election of Fletcher Bowron and his reformist platform in 1938, the city's vice operations suffered a major blow. From the late 1930s into the 1940s, as Bowron's city hall deployed the police force in its zealous crusade against the Los Angeles underworld, police brutality and the infraction of civil liberties came to dwarf corruption as matters of public concern.

It was in this rather lawless environment that William Parker, a devout Catholic and an autocratic moralist, mastered the political skills that would help him maneuver his way to a position of power. He joined the force in 1927 and rose through the ranks quickly. While acting as Chief Davis's administrative assistant, he helped rewrite Section 202 of the city charter, which vested and codified the rights of LAPD officers and which, in essence, guaranteed the chief of the department lifetime tenure, free of accountability to city hall or to the general populace. Upon his return from service in the war, Parker, upholding an ideology in line with the reactionary ethos of postwar Los Angeles, was within easy reach of the chief's office. In 1949, he assumed the position as the head of the Internal Affairs Division, a new division responsible for investigating complaints of police misconduct and for meting out appropriate disciplinary measures. By internalizing this function, the LAPD in effect shielded itself from outside intervention. When at last Parker was offered the job, the position of LAPD chief was perhaps the most powerful—certainly the most autonomous—in the city of Los Angeles, largely through Parker's own efforts and design. In 1950, he seized total control over the department, reorganizing divisions, implementing scientific and technological improvement in police work, recruiting drill instructors from elite military academies to train police cadets and to put into place a military code of conduct, generally raising the standards of police comportment, and remaking his men (and a handful of women) in his own image. Parker's value system permeated every aspect of the LAPD and shaped a police culture that survives to this day.[11]

First and foremost, Parker envisioned the role of the police department to be one of social control. Upon taking the mantle of the LAPD chief, Parker, who often resorted to barely veiled white supremacist rhetoric, proclaimed that "Los Angeles is the white spot of the great cities of America today" and pledged to take whatever actions necessary to preserve the status quo.[12] In an article in which he advocated the use of wiretap surveillance for effective policing, Parker wrote, "Policemen consider themselves as a 'containing element'—a thin line of blue which stands between the law-abiding members of society and the criminals who prey upon them."[13] The chief made his thoughts on who belonged on each side of that thin blue line abundantly clear in statements like the following: "It's estimated by 1970 that . . . 45% of the metropolitan area of Los Angeles will be Negro. . . . Now how are you going to live with that without law enforcement? This is the lesson that we refuse to recognize, that you can't convert every person into a law abiding citizen. If you want any protection in your home and family in the future, you're going to have to stop this abuse, but you're going to have to get in and support a strong police department. If you don't do that, come 1970 God help you!"[14] Rather than acknowledge police complicity in the racial conflicts of the 1940s, the chief maintained that stronger law enforcement was the best deterrent against such occurrences. Parker acceded to a position of power within an inherently racist society, and by condoning and even encouraging the aggressive practices already rampant among police officers, he helped institutionalize racism in the LAPD.

The LAPD had been linking race and crime for some time, starting in 1923 to compile and annually publish statistics on the number of people arrested for specific crimes, broken down into specific races.[15] The "Arrests by Charge and Race" tables published in the LAPD *Annual Reports* between 1945 and 1949 show some surprising figures (some of the data from those tables appear in table 3.1).

The African American population, making up less than 10 percent of the city's whole, was responsible, according to the LAPD arresting officers, for approximately a third of the homicides, rapes, and narcotics infractions. Black prostitution and vice arrests made up about 40 percent of the city's total; assault, more than half. Even though blacks earned significantly less than their white counterparts and cars were an unattainable luxury for most, blacks constituted a third of the traffic apprehensions.

The stories involving the police that appeared regularly in the *California Eagle,* a weekly paper serving the African American community, give some indication of the frequency and the degree of violence of the encounters between the LAPD and black Angelenos.[16] In one well-publicized case in January 1952, singer Jimmy Witherspoon, headlining a show at the Club Alabam, was picked up on his way home on charges of drunk driving, was beaten, and then was kept at the police station all night. The officers refused his request for a sobriety test, denying him the opportunity to disprove the charges brought against him.[17] The high rate of police brutality incidents

Table 3.1. LAPD arrests of blacks in relation to the general population, 1945–49

	1945				1946				1947				1948				1949			
	M[a]	F[b]	T[c]	%[d]	M	F	T	%	M	F	T	%	M	F	T	%	M	F	T	%
Assault	657	147	1,590	51	805	155	1,908	50	741	224	1,852	52	1,069	300	2,375	58	964	286	2,237	56
Disorderly conduct	62	15	408	19	63	9	462	15	47	17	323	20	45	15	339	18	53	18	382	19
Gambling	6,224	304	9,450	69	5,418	245	9,225	61	5,438	253	9,614	59	5,510	309	9,766	60	4,562	346	7,631	25
Homicide	52	12	190	34	53	16	241	29	75	18	264	36	41	14	191	29	42	5	184	26
Liquor	143	55	475	42	116	44	518	31	89	32	567	21	28	15	559	8	21	8	362	8
Narcotics	225	25	721	35	344	48	1,058	37	462	55	1,458	35	463	60	1516	34	431	56	1,372	35
Prostitution/vice	546	825	3,796	36	752	1,090	4,391	42	464	816	3,038	42	372	750	3,001	37	323	664	2,607	39
Rape	146	—	390	37	133	—	439	30	169	—	543	31	161	—	514	31	144	—	469	31
Robbery	2,166	70	3,279	68	1,752	72	3,978	46	2,202	1581	4,926	77	1,759	77	4,431	41	1,282	61	3,613	37
Traffic violation	966	10	2,571	38	718	21	2,795	26	960	12	2,987	33	1,856	29	5,147	37	2,653	46	7,074	38
Vagrancy	173	14	675	28	107	11	939	13	138	26	1,282	13	173	27	1,520	13	240	31	1,437	19

M = black male arrests

F = black female arrests

T = total number of arrests

% = percent of black arrests/total number of arrests

Source: Los Angeles Police Department Annual Reports for 1945 through 1949, published by the department. M, F, and T numbers are from "Arrests by Charge and Race."

in black Los Angeles stemmed in large part from the LAPD's practice of proactive policing, which involved apprehending anyone who seemed suspicious, even before any crime was perpetrated. Racial bias often influenced the judgment of the almost exclusively white police on the highly subjective determination of who "appeared" suspicious.

Starting in 1950, the annual reports no longer contained the "Arrests by Charge and Race" tables. However, racial profiling was certainly not on the wane in Chief Parker's police force. Parker defended his stance on this issue: "The demand that the police cease to consider race, color, and creed is an unrealistic demand. Identification is a police tool, not a police attitude."[18] The reports from the Parker era instead display tables that break down the number of arrests by police divisions, and these show evidence of intense police activity in certain areas of the city. Witnesses noted a marked increase in the harassment of the clientele patronizing Central Avenue establishments after Parker's accession, and tables 3.2 and 3.3 show the high numbers of arrests in the Newton Street station, white and black, in relation to the significantly lower numbers in Hollywood, a white area with a similar nightclub economy.

Especially notable are the figures for the number of arrests per one hundred thousand people living in the division. The Newton Street Division ranked either first or second every year in the entire city (second only to Central Division, adjacent to Newton to the north), and the number for the Hollywood Division was about half that of Newton. The number of arrests peaked in 1957—when a resident or visitor in this precinct could expect a one in ten chance of getting arrested—and dropped off thereafter. Increasing reports of false arrests and police harassment prompted action on the

Table 3.2. LAPD vice arrests, 1950 and 1952

	1950				1952			
	Newton St.	% total	Hollywood	% total	Newton St.	% total	Hollywood	% total
Prostitution	316	12.8	98	4	282	13.6	94	4.5
Liquor	39	8.8	35	7.9	20	4.8	44	10.5
Sex perversion	49	2.1	406	17	12	1.0	179	15.5
Other sex	3	6.7	5	11.1	85	1.6	26	41.2
Bookmaking	117	11.8	81	8.2	85	18	29	6.2
Other gambling	1,876	44.5	37	.9	2,091	46.8	29	.6
Total	2,400	22.8	662	6.3	2,491	28.7	401	4.6
Number of crimes per 100,000 inhabitants	5589.61		2,865.75		5,575.8		2,856.3	

Source: Los Angeles Police Department *Annual Reports* for 1950 and 1952, published by the department. Percent total numbers represent total arrests in Los Angeles.

Table 3.3. LAPD arrests by divisions, 1954–57

	1954				1955			
	N[a] / 100[b]		H[c] / 100		N / 100		H / 100	
Assault	1,146	1,397.7	128	82.9	1,026	1,235.7	147	93.5
Auto theft	563	686.7	628	406.6	597	719	657	417.7
Burglary	1,458	1,778.2	1,172	758.9	1,668	2,008.9	1,235	785.2
Homicide	14	17.1	25	5	18	21.7	4	2.5
Larceny	2,601	3,172.2	3,359	2,174.9	2,343	2,821.9	3,456	2,197.2
Rape	82	100	25	16.2	115	138.5	65	41.3
Robbery	338	412.2	207	134	295	355.3	226	143.7

	1956				1957			
	N[a] / 100[b]		H[c] / 100		N / 100		H / 100	
Assault	1,153	1421.4	159	99.7	1,110	1,338.1	170	104.5
Auto theft	940	1,158.8	710	445.4	1,036	1,248.9	958	589.1
Burglary	2,039	2,513.6	1,597	1,001.8	2,290	2,760.5	1,713	1053.4
Homicide	16	19.7	5	3.1	15	18.1	6	3.7
Larceny	2,832	3,419.2	4,413.5	2,593.9	2,903	3,499.9	4,374	2,689.9
Rape	161	198.5	94	59	167	201.3	80	49.2
Robbery	429	528.9	253	158.7	505	608.8	268	164.8

[a] N = Newton Street Division
[b] H = Hollywood Division
[c] / 100 = number of arrests per one hundred thousand people living in the division
Source: Los Angeles Police Department *Annual Reports* for 1954 through 1957, published by the department.

part of the National Association for the Advancement of Colored People (NAACP), resulting in a grand jury probe. The NAACP "placed the blame for such abuses squarely on Chief William Parker."[19]

Parker's Police Officers and Black Musicians

Several musicians hypothesize that it was the racial mixing of crowds at Central Avenue clubs that provoked the intense police activity in the area. For Parker and the city's conservative power elite, racial intermingling was an undesirable trend that necessitated strong defensive measures. They were powerless to fight the Supreme Court ruling of 1948 that struck down segregated housing as illegal, but Central Avenue, a concentrated area within the jurisdiction of the LAPD, could be made subject to police control. Ernie Andrews recalls, "You had a chief of police downtown who was tough, he was tough. He just didn't want all of this love, peace, and happiness going along with all these various people, white, black, blue or indifferent. He didn't want this mockery, so he broke up all of that."[20] Bassist David Bryant remembers that glamorous Hollywood stars were frequent visitors on the Central Avenue scene, drawing even more attention from the police: "All the stars and all the [white] people would come over to Central Avenue and listen to the music, man. So [the police] didn't like the mixing, so they rousted people around and stuff, and that's how they closed it up."[21]

By holding the thin blue line taut and impermeable between whites and nonwhites, the police positioned themselves to safeguard the virtue of Hollywood icons such as Rita Hayworth, Lana Turner, and Ava Gardner, regular patrons at the clubs, as well as the countless white middle-class women who ventured into the area looking for excitement and good music. Judith Butler, writing about the LAPD in more recent times, argues:

> The fear is that some physical distance will be crossed, and the virgin sanctity of whiteness will be endangered by that proximity. The police are thus structurally placed to protect whiteness against violence, where violence is the imminent action of the black male body. And because with this imaginary schema, the police protect whiteness, their own violence cannot be read as violence; because the black male body . . . is the site and source of danger, a threat, the police effort to subdue this body, even if in advance, is justified regardless of the circumstances.[22]

Art Farmer bears out her theory: "The police, as far as they were concerned, the only thing they saw anytime they saw any interracial thing going on was crime. . . . It was a crime leading to prostitution and narcotics."[23] Clora Bryant recalls that the police were not above abusing the very women they purported to protect: "They would stop the women and pat them down and call them nigger lovers and all that kind of stuff." The police, in this instance, disturbed rather than maintained peace and order, even molesting innocent, law-abiding citizens. Bryant describes the humiliating pat-downs: "They'd have the men patting the women down up against the wall. The men spread their legs, and they'd be patting them all over." She sums up, "You know, that's what stopped Central Avenue. It was the insults, the heckles, raiding the after-hours places."[24]

The LAPD's tactic of intimidation on the Stem, the cultural heart of African American Los Angeles, was part of a larger effort to suppress the voice of a minority population and thus to block the channels of mass protest. During the postwar years, the Los Angeles establishment reacted to the perceived danger of African American music by attempting to minimize its presence within the city. Black bands were signed to play in the city's white clubs only after 1944, lagging several years behind their counterparts in New York. Their popularity among mainstream audiences was immediate and provoked a conservative backlash. The comedic antics of Slim Gaillard and Harry "the

Hipster" Gibson, who lampooned and translated the more inaccessible bop style for mainstream audiences (and, incidentally, shared the stage at Billy Berg's with Coleman Hawkins's and Dizzy Gillespie's bands), came under the negative scrutiny of the morally righteous and were banned by the radio station KMPC: "Said Program Director Ted Steele: 'Be-bop . . . tends to make degenerates out of young listeners.'"[25] Between 1948 and 1949, both the Shrine and the Philharmonic auditoriums proscribed further staging of bebop concerts, citing the obstreperousness of bop fans. The industry rag *Variety* reported: "Board of directors [of the Shrine] was more than somewhat upset by bop addicts who attended a Dizzy Gillespie bash early in January. Squad of cops had to quiet youngsters of both sexes, who stampeded up on stage and began snake dancing in the aisles."[26] Despite city council exhortations not to attend a 1949 Paul Robeson concert, seventeen thousand Angelenos showed up to hear the singer in Wrigley Field. Meanwhile, the council chose not to intervene in a meeting of thirty-five race baiters who gathered at the corner of Sixty-sixth and Compton to call for the expulsion of all blacks and Jews from Los Angeles. Observers noted "a parallel between the action of the city council in asking the public not to attend the Robeson concert, and the freedom without council interference with which a meeting based upon the philosophy of the Ku Klux Klan was held on a street corner."[27]

Central Avenue was an important site of black musical innovation. It was one of the birthplaces of rhythm and blues, a new genre that grew out of the meeting of rural blues, gospel, and jazz. Artists such as T-Bone Walker, Nat King Cole, Ivory Joe Hunter, Charles Brown, Joe Turner, Joe Liggins, Little Esther Philips, and Big Mama Thornton sang alongside jazz musicians and itinerant bluesmen at the Club Alabam, Elks Hall, and the Last Word on Central Avenue, as well as at the Barrelhouse in nearby Watts.[28]

Pious moralists alleged that R&B corrupted young minds with lewd, overly sexual imageries and lyrics and tried to banish the new music from the city. R&B artist Big Jay McNeely recalls his popularity with white Los Angeles youths and the resultant trouble with adults: "I developed a tremendous white audience. And [the adults] didn't understand, because I was acting so wild. They didn't know if I was using stuff or not, because they'd never seen the white kids act this way." The police tried to stop him: "I was drawing five or six thousand kids every week. . . . That's when I got locked up and put in jail. I was outside blowing my horn, and a guy came by off duty. . . . He said I was disturbing the peace. . . . So, eventually, they just banned me out of the whole city. I couldn't play at all."[29]

Greek American Johnny Otis, bandleader and talent promoter active in the Central Avenue scene, also remembers the police harassment at R&B concerts: "The Los Angeles police hounded us in the early days of R&B. They hated to see white kids attending the dances along with Black and Chicano youngsters. . . . At first, the cops would stand around glaring at the kids and harassing them with bullshit questions, checking their ID's and so on. This was damaging enough, but eventually they began to use ancient blue laws against us." These particular blue laws prohibited fifteen-year-olds from dancing with sixteen-year-olds, sixteen-year-olds with seventeen-year-olds, and so on. Eventually, Otis's band was forced to move its Saturday night dances to the American Legion Stadium in El Monte, a small town outside of Los Angeles. The El Monte city fathers revoked its dance license as well; it was reinstated only when the band agreed to pay off the firemen and police. According to Otis, the perceived danger of R&B lyrics was far greater than its actual content: "With the exception of a few blue records with naughty lyrics, most releases in the early days were simply about love or good times. The reason the establishment was so uneasy about the new R&B discs was the radically new sound. . . . The straight-laced American moralists saw the new music as alien and subversive."[30]

Nightclubs helped foster the narcotics trafficking trade, which also provoked police crackdowns. Marijuana had been on the streets in previous decades; heroin was introduced into the Central Avenue area in the postwar years, hitting musicians first and perhaps the hardest.[31] As part of his rigorous antivice campaign, Chief Parker advocated a strong police response to any violation of narcotics laws. The 1952 LAPD *Annual Report* announced:

> Los Angeles has a narcotic problem. Drug addiction is on the increase, both among adults and children. Adult narcotic arrests have risen about 600% in the past ten years. Juvenile narcotic arrests have shown an even greater increase. . . . The Los Angeles Police Department has used specialized narcotic officers since 1920. The present Narcotic Division of the Detective Bureau is rated as the finest municipal squad of its type in the nation. Its around-the-clock battle has limited the spread of this vice and demonstrated that cooperative community efforts can win against the dope peddler.

The report continues in an alarmist fashion, equating drug use with immorality and warning of its viral propensity: "Because morality deteriorates with drug use, there are few barriers left to anti-social activity. This is doubly dangerous to the community because *addiction is contagious*—it spreads from person to person. If the spread of this disease-like vice is not controlled, it will multiply at a frightening rate, infecting all age groups, social levels, and races."[32] The police zeroed in on Central Avenue in their attempt to quarantine the drug epidemic from the larger Los Angeles population. Whether the LAPD ameliorated or worsened the drug problem is debatable.

According to the musicians on the scene, the LAPD's campaign against drugs was draconian if not outright illegal. Art Farmer remembers, "If you had one marijuana cigarette, you could get ninety days. . . . And if you had one mark on your arm you'd be called like a vagrant addict. I don't know if that still exists or not, but that was automatic: ninety days." The police would target known users repeatedly in order to get the arrest numbers up. According to Farmer, the musicians would "get hooked and they'd get arrested by the police. You go to jail, you come out, you have a record, and if the police want a promotion . . . they know who to come to. . . . And sometimes they might even manufacture some evidence, because you already have the record."[33] Miles Davis, who was arrested on drug charges during his stint in Los Angeles, later recalled, "They were especially bad on musicians in L.A. . . . because as soon as you said you were a musician, all the white policemen would think you were a junkie."[34]

Police harassment, which precipitated club closures and created a hostile and antagonistic environment, may have aggravated the narcotics problem by taking away the livelihoods and the dignity of Central Avenue musicians. Horace Tapscott, trombonist and leader of the Pan-Afrikan People's Arkestra, insists that the hard drugs began to pervade the Central Avenue scene only in 1951, when the clubs were already in decline, and that "it didn't have to do with just narcotics. It had to do with more than narcotics. It had to do with everyday living in the kind of society . . . during those early fifties for black people, and the black male in particular."[35] Farmer echoes his sentiment: "The prejudice thing might have led to the narcotics in some cases, you know, just feeling like the avenues are blocked anyway, so we might as well get high."[36]

Another possible incentive behind the police crackdown in Central Avenue was economic. Clora Bryant offers her theory: "Central Avenue closed up when they found out how much money was being dropped over there and city hall started sending the cops out there to heckle the white people." She continues, "They found out there was more action on the Avenue than the clubs were getting out West—out northeast, you know, Hollywood."[37] Other musicians corroborate the importance of the money the white patrons pumped into Central Avenue. Responding to the question of how much white customers contributed to the Central Avenue economy, jazz sideman Frank Morgan replies, "At least 60 percent of it, maybe more. The prices certainly weren't geared to the people of the local community. You know $10 and two-drink minimums. It was stickup prices."[38] Saxophonist Marshall Royal describes the Apex, one of the largest clubs on the avenue, as "a black-owned place that would have 90 percent white [audiences]. The blacks didn't have the money to spend."[39] Tapscott believes city hall was behind the movement to shut down Central Avenue from the start. In addition to sending cadres of policemen into clubs, "they started rezoning the areas in the district, which would call for this and not call for that, certain beverages, and this type of establishment in the block or in the neighborhood . . . you know, anything to become a nuisance."[40]

Through the late 1940s and into the 1950s, the LAPD and city hall succeeded in siphoning money away from Central Avenue and South Central. The Plantation Club, opened during the height of the boom on the avenue in 1942, closed its doors in 1947, reopening briefly in 1949, only to shut down again for good shortly thereafter. When one of the largest and oldest nightspots, Club Alabam, closed temporarily in the late 1940s, theater critic Gertrude Gipson mused, "We'd sure like to see the Alabam in operation again. Think it would sorta do something to the many nitelifers who seemingly have hibernated."[41] In 1950, the Downbeat Club was out of business, and the nightlife moved underground into smaller late-night joints, prompting Gipson to note: "Avenue deader than dead, with little or no entertainment to offer. . . . Seems as though unless you are a stay-up-later, you miss out on all the fun. . . . Jack's Basket Room holding down the late crowd on the avenue."[42] In May 1951, "Jack's Basket Room [was] under renovation in more ways than one with the new law in effect concerning early morning spots,"[43] and a few months later, it was reported as defunct.[44] New clubs farther west, such as the Oasis, Club Milomo, the Rubiayat Room, and Club Morocco on Western Avenue, began to receive more extensive coverage in the papers in the early 1950s. *Los Angeles Tribune* critic Lillian Cumber noted the general trend: "Night club traffic fast moving westward."[45] Club Alabam reopened in November 1951 to great fanfare, but by late 1952, the *Eagle* gossip column was already hinting at the club's near-future demise, recounting owner Joe Morris's complaint that "he is making everything but loot."[46] The fate of the Dunbar Hotel, the luxury hotel patronized by hundreds of African American luminaries since its founding in 1928, was tied to the boom and bust of Central Avenue. Having presided over the scene from its central location at the corner of the avenue and Forty-second Street, it struggled to stay open through the neighborhood's economic decline of the 1950s and 1960s. Its closure in 1974 sounded the final death knell of the Stem.

Short- and Long-Term Consequences of LAPD Policies

With his expansionist ambitions for the police force, Chief Parker instituted a public relations machinery, establishing the Public Information Division, entrusting several of his top men to consult on Jack Webb's television show

Dragnet, and even appearing on television himself to field criticisms and questions about the department on the weekly show *The Thin Blue Line.*

The change is visible in the appearance of the 1950 *Annual Report,* now with glossy photographs and brochure-ready text touting the professionalism of the new Parker LAPD and its significant value to the community:

> Our stockholders, the citizens and taxpayers, have a 20,000,000 dollar-per-year investment in the department. They are entitled to expect the best possible return on that investment. Their dividend is a police service which gives them the greatest protection for the least cost. To merit the confidence of the people of Los Angeles, we must see to it that they have top-notch service for their tax money. In order to do this, we must be constantly aware of the changes in the city's needs and be prepared to make changes and improvements in our organization necessary to keep pace with the city.
>
> We believe we did exactly that in 1950.[47]

The pictures show attractive policemen, predominantly white, looking out for the welfare of children and housewives, also predominantly white. Even at the risk of infringing upon the civil rights of minority populations, the police protected its white constituency, keeping in check, in Parker's own words, the "primitive Congolese" incapable of obeying the rule of law.[48] To this constituency, the demise of Central Avenue represented a victory in the war against miscegenation, vice, narcotics, and related crimes. The high arrest numbers in the Newton Street Division, for example, were proffered as evidence both that the area was a high-crime district and that the LAPD was doing its job efficaciously.

The LAPD propaganda gained the department additional funding—especially for salary increases and more officers (see table 3.4)—and helped it become more autonomous and more attractive to higher-quality recruits. Within the first decade of Chief Parker's tenure, the budget increased almost twofold, and the size of the force grew by 13 percent. By 1956, the LAPD was the best-paid police department in the United States.[49]

Chief Parker received many individual honors as well. In August 1951, the Los Angeles Chamber of Commerce recognized the LAPD for its exceptional efficiency and granted the chief an award for his leadership. In February 1953, the Los Angeles Junior Chamber of Commerce elected Parker "Citizen of the Year." Throughout his tenure, the Los Angeles establishment—in the form of the Chamber of Commerce, the Merchants and Manufacturers Association, the *Los Angeles Times* and *Examiner,* the mayor and city council—valorized Parker. In 1958, Jack Webb, who played Sergeant Friday on *Dragnet,* wrote a hagiographic biography of the chief, *The Badge.* In 1966, Parker suffered a fatal heart attack at an awards ceremony held by the Second Marine Division

Table 3.4. LAPD Expenditures, salaries, numbers of officers, 1950–1959

	Total LAPD expenditure	Salary for police	Allotted number of officers
1950	21,599,298.23	17,727,656.81	4,158
1951	21,747,111.11	17,605,424.12	4,494
1952	28,748,660.12	18,816,576.80	4,494
1953	26,214,277.97	20,869,524.33	4,494
1954	27,379,924.99	21,807,032.22	4,494
1955	29,669,235.32	23,476,411.60	4,494
1956	30,359,434.55	23,811,534.05	4,560
1957	34,159,209.83	26,699,328.03	4,575
1958	36,868,995.33	28,963,060.16	4,708
1959	41,482,009.27	32,294,677.01	4,708

Source: Los Angeles Police Department *Annual Reports* published by the department for the years 1950 through 1959

Association, collapsing just as more than one thousand marines were giving him a standing ovation for his services to the city.[50] The *Los Angeles Times* featured front-page stories on the chief for four days following his death and published numerous tributes, including those from Mayor Sam Yorty, Governor Pat Brown, the attorney general, and city council members.[51]

Although the short-term benefits were many for Chief Parker and his force, the LAPD's success in shutting down Central Avenue proved to be a Pyrrhic victory, with long-term consequences that were disastrous for both the city and the police department. With unemployment at 14 percent among the general black population in the late 1940s and increasing thereafter and with no big spenders pouring cash into the clubs, the stores that lined Central Avenue began to shut down one by one.[52] By eviscerating the cultural heart of the area, the LAPD stamped out the glamour and pride that had once flourished and exacerbated the economic slowdown of South Central. The bitterness and hopelessness that filled the void caused more people to turn to drugs and crime, in effect creating a high-density crime ghetto. Parker's earlier characterization of South Central became a self-fulfilling prophecy thanks in part to his own policies. The tensions created by South Central's worsening socioeconomic conditions and increasingly combative relationship with the police department snowballed and culminated in the Watts riots in 1965. A police arrest set off the riots, and after seven days of burning, looting, and violence that came to an end only after the National Guard was called in, thirty-four people were dead, four thousand had been arrested, and the damage totaled more than $40 million. An independent study from 1967 encapsulated what South Central residents already knew: "[Chief Parker] began to look at the Negro community as an implacable foe." It concluded that "the police in their uniforms seem like the troops of an occupying country to the Negro."[53]

The horrifying outcome of the 1965 riots did not alter the conduct of the LAPD nor its chief. The *Los Angeles Times* reported: "Commenting on . . . allegations of police brutality, Parker retorted that the riots might not have occurred if police hadn't been handling Negroes with 'kid gloves.'"[54] Police brutality continued to be a problem after Parker's death, as his successors helped sustain the macho police culture Parker had done so much to cultivate. As late as the 1990s, violence and anger directed against the LAPD blew up in the African American community following the Rodney King verdict.[55] Mike Davis characterizes Los Angeles in the late twentieth century as the full-fledged realization of Michel Foucault's "carceral city."[56] The panoptic gaze of the establishment has become inescapable with the "imbrication of the police function into the built environment," and the boundaries between the races and classes have become even more rigid with the erection of physical barricades in certain neighborhoods, including along Central Avenue, creating conditions for de facto apartheid.[57]

Central Avenue's Musical Legacy

In terms of American musical heritage, the untimely demise of the Central Avenue scene helped distort the history of jazz and popular music on the West Coast. The brilliance on the Stem was extinguished before the rest of the world had a chance to admire it, so that when the New York critics finally condescended to designate a style of "West Coast jazz," the players from Central Avenue were nowhere to be found and the white purveyors of "cool" jazz came to represent the California scene.

Even before its premature demise, racial preference and East Coast snobbery had conspired to bring about the critical neglect of the Central Avenue music scene. In the years of bustling activity on the Stem, from the early to mid-1940s, Hal Holly's column "Los Angeles Band Briefs" in *Down Beat* reported regularly on the music played by visiting artists at clubs on the Sunset Strip, on Wilshire Boulevard, and in Culver City and very rarely mentioned local talent or Central Avenue clubs. In 1952, when *Down Beat* critic Charles Emge wrote of bop's ascendancy in the Southland, he bypassed the contributions of Central Avenue musicians altogether. He avowed: "The bop movement, or progressive jazz as the musicians probably would prefer to have it tagged, has reached its peak of commercial success at Hermosa Beach where Howard Rumsey, a onetime Kenton bass player, starting with Sunday afternoon sessions a couple of years ago, has gradually built his affairs into a full-time operation."[58] Nesuhi Ertegun, writing for the *Record*

Changer, likewise ignored Central Avenue musicians and credited Rumsey with bringing much-needed innovation to a provincial and backward jazz culture: "It should be remembered, too, that Howard Rumsey more than anyone else made modern jazz a popular success on the West Coast. When in 1948, at a time when practically no modern jazz was to be heard there, he began to present the finest musicians of the new style at the Lighthouse in Hermosa Beach."[59] *Metronome's* Teddy Charles reported that the "young cats [on the Coast] are five or six years behind the eastern level of development," attributing the inferiority of these musicians to "the easy living, goof off environment, etc., in Southern California."[60] In *Billboard's* retrospective on the Los Angeles scene, Dave Dexter anointed Stan Kenton California music's "distinguished messiah" but otherwise remained consistent in omitting any mention of Central Avenue clubs and musicians.[61]

Contrary to the descriptions of West Coast musical life promulgated by the mainstream press, jazz history was being made in the South Central ghetto of Los Angeles throughout the 1940s and early 1950s. In 1945, a few months before Gillespie and Parker's historic stint at Billy Berg's club in Hollywood, Howard McGhee introduced bebop to Central Avenue audiences at the Downbeat, and his later eight-piece lineup included such giants as Charlie Parker and Sonny Criss on alto, Teddy Edwards and Gene Montgomery on tenor, and Roy Porter on drums. Local saxophonist Dexter Gordon, in addition to recording with visiting virtuosos Gillespie and Parker, preserved for posterity a taste of the excitement generated by his legendary cutting sessions with Wardell Gray in the 1947 Dial release *The Chase.* Gray's 1952 Prestige recording featured up-and-coming Angeleno trumpeter Art Farmer and pianist Hampton Hawes. Another rising local star, Charles Mingus, gigged with Buddy Collette in various clubs on Central Avenue and composed the tunes that a decade later would earn him national recognition. Innovators Eric Dolphy and Ornette Coleman languished in semi-obscurity during the 1950s, their avant-garde styles shunned by the resident bands of the now-dominant westside clubs.

Christening the "West Coast sound," a 1953 Contemporary Records release of that name bypassed the contributions of the Central Avenue musicians and heralded the advent of a new group of jazz musicians, primarily white studio players, who congregated at the Lighthouse Café in Hermosa Beach. The musicians on this recording—Shelly Manne, Bud Shank, Joe Mondragon, and Shorty Rogers—as well as others associated with the California cool sound (including Howard Rumsey, Stan Kenton, Gerry Mulligan, and Chet Baker) played a style of jazz that prioritized composing over improvising and contrapuntally intricate ensemble work over solos. With the black bebop-influenced styles of the Central Avenue musicians suppressed, the carefully crafted arrangements of the white westside musicians became emblematic of California jazz, marketed by recording companies as jazz "tanned by the seaside and tempered by the cool Pacific breeze."[62] The diversity of the musical offering in pre-1953 California was nullified by the reductive rubric of "West Coast jazz," with its implications of provincialism and marginality.

Having gigged in clubs on and around Central Avenue with Benny Carter, Charlie Parker, and Charles Mingus, as well as at the Lighthouse with Chet Baker and other cool jazz players during his visits to California, Miles Davis experienced firsthand the unequal treatment the critical establishment, as well as the police, accorded musicians of different races. At the height of the West Coast jazz hype, Davis expressed his frustration at how white critics, not unlike the police, used drugs to besmirch black musicians and boost the white Californian players as the saviors of jazz: "A lot of white critics kept talking about all these white jazz musicians, imitators of us, like they was some great motherfuckers and everything. Talking about Stan Getz, Dave Brubeck, Kai Winding, Lee Konitz, Lennie Tristano, and Gerry Mulligan like they was gods or something. And some of them white guys were junkies like we were, but wasn't nobody writing about that like they was writing about us." Specifically, the success of Chet Baker, who had beat him and Dizzy Gillespie in the *Down Beat* poll for Best Trumpet of 1953, rankled Davis: "What bothered me more than anything was that all the critics were starting to talk about Chet Baker in Gerry Mulligan's band like he was the second coming of Jesus Christ. And him sounding just like me—worse than me even while I was a terrible junkie."[63] Although clubs in Los Angeles, especially those on Central Avenue, offered spaces for interracial music making, racist attitudes colored critical reception, which then hurt the relationships between the musicians.

Today the clubs on Central Avenue are defunct, and graffiti-ridden store-fronts and sweatshops stand mutely where legendary musicians once played. Hatred of the police is a central tenet of the hip-hop culture that has thrived in South Central in the place of jazz and jump blues. Fifty years ago, the music coming out of the Central Avenue clubs, feared by the white establish-ment, celebrated love and good times. In the current hip-hop era, the music that blares out of boom boxes exhorts gangstas to kill cops and to put an end to the oppression of a downtrodden community. Although the collapse of the music scene was not the only factor leading to the deterioration of the area, it precipitated the downward turn and stemmed out of the same racist impulses that affected every aspect of life in postwar Los Angeles. As blues singer Jimmy Witherspoon laments, "It's all gone now . . . nothing left but crack and hardship."[64] Even the memories of Central Avenue's musical heyday are fading away into oblivion, as the old-time musicians pass on to another world.[65]

4. Noir Entanglements

Black Music, White Women, and the Dark City

Because of the location of the film industry in Los Angeles, the battle between black music and the Anglo establishment did not remain a mere local conflict but rather was transferred onto celluloid and broadcast around the world. Throughout its checkered history, Hollywood has held up a mirror, as distorting and one-sided as it may be, that has captured in filmic images and sounds the vicissitudes of race relations in Southern California.

At one time, Hollywood was a relative latecomer to the movie business, entering the field of competition over two decades after Thomas Edison had invented the moving picture technology. According to Lary May, Los Angeles was the ideal setting for the budding mass media industry, with its cheap land, closed shops, moderate climate, and, not least of all, its claim on the myth of a new West, free from the hierarchical and tradition-bound social constraints of the East. Here, immigrants and children of immigrants, mostly of European Jewish origins, could create spectacles that offered working and middle-class Americans glimpses of the liberating possibilities of modern and urban life. In the wake of Mary Pickford and Douglas Fairbanks's phenomenal success, Hollywood stars embodied enticing alternatives to the Victorianism of old, replacing self-denial with conspicuous consumption, the Protestant work ethic with the celebration of leisure and recreation, and nineteenth-century Anglo-Saxon values with modern notions of the melting pot.[1]

Throughout the 1920s and 1930s, American popular culture both spurred and responded to the democratizing, pluralizing tendencies of the times. Even under the watchful eyes of censors and moral crusaders, Hollywood produced films that were inspired by the lower classes and vernacular arts, championed new models of femininity, and even occasionally allowed for romantic relations between whites and nonwhites. In popular music and dance, first the jitterbug and then swing swept across the nation, bringing together black and white musicians and fans in limited but potentially revolutionary contexts. World War II swung the pendulum back: in the place of Benny Goodman's integrated bands, Glenn Miller's patriotic, all-white orchestra came to symbolize nostalgia for an imagined America; wartime consensus was made manifest in films that showed ethnic minorities only if they assimilated seamlessly into an idealized Anglo-Saxon mold.[2]

The social, political, and economic instability of the postwar period made its impact felt on the country as a whole and on the film industry more specifically. Those coming home from the battlefront adapted with difficulty to civilian life in a country that had been altered irrevocably in the war years. Soldiers returned to urban centers ravaged by racial strife, caused in large part by widespread migration to the cities by minorities during the boom and the resultant white panic. Women, having grown accustomed to working outside of the home, retreated to the domestic sphere and gave up their newly earned independence only with great reluctance. The economic boom of the war years sagged as war production came to an abrupt halt.

The problems confronting postwar America were magnified many times over in Los Angeles. Because the region had won the lion's share of government contracts during the war, the economic slowdown that followed was felt more excruciatingly here than in the rest of the country. New Angelenos, who had arrived in the city during a time of tremendous expansion, now found themselves without work and often targeted in the establishment's crusade to conserve the city's prewar socioeconomic status quo. The Zoot Suit riots of 1943 and the wartime internment of Japanese Angelenos were only the most sensational occurrences in a city torn asunder by police brutality against minorities, white flight into new municipalities designed to be exclusive domains of the white bourgeoisie, and the subsequent ghettoization of the inner city occupied by the nonwhite poor.[3] Added to this widening rift in the social fabric was the paranoia that settled on Hollywood as the House Un-American Activities Committee (HUAC) hearings of 1947 and 1951 to 1952 destroyed careers and relationships and ushered in an era of industry-wide blacklists. The Supreme Court ruling of 1948 ordering the breakup of the studio system, and the decline in ticket sales following the advent of television led inexorably to the end of Hollywood's Golden Age.

A new genre, film noir, articulated the anxieties that pervaded American society in the Cold War period. Gone was the utopic picture, circulated by real-estate speculators and boosters, of sun-drenched Los Angeles as the place where dreams come true, and installed in its vacuum were the images of a dystopic netherworld of moral contingency and fallen heroes. According to Mike Davis, noir (literary and cinematic) is only the most outstanding example from a tradition of critique that has shadowed L.A.'s booster culture from the very beginning: "A fantastic convergence of American 'tough-guy' realism, Weimar expressionism, and existentialized Marxism—all focused on unmasking a 'bright, guilty place' . . . called Los Angeles."[4] Hollywood's new West, which in the second decade of the twentieth century seemed to offer infinite possibilities for self-fulfillment, devolved in the noir decade into a deadly site of uncontrolled passions and potential annihilation.

Black Film, Black Music

Starting with the striking visual clash between light and dark that defines the noir genre, binary oppositions permeate every level of the filmic discourse, from overt plays of contrasts to symbolic representations of difference. Good confronts evil, utopia and dystopia lie in close proximity, male and female subjectivities collide, night intrudes upon day, self and other occupy a realm in which reality is distorted beyond recognition by shadows and fantastic visions.[5] Noir's peculiar black and white world was produced through visual and narrative elements emphasizing polarity. Soundtracks amplified these chiaroscuro effects by exploiting music's connotative and affective properties. Specifically, black music—jazz and other related popular idioms—was used in film noirs of the mid-1940s to the early 1950s as an aural foil to the Wagnerian orchestral film scores that constituted the norm in the soundtracks of the classic film era. As a marker of difference, of darkness, black music was reserved for moments of heightened drama, for scenes in which the noir side of the binary schemata exerted its dominance. In particular, black music came to signal female transgressions, anticipating, accompanying, or even prodding the female protagonist to succumb to the evil forces immanent in her surroundings.

From the very beginning of the film industry, African Americans and other nonwhites were underrepresented and rarely accorded subjectivity in movies. The internal censorship body created by the Motion Pictures Producers and Distributors of America in 1930, the Production Code Administration, expunged pejorative references to ethnic and racial groups from Hollywood productions, leaving behind only bland stereotypes of nonwhite characters at the periphery of filmic narratives. Depression-era social movements and the wartime demand for national unity had helped bring about some measure of progress in race relations, but once the fighting ceased, many of the recently implemented liberal policies in the political and cultural arenas were scaled back. Hollywood, facing declining profits, likewise retreated from the more integrationist movies of the war era to fall back on familiar strategies of racial exclusion.[6]

While the actual presence of African Americans remained minimal on the screen, black music was featured regularly in movies starting as early as 1927 with Al Jolson performing in blackface in the first "talkie," *The Jazz Singer.* In musicals (*High Society,* 1956), biopics of musicians (*Young Man with a Horn,* 1950), and historical treatments of musical styles (*The Birth of the Blues,* 1941), black music was appropriated, "whitewashed," and repackaged by Hollywood filmmakers who seemed unable or unwilling to acknowledge the centrality of African Americans in the creation of America's popular music.[7] The cooptation and misrepresentation of certain genres of music point to deeper tensions. Caryl Flinn argues, "Because music's relationship to the image is constructed, it is clear that it must be constructed and arbitrated *by* something—and one would assume that ideology provides such an arbitrating force." Flinn further posits that "the ideology of race can affect scoring practices" and that "the presumed norm around which this early film music was organized . . . was not universal, but decidedly white and masculine."[8]

As Robert Porfirio points out, jazz had been associated with the triad of death, drugs, and sex from the very beginning of the film noir cycle. Porfirio describes a classic scene from *Phantom Lady* (1944) in which jazz is equated with sex. The heroine, "Kansas," poses as a tart and pretends to be interested in drummer Cliff Milburn in order to glean information from him that could save the life of her boss, the true object of her love. Her pursuit of Cliff sends her into an underground jazz jam session, and the ensuing sequence, comprised of frenetically fast music and visual tricks betraying German expressionist influence, communicates unambiguously how far the virtuous heroine is willing to transgress normal boundaries of propriety to help her boss. Cliff's drum solo crescendos into a frenzied musical orgasm—real for Cliff, feigned for Kansas. Other films use jazz in analogous ways. In *D.O.A.* (1950), protagonist Frank Bigelow is poisoned in a bar that features a jazz combo. As black musicians grimace comically and palpitate to the rhythmic excitement generated by the music, unknown blonde women make sexual advances on Bigelow, and a mysterious stranger slips a deadly substance into his glass of bourbon.[9] Ava Gardner's femme fatale character in *The Killers* (1946), Kitty Collins, appears in three notable scenes that are accompanied by a jazz piano: her first scene, in which she meets Swede, the protagonist; her second, in which Swede becomes her fall guy and takes the rap for her misdemeanor; and her penultimate scene, in which her duplicity in her relations with Swede becomes apparent. In *Detour* (1945), the main character, Al, a jazz pianist, begins his nostalgic flashback with the pleasurable memory of his fiancée, Sue, singing the song "I Can't Believe That You're in Love with Me." Instead of meeting up with Sue in Los Angeles as anticipated, he has the bad luck of running en route into Haskell and Vera, who prove to be insurmountable obstacles in his quest for a happy reunion with Sue. In the prisonlike motel room he is forced to share with Vera, Al is tormented by a discordant saxophone melody that drifts in through an open window. Sue's mellifluous music has been transformed into a saxophone's pained wail as Al struggles to escape the clutches of Sue's evil counterpart, Vera.[10]

During and immediately following World War II, black music often provided the backdrop against which the various constituents of Los Angeles culture questioned and negotiated the existing social parameters. The racial mixing on South Central's Central Avenue, as well as the prosperity endowed on the surrounding neighborhood by nightclub patronage, threatened a power structure that sought to maintain ideological control through the segregation and impoverishment of minority communities. As outlined in chapter 3, the growing polarization in the city as a whole—of whites on the one hand and nonwhites on the other—was forcibly replicated and maintained in this musical hub through the deployment of the police and other technologies of social control.

At the peak of Central Avenue's musical efflorescence, members of the Hollywood aristocracy regularly patronized the clubs along its main strip to delight in the exoticism of black music and dance and found themselves embroiled in the turf battles between the police and musicians. For many Hollywood insiders, then, black music carried connotations of difference, fear, and violence—a potent combination ripe for filmic exploitation.[11]

In her seminal work on film music, Claudia Gorbman proposes that "music signifies in films not only according to pure musical codes, but also according to *cultural* musical codes and *cinematic* musical codes," cultural codes that are informed by preexistent cultural associations of certain musical styles and cinematic codes set up by the filmic context.[12] Black music's place in the sociocultural life of Los Angeles encoded associations of danger and excitement into its sounds; the exploitation of these cultural codes in specific filmic contexts assigned it additional levels of meaning. Through analyses of the interplay and elaboration of the different levels of musical codes—musical, cultural, and cinematic—in *Double Indemnity* and *The Postman Always Rings Twice,* two classic film noirs, and *The Blue Gardenia,* a later and lesser known work, I argue that black music played an integral role in film noir by projecting onto the soundtrack the fears of the white masculine subject as he loses his bearing in his environment and in his relationships with feminine and racial others. Whether or not these filmmakers intended to critique Cold War conservatism, they used black music in various subtle and not so subtle ways to express the complex of feelings—from pleasure to revulsion—surrounding urbanity, modernity, and sexuality in the noir decade. These films, distributed and exhibited in theaters around the country, popularized and national-ized attitudes about race and ethnicity particular at first to California. By participating in a discourse that reasserted the polarization between racial groups and genders, film noir helped propagate an ideology that justified the suppression of black music, associated with danger and miscegenation, and the suburbanization and containment of white women.

Two Women, Two Musics in Double Indemnity

Both *Double Indemnity* and *The Postman Always Rings Twice* are based on the prewar novels of James M. Cain. *Postman*, published in 1934, together with Horace McCoy's 1935 *They Shoot Horses, Don't They?*, established a new type of *roman noir*, the Los Angeles novel, "a regional fiction obsessively concerned with puncturing the bloated image of Southern California as the golden land of opportunity and fresh start."[13] Cain, McCoy, and later Los Angeles novelists such as Raymond Chandler, Nathanael West, and Dashiell Hammett charac-terized the city as a place of broken dreams, peopled by scheming deviants and desperate losers. Their impressions of Depression-era L.A. became fodder for the film studios, which starting in the mid-1940s produced a string of dark, cynical pictures that compose the film noir cycle.

Billy Wilder's *Double Indemnity* (1944), based on Cain's novella written in 1935, helped launch the noir trend with its box-office success and critical ac-claim. As the original "black film," Wilder's picture displays all the hallmarks of the new genre: sex, murder, deceit, betrayal, and stylized visual effects playing up the contrasts between light and dark. Another defining feature of film noir, which has received less notice and commentary and is evident in *Double Indemnity*, is the distinctive style with which race and ethnicity are transmuted and exploited.

In "The Whiteness of Film Noir," Eric Lott, attempting to redress the lack of critical attention on "film noir's insistent thematizing of spiritual and cin-ematic darkness by way of bodies beyond the pale," writes: "Film noir is re-plete with characters of color who populate and signify the shadows of white American life in the 1940s. Noir may have pioneered Hollywood's merciless exposure of white pathology, but by relying on race to convey that pathology, it in effect erected a cordon sanitaire around the circle of corruption it sought to penetrate. Film noir rescues with racial idioms the whites whose moral and social boundaries seem in doubt. 'Black film' is the refuge of whiteness."[14] Lott catalogues the various ways in which blackness is deployed as a symbol of moral decay in *Double Indemnity*. For example, as the protagonist, Walter Neff (Fred MacMurray), narrates the events that have led to his moral degeneration, the blood stain from his shoulder wound, which appears black on screen, grows ever larger. Lott also calls attention to the ethnic and racial others who stand at the margins of the unfolding drama—Charlie the black garage attendant and Lou Schwartz (which, incidentally, means "black" in Yiddish), Neff's Jewish colleague, who serve as alibis; the black custodians who work in the insurance company offices in the dark of the night; the Greek American Sam Garlopis, who tries to swindle the insurance company with a fraudulent claim—to argue that "moral rot is quite unself-consciously aligned with nonnormative Americanness in *Double Indemnity*."[15]

Most significantly, the femme fatale, Phyllis Dietrichson (Barbara Stanwyck), is shown from the beginning to be linked to ethnic and racial signifiers. She first appears at the top of the stairs having just come in from sunbathing, darkening her skin. As she descends the stairs, the camera zooms in on the "slave bracelet" she wears on her ankle, an object that becomes the fetishistic focal point in several later scenes. In the end, Phyllis is discovered to be a "black widow," a woman who marries and murders wealthy men for financial profit.[16] The white male protagonist's submission to her evil schemes and his subsequent downfall are signaled through the increasing use of shadows and other visual devices emphasizing darkness, through the mise-en-scène, and, I would add, through the deployment of cultural codes conveyed in different types of music.

Miklós Rózsa's score plays in the background for approximately half of *Double Indemnity*. In addition, there are two scenes in which the music is diegetic, that is, in which music plays within the realm of filmic action (so that the characters, as well as the audience, hear the music). Because the diegetic soundtrack consists of familiar works, it stands in relief against Rózsa's original score. In the first scene containing diegetic music, Neff sits on the grass with Lola, the murdered Dietrichson's daughter (and Phyllis's stepdaughter), in the Hollywood Hills. An orchestra in the Hollywood Bowl concert shell, looming in the distant background, plays Schubert's Unfinished Symphony. Glancing over at Lola, Neff notices her tear-stained face and asks what is troubling her. She tells him that she has been following her ex-boyfriend Nino Zachetti and has caught him visiting Phyllis's house night after night. She suspects he is having an affair with Phyllis and was an accomplice in her father's murder. She begins to cry again and admits that she still loves Nino. The camera rests on Neff's face, and as the music continues in the background, his voice-over articulates his thoughts at this moment: "Zachetti. That's funny. Phyllis and Zachetti. What was he doing up at her house? I couldn't figure that one out. I tried to make sense of it and got nowhere." Lola emerges, at this point in the narrative, as a "good kid," in Neff's words, and Phyllis, by contrast, as a duplicitous and treacherous woman.

The screenplay indicates that César Franck's D-Minor Symphony was originally intended as the background music in this scene.[17] Rózsa's later recollections suggest that the Schubert symphony may have served as an inspiration for the film's score: "When Billy [Wilder] and I discussed the music, he had the idea of using a restless string figure (as in the opening of Schubert's Unfinished Symphony) to reflect the conspiratorial activities of the two lovers against the husband; it was a good idea and I happily accepted it as a basis to work on."[18] Both the Franck and the Schubert symphonies are in minor keys and portray somber emotions with broad strokes in a Romantic style. Since the scene is borne out of Neff's memory, the music reflects his state of mind during his conversation with Lola. Even as he maintains a stoic visage, the music evinces Neff's inner agitation caused by Lola's distress and her revelation of Phyllis's perfidious actions.

The scene makes use of most of the development section of Schubert's first movement, starting in measure 117 with the pianissimo descent of the low strings and ending in measure 196 following a double sforzando chord right before the lead-in to the recapitulation. The music sets up a mood of anticipation that builds to an agitato climax. The upper strings enter with a four-measure theme, a gesture of yearning, which repeats over a foreboding tremolo in the low strings; the strings are then joined by the winds, climbing higher and higher and growing in intensity until they arrive on a C-sharp minor chord in measure 146. The use of hemiola beginning in measure 134 adds to the feeling of dislocation and anxiety. After a diminuendo over four bars, the offbeat accompanimental figure, first heard with the lyrical, major-key second subject, provides a short respite from the tumultuous fulmination of the rest of the development. This tender gesture can be heard as an expression of Neff's feeling of genuine affection for the distraught young woman. The four measures of a loud chord, followed by a diminuendo, alternate with the four measures of the quieter second-subject accompanimental figure twice more. Finally, the orchestra pulls out all the stops and plays the opening theme in fortissimo in various guises as Neff tries to come to terms with Phyllis's infidelity and his own guilt.

The second scene with diegetic music takes place in Phyllis's house. The first time Neff sees the residence, he describes it as a Spanish-style home, typical in Los Angeles during this time, and notes the sweet smell of honeysuckle emanating from it. In the last scene in the house, now enveloped in nocturnal darkness, Neff sheds any vestigial illusions he may have had about the sincerity of Phyllis's love for him, and the house, a metaphor of the California Dream with its Spanish pretensions and mortgaged grandeur, has become a deadly trap. As Neff confronts Phyllis, sitting in darkness and armed with a gun hidden under the cushion, the lilting melody of the popular tune "Tangerine" wafts in through the window.

The breezy dance tune seems at first listen to provide a background mood ill-suited to the dark and tense face-off between the two characters, suggesting that it was perhaps chosen for what Michel Chion calls music's "anempathetic" qualities, music's ability to exhibit "conspicuous indifference to the situation, by progressing in a steady, undaunted and ineluctable manner: the scene takes place against this very backdrop of 'indifference.'"[19] Closer scrutiny, however, reveals hidden meaning in the song that makes it particularly relevant for this scene. Although the swing band rendition of "Tangerine" used here is instrumental, audiences viewing the film in 1944 would have most likely remembered the lyrics for this song, a big hit in 1942, when it made its screen debut in Paramount's musical *The Fleet's In,* with the Jimmy Dorsey Orchestra performing the song.[20] The song, composed by Victor Schertzinger with lyrics by Johnny Mercer, portrays a captivating woman:

> South American stories tell of a girl who's quite a dream
> The beauty of her race.
> Though you doubt all the stories
> And think the tales are just a bit extreme,
> Wait till you see her face.
>
> *Refrain*
> Tangerine
> She is all they claim
> With her eyes of night and lips as bright as flame
> Tangerine
> When she dances by
> Señoritas stare and caballeros sigh.
> And I've seen
> Toasts to Tangerine
> Raised in ev'ry bar across the Argentine,
> Yes, she has them all on the run
> But her heart belongs to just one
> Her heart belongs to Tangerine.[21]

Tangerine is Phyllis's fictional alter-ego, a woman of irresistible and dangerous beauty, who entices all yet loves only herself. Her allure and inaccessibility reside in her racial exoticism; her face contains, with its "eyes of night and lips as bright as flame," noir's opposing tropes of light and dark. In a filmic discourse that flattened the individuality of nonwhite characters into one-dimensional caricatures—the other to the white male subject with whom the audience should identify—the differences between various ethnic signifiers are collapsed and conflated. Phyllis Dietrichson is at once black and Latin, just as *Lady from Shanghai*'s Elsa Bannister embodies both Chinese and Mexican qualities.[22] The band plays the tune like a sentimental dance number, inflected by the sweet style of contemporary popular music.[23] The swing song, with its connections to black culture, carries conventional associations of jazz with the dancing body and therefore with excessive sexuality.[24] It was Neff's sexual desire that led him to this confrontation, and the sexual ambience created by the black music, like the smell of honeysuckle in the air, finally discomfits him with its cloying sweetness.

It is not the sound of the music alone that provides affective cues. The relationship of "Tangerine" to the Schubert symphony—its status as the other to the normative music redolent of European Romanticism—is just as crucial in setting up expectations of danger and signaling malevolent intentions. The film contextualizes its source music in such a way that the cultural codes associated with each style, informed by a racist bourgeois ideology, become prioritized. The Schubert symphony personifies Lola, a young woman with a genteel background, whose virtue must be protected. "Tangerine" is identified with Phyllis, a social climber and a self-serving seductress. Lola's apparent goodness provides the foil to Phyllis's ever more discernible evil, just as the Schubert excerpt acts as a foil to the jazz tune. In the perennial opposition between the female archetypes of "the deadly seductress and the rejuvenating redeemer," Lola is clearly identified, by Neff's words and visual imageries, as the woman for whom we should feel sympathy.[25]

Although Neff is badly wounded in the "Tangerine" scene, he lives long enough to tell his story and thereby retains subjective control over the narration. It is his interpretation of events, his views and perceptions, that are imparted with the appropriate use of lighting and music. Moreover, even though Neff's body collapses at the end of the film, the white masculine subject position remains intact and is merely transferred to another white male. Claims agent Barton Keyes, Neff's colleague and father figure, appears toward the end of Neff's confession into a Dictaphone. Throughout the film, Keyes's character is established as the upholder of societal norms, the guardian of rules and laws, charged with the task of proving that Dietrichson was murdered and of delivering the guilty party to justice. Keyes is more "male" and "white" than Neff—earlier in the film, we hear that he has shunned women and marriage and see him putting the Greek Garlopis in his rightful ethnic place. By addressing his confession to Keyes and collapsing in his arms, Neff hands Keyes the subject baton, ensuring that law and order will prevail. With this final gesture, *Double Indemnity* allays the anxieties and fears stirred up during the course of its narration, showing the triumph of good over evil, reinscribing traditional gender and racial hierarchies, and bringing closure to the dark tale with the dawning of a new day.[26]

Erasure and Reconstitution of Ethnicity in *The Postman Always Rings Twice*

Cain's other Los Angeles crime novella, *The Postman Always Rings Twice,* is at its very core a story driven by racial subtexts. In the first conversation between the two principle protagonists, Cora insists upon her whiteness even as Frank agrees upon it from the first:

> "You think I'm Mex."
> "Nothing like it."
> "Yes you do. You're not the first one. Well, get this. I'm just as white as you are, see? I may have dark hair and look a little that way, but I'm just as white as you are. You want to get along good around here, you won't forget that."
> "Why, you don't look Mex."
> "I'm telling you. I'm just as white as you are."

Frank postulates that "it was being married to the Greek that made her feel she wasn't white."[27] After they fall in love, Cora explains her attraction to Frank, implicitly contrasting him to her husband, Nick Papadakis, with his repulsive ethnic characteristics: "And you're hard all over. Big and tall and hard. And your hair is light. You're not a little soft greasy guy with black kinky hair that he puts bay rum on every night."[28] When Nick presses Cora to give him a child, Cora makes up her mind to get rid of him and tells Frank, "I can't have no greasy Greek child, Frank. I can't, that's all. The only one I can have a child by is you."[29] Their love affair and the resultant murder of Cora's husband, the central narrative events of the novella, grow directly out of Cora's need to whiten her own racial identity, as well as that of her offspring, by attaching herself to the unmistakably Anglo Frank and by distancing herself from the darkness embodied in Nick's person.

Such an overt dramatization of racial tension, even if based on observations of actual social relations in Los Angeles during this time, would have violated the spirit of race blindness regulated and enforced by Hollywood's Production Code. In the film version of *Postman,* race and its concomitant social fears were elliptically exploited at the subtextual level. In the 1946 MGM film adaptation directed by Tay Garnett, Cora is played by Lana Turner and Nick by Cecil Kellaway, appearing as just an ordinary white guy, older and less physically attractive than John Garfield's Frank, but white nevertheless and even bearing the respectable WASP last name of Smith (which was Cora's maiden name in the book). In her first appearance, Cora lights up the screen in an all-white outfit that shows off her curves and long legs. Her blond hair, which surrounds her irradiated face like a halo, is a conventional marker used in film noir to at first suggest purity and whiteness and later sexual promiscuity and feminine depravity.[30] With the absence of the racial subtext, Cora's lust for sex and money becomes the propelling force that advances the story.

Although Nick's ethnicity is bleached out from the actual person, his music marks him as an alien other, a threat to the happiness of the beautiful protagonists. At key moments in the film, Nick is moved to sing. The first time he sings, the three main characters are gathered together for the evening. There is already a sense of growing tension as stolen looks and body language betray the magnetic attraction between Frank and Cora. In the book, Nick sings an unnamed song with "a big tenor," not unlike Caruso.[31] In the film, he pulls out his guitar and at Cora's prodding launches into an amateurish and amiable performance of "She's Funny That Way." He sings:

> I'm not much to look at,
> Nothing to see.
> Just glad I'm living,
> Lucky to be.
> I've got a woman crazy for me,
> She's funny that way.

The song is immediately recognized by Frank and the viewer as an ironic commentary on the developing situation. Nick is indeed "not much to look at"; contrary to the song lyrics, however, Cora is obviously not crazy for him and is visibly flustered by Frank's attentions.

Analyzing the soundtracks of contemporary cinema, Anahid Kassabian notes that popular music produces meaning differently than classical music in the context of film: "Pop songs sometimes enter into meaning production through language . . . , but most often depend broadly on the identities of the musical genre's audience and on identification processes between the music and the perceiver that took place before the film."[32] Since appearing as a hit song in 1928, "She's Funny That Way" (Richard Whiting/Neil Moret) had become a frequently played jazz standard. In 1944, Ike Quebec scored a hit record with this tune; in 1945, Bill Harris followed with another jazz hit record featuring this song; a year later, a recording of the Jazz at the Philharmonic concert with Billie Holiday's rendition was released.[33] These musical precedents have attached themselves to the song, coding it as "black" for the film's contemporary audiences. Nick's recitation of the song marks him as the other, the odd man out in the threesome. After he sings, Nick pushes Frank and Cora closer together, urging them to dance with one another, and accompanies the Latin tune playing on the jukebox. Again an exotic music facilitates and naturalizes the coupling of Frank and Cora and the exclusion of Nick (and as in *Double Indemnity*, the exotic music consists of the conflation of black and Latin sounds and associations).

A little later in the film, Nick sings "She's Funny That Way" in the shower, right before Frank and Cora's first attempt to murder him. The irony of the text is amplified under such extreme circumstances—she's so crazy about him she tries to kill him! His singing becomes increasingly boisterous and, during his third singing bout, comes to approach nonsensical gibberish because of his drunken state. As he pauses for breath in his last absurd musical performance, Frank deals him a murderous blow, rendering Nick's exclusion and silence absolute. The coded music, then, acts as a surrogate for the more explicit ethnic markers in the novella and, in the morally skewed world of Frank and Cora, justifies their affair and crime.

In the end, Cora meets a violent death as well, as the car Frank is driving collides into an oncoming truck. Having sated her sexual lust, Cora had taken complete control, making over her deceased husband's roadside diner to bring in big profits and threatening to withdraw her love from Frank. The liberated woman is destroyed and Frank is sent to the gas chamber for her murder. As in *Double Indemnity*, the narration is in the male protagonist's voice and in the confessional mode. Representatives of the patriarchal order provide the restorative closure at the end: District Attorney Sackett (who was the Jewish Katz in the novella) takes control over Frank's body, and a white Catholic priest, the auditor of Frank's confession, claims guardianship of his soul.

Bending Noir Conventions in *The Blue Gardenia*

Released in 1953, Fritz Lang's *The Blue Gardenia* departs from the film noir conventions detailed above in several significant ways. Lang purportedly made the film immediately following a dry spell that he attributed to a McCarthyist attempt to blacklist him. Although never a registered member of the Communist Party, Lang had shown a predisposition toward social critiques in his films and was therefore vulnerable in the cultural battles being waged in the film industry, which culminated with the HUAC hearings. In response to the comment that *The Blue Gardenia* "is a particularly venomous picture of American life," Lang explained, "The only thing I can tell you about it is that it was the first picture after the McCarthy business, and I had to shoot it in 20 days. Maybe that's what made me so venomous."[34] In *The Blue Gardenia,* protagonist Norah Larkin (Anne Baxter) is unsure of whether she is actually guilty of the murder of Harry Prebble (Raymond Burr)—not unlike Lang, who believed he was punished for a crime he did not to his knowledge commit.

The noir elements that permeate *The Blue Gardenia* follow noir conventions in form but not entirely in substance. The most pronounced departure, and one that E. Ann Kaplan has examined in depth, is the foregrounding of a feminine discourse, running in parallel to the masculine one. The feminist angle makes for significantly different characterizations of the protagonists and brings to the film a tone of progressive critique.[35] As Kaplan points out, the women's world that Norah shares with her female roommates and co-workers is brightly lit, warm with camaraderie, whereas the men's world, Prebble's apartment and Casey Mayo's office in particular, is menacing, shot in stylized noir fashion to emphasize weird shapes and shadows. Dubbed the "Blue Gardenia"—a symbol of exotic femininity—Norah is portrayed by the male-controlled police and press as a typical femme fatale: clad in black taffeta, sexually promiscuous, and frustratingly unknowable.[36] Having followed the story through Norah's eyes, the viewer comprehends that she in fact contradicts the femme fatale archetype in all the important ways: she is generous and affectionate with her friends, was unduly devoted to a man who ended up abandoning her, and if she had actually killed Prebble, it was in an act of self-defense, not of self-advancement. The male protagonist, Casey Mayo (Richard Conte), on the other hand, is shown to be an attention-monger who does not hesitate to trick Norah into ensnaring herself by pretending to be a sympathetic friend.

In the end, Mayo does play a hand in discovering the truth, thereby proving Norah's innocence. Waiting at an airport for a flight, Mayo notices the piped music playing in the background and asks his companion, Al, "What's that?" Al responds, "Music. They can everything these days." The music is in fact Richard Wagner's "Liebestod," Isolde's love-death aria, which triggers Mayo's memory. He remembers that in Norah's recounting of the events that transpired on the evening of Prebble's death, a phonograph recording of "The Blue Gardenia" was playing while she was in the victim's apartment, yet when the maid discovered Prebble's body the next morning, Wagner's "Liebestod" was on the phonograph instead. Mayo and the police trace the Wagner recording back to a record shop where they find the real killer, Rose (another flower name), a woman seen earlier on the phone with Prebble. Janet Bergstrom suggests that Rose stands in as Norah's double, resembling the heroine in superficial details. According to the criminal justice system, merciless and arbitrary in Lang's representation, it is only because Rose is guilty that Norah can be innocent. Music, the only hard evidence pointing at the truth, proves to be the essential differentiator between the two women.[37]

Music, like other elements in this film, is used in both conventional and subversive ways. As in *Double Indemnity*, two different musical works (one European, the other black) are identified with two women (one guilty, the other innocent). In this case, however, the European work, Wagner's über-Romantic "Liebestod," is associated with the guilty Rose, who personifies the stereotype of the scorned woman, and Nat King Cole's song "The Blue Gardenia" with Norah, who is not only innocent of murder but is presumably sexually chaste as well. Further, although both pieces are heard on recordings in Prebble's apartment, the Wagner is shown to have originated in a record shop and is thus reduced to a commodity (and even airport Muzak), whereas "The Blue Gardenia" is first heard in a live performance by Cole in the nightclub scene.

Cole's performance is remarkable in and of itself. In a genre that has consistently minimized black presence, Cole is given almost three minutes of face time on the screen, and his name appears prominently in the opening credits of the film. Before the rock and roll invasion of the mid-1950s, Cole was one of the biggest African American crossover sensations, with mainstream hits like "Mona Lisa" and "Unforgettable" to his credit. Krin Gabbard contends that Cole's physical presence on television and on the big screen could be tolerated only after his music had been erased of all traces of jazz, that is, "blackness," and his public persona had been emasculated and stripped of any sexual suggestiveness.[38] Cole himself attributed his universal popularity to his abandonment of jazz and the adoption of a style that owed more to white arrangers like Pete Rugolo, trained by Darius Milhaud, than to contemporary black bebop or rhythm and blues musicians.[39] "The Blue Gardenia," then, is "whitewashed" music sung by a black musician in "whiteface."

But that is not really the whole story. Being a black celebrity in the postwar era and having broken the color barrier, Cole could not help but find himself enmeshed in the racial conflicts that plagued pre–civil rights American society. In 1948, when Cole and his wife, Maria, were considering buying a home in the affluent neighborhood of Hancock Park in Los Angeles, Hancock Park residents organized to block their purchase and hassled the couple with racial epithets and displays of violence. In a well-publicized showdown, the

Coles stood their ground and bought their dream house, while their new neighbors unsuccessfully tried to challenge and reverse the recent ruling of the U.S. Supreme Court finding housing covenants unconstitutional.[40] A few years after his appearance in *The Blue Gardenia,* Cole was again caught in the middle of a race incident when he was attacked onstage by members of the White Citizens Council during a 1956 concert in Birmingham, Alabama. In the storm of controversy that followed, Cole tried to maintain political neutrality, but as one of the few African Americans in the national cultural limelight, he was eventually pressured to take a stance in support of the burgeoning civil rights movement.[41] His personal history therefore embraces contradictions and ambiguities that defy hard and fast racial or political categorization.

Because "The Blue Gardenia," a rather generic love ballad, was composed especially for the film and sung by an artist who occupied an ambiguous position racially in public life, the song proves to be capable of taking on multiple meanings, acting as a "sliding signifier" in the film.[42] The song is first heard in Cole's live performance in the nightclub scene, presented by a black body in an environment replete with exotic markers. The club, also called The Blue Gardenia, is decorated in a Polynesian style, the waiters are Asian, the flower seller is a blind woman, and Norah imbibes a tropical drink called Polynesian Pearl Divers with uncharacteristic abandon. When a detective claims that the waiter remembers Norah as being blonde because, "to Oriental men, all beautiful women are blonde," it is unclear whether Lang is making an ironic statement or merely perpetuating a pernicious stereotype. The second time the song is heard, Norah and Prebble are back in his apartment. The music grows more menacing as Prebble's sexual advances become increasingly aggressive and finally escalate into violence. So far, the black music is associated with alcohol, sex, and violence in conventional ways. The next hearing of the song, however, turns around the associative meaning of the song. As Mayo and Norah talk in the café, the song plays on the jukebox, and this time, the song indicates a real developing tenderness on Mayo's part for the troubled heroine. The song, heard without the disturbing visual presence of a black body, becomes just a romantic ballad and nothing more.

Lang makes ambiguous the narrative ending as well. Norah's innocence is restored, but we are left in doubt about the validity of a society in which an innocent woman escapes sexual violence and capital punishment only by sheer luck. Although there are hints of a blossoming relationship with Mayo, it is the women's world to which Norah returns triumphantly in the end. By adopting noir conventions, including the use of certain types of music, and then subsequently negating their traditional signification, *The Blue Gardenia* offers the possibility, even if only a limited one, of an oppositional stance, of a point of view that resists and subverts the dominant ideology. *The Blue Gardenia,* released nine years after *Double Indemnity* and only a year after the latest round of the HUAC inquisition, shows the fissures in the ideological construction of the film noir cycle, portraying a world where the lines demarcating the two halves of the dualistic order are blurred and penetrable.

Confronting socioeconomic conditions that marked a rupture from the prewar period, Hollywood manufactured and purveyed an ill-defined but palpable mood of anxiety and fantastical imaginaries of psychosis with the film noir cycle. At first glance, these dark films seem to affirm the conservative ideology that prevailed in Los Angeles during the second half of the 1940s and into the 1950s. Ethnic and racial others were pushed aside to the barely visible periphery, their actual presence sublimated into music and other less visible signifiers conjoined to the sexuality and destruction of fallen women. The wartime incursion of women and racial minorities in the public sphere was felt as a serious threat to the sacrosanct institution of the white middle-class family, and film noir provided a fantasy outlet in which beautiful women and black music titillated but in the end were summarily disposed of.

But as Mike Davis and others argue, noir was also a means of critiquing the existing power structure and calling attention to the feelings of alienation engendered by the threatening cityscapes of Los Angeles and other modern metropolises. Many of the artists involved in the production of these films, including Billy Wilder, John Garfield, and Fritz Lang, leaned in different degrees to the political left and employed signature noir techniques to get around the increasingly meddlesome scrutiny of the censors. Even cold-blooded killers like Cora Smith and Phyllis Dietrichson win our grudging admiration with their ability to rise above the limitations of a patriarchal system that offers them few real choices. Walter Neff opts for what looks to be the only way out of a life-draining existence in a city overtaken by corporate malfeasance and indifference. In another film noir classic, *Sunset Boulevard* (1950), Wilder, turning a critical eye to the film industry itself, tells a story in which the alluring but ultimately empty promises of the new West—fame and glory—drive the protagonists to madness and death. Often in noir, seemingly ordinary people find themselves in hostile situations and environments they can escape only by resorting to crime.[43]

Even with these inherent ambiguities, film noirs treat certain themes with insistent frequency and consistency. The reiteration of the link between black music and taboo sexuality, for one, serves to reinforce the conservative regional and national agenda of the Cold War era. Even as film noir directors and cinematographers experimented with new techniques, the sound departments of the major studios were notoriously slow in keeping up with innovations in the musical field. As excoriated by émigré composer Hanns Eisler in *Composing for the Films,* film soundtracks during this time remained largely conservative, recycling clichéd phrases overflowing with pseudo-Romantic sentiments. Eisler lamented in 1947: "Every genuine innovation meets with opposition that manifests itself not as censorship, but as inertia, as the rule of 'common sense' in a thousand little matters, or as respect for allegedly irrefutable experience."[44] The black music employed in Hollywood was almost always old-fashioned (it is interesting to note that black musicians like Louis Armstrong and Nat King Cole appeared on film rather than the younger and more modern Dizzy Gillespie or Charlie Parker), mediated by white studio musicians and arrangers, and conformed to dominant ideological constructions. Aesthetically and politically, then, music in film noirs was often animated by an intransigent spirit of reactionary conservatism that undermined the more progressive critical messages of the filmmakers.

The music discussed in the above films was chosen to add texture to the narration and the visual spectacle through its association with cultural and racial codes. The music's conjunction with filmic images of fallen women and menacing cityscapes in turn multiplied its associative meanings. Black music thus became both accessory and victim in the postwar project of reconstituting the patriarchal power structure in Southern California and the rest of the United States.

5. From the Mission Myth to Chicano Nationalism

The Evolution of Mestizo Identities and Music

From the beginning of the United States' occupation of California, race relations in this western outpost were much too complex to be cast as simply another iteration of the black/white conflict. Indigenous peoples and Spanish colonialists preceded the American entry into the region, and their descendants, along with immigrants from Latin America and other parts of the world, contributed their rich musical heritage to the Californian mix. As their numbers grew, so did the reaction of the Los Angeles oligarchy to their perceived threat. The Anglo establishment's attempts to manage and neuter mestizo culture, as well as the Chicano resistance to such control, involved intricate negotiations and power struggles with other racial and immigrant communities that settled in Southern California.

Two versions of the story of the encounter between indigenous peoples and Europeans get told in California. In the boosters' version, the Spanish missionaries and their Indian neophytes lived together harmoniously until the arrival of the Americans ended their halcyon way of life. This mission legacy continues to be commemorated in pageants and multicultural fairs that reenact California's arcadian past. In the other version, missionary life was hardly the stuff of pastoral romance, and its legacy consists not of long-ago legends but rather lives on in the mestizos' descendants in Mexico and California. The second version is much more complicated and unfolds in unpredictable ways. At times, it makes for an interesting counterpoint to the more static version of the boosters, but generally, it proceeds independent of the other, punctuated by the very real sociopolitical clashes the mestizos have experienced in their continued and shared history with other Californians.

In this chapter, I follow the second version of the story, tracing the evolution of the mestizo identity from Mexican to Mexican American to Chicano through music. From the *corridos* of the early immigrants to the protest rock of the 1970s, music has played a significant role in constructing mestizo identities, which belie the Los Angeles establishment's portrayal of a romanticized mission culture and resist the ideology of assimilation and white supremacy. Mexican American music, drawing upon its mixed heritage, provides a valuable and alternative model of multiculturalism—one that foregrounds political struggles, recuperates history, calls attention to real economic and social disparities, and challenges the status quo.

Mexican Americans occupy a unique position in American society for several reasons. Because of the proximity of Mexico to the United States, Mexican immigration is uniquely characterized by both continuity and circularity that sustain the connection of the immigrants to the motherland. California's shared border with Mexico and sizable labor needs ensure the steady stream of Mexican immigration, while the distance of Californian cities from Mexico's heartland provides the requisite space for the growth of an independent Mexican American culture. The relationship of Mexican Americans to the region is further complicated by the fact that the ancestors of Mexicans inhabited California long before the arrival of Anglo Americans. Even with such ancestral claims, however, Mexican immigrants often confront insurmountable obstacles in achieving economic mobility—accessible to European immigrants within the course of several generations—linking them more closely to the African American rather than the European immigrant experience. Like African Americans, Mexican immigrants have been and continue to be "racialized," marked as a racial other, by the white power structure, even as they enjoy certain privileges unavailable to blacks because of their lighter skin color. As George J. Sánchez succinctly puts it, "To be Chicano, in effect, is to be betwixt and between."[1]

The Back Story: The Real and Imagined Music of Early Mexican Immigration

In the early decades of the twentieth century, Mexicans crossed the border with increasing frequency and set up communities that retained Mexican cultural practices. Around the same time that new aqueducts brought irrigation into the Imperial Valley, making available vast tracts of land for large-scale farming, the 1910 revolution in Mexico was destroying the livelihoods of many Mexicans. In order to successfully launch their ambitious agricultural schemes, Californian entrepreneurs needed cheap labor in abundance and actively recruited Mexican workers. With the drastic decline in immigration

from European countries following World War I and the growth of manufacturing industries in the Southland, Mexicans also found employment
in urban areas. When jobs disappeared during the Great Depression, the
United States government sponsored a repatriation program, expelling approximately half a million Mexicans from the Southwest in order to reduce
its welfare rolls. World War II shifted the tide once more. As California
became the site of many war-related industries, Mexicans were once again
recruited, many as contract workers or *braceros,* to help launch yet another
Californian boom. From that point on, the flow of Mexicans into California
has been steady, and Mexican Americans now make up the largest nonwhite
group in California.[2]

The Californios, the original descendants of the Spanish and Indians, were
few in number relative to the Anglos who arrived in the second half of the
nineteenth century and did not pose a real threat to the new controlling power. The Mexican mass migration during the second decade of the twentieth
century also failed to attract much attention from white Los Angeles because
Mexicans were thought of as temporary sojourners rather than permanent
settlers. However, in the 1940s, with the removal of the earlier scapegoat, the
Japanese Americans, and the encroachment of the Mexican community into
new areas of Los Angeles, the Anglo power elite took notice of their growing
numbers and instigated an active campaign of discrimination.

Two events during this decade marked the outbreak of anti-Mexican
hostilities in Southern California. In the Sleepy Lagoon case of 1942, the
murder of a young Mexican American was pinned on a Mexican gang, and
the mainstream media and the judicial system seized this incident as an opportunity to vilify Mexican youths as criminal gangsters. The Zoot Suit riots
of 1943 began when a fight broke out between a handful of Mexicans and
white servicemen, setting off mass beatings of Mexican and black youths by
the police and members of the U.S. Navy.[3] By 1945, the relationship between
the LAPD and the Mexican American community had deteriorated to one
of deep suspicion and antagonism.[4] Through this period, many Mexicans
in Los Angeles lived in substandard housing, received wages at exploitative
levels, and were denied educational and professional opportunities. The
mainstream media distorted the outward signs of their poverty to concoct
and disseminate the negative stereotype of Mexicans as unhygienic, primitive, and violent.

Ignoring the problems of the Mexicans living and working in their midst
under inhospitable conditions, Anglo Angelenos celebrated their Spanish
legacy and maintained an idealized vision of mission life in a more innocent
and remote past. In *North from Mexico,* the first sympathetic account of Mexi-

cans written by an Anglo historian, Carey McWilliams chronicles the Fantasy Heritage current in Los Angeles in the first half of the twentieth century:

> Long, long ago the borderlands were settled by Spanish grandees and caballeros, a gentle people, accustomed to the luxurious softness of fine clothes, to well-trained servants, to all the amenities of civilized European living. Inured to suffering, kindly mission *padres* overcame the hostility of Indians by their saintly example and the force of a spiritual ideal, much in the manner of a gentle spring rain driving the harsh winds of winter from the skies. . . . All in all, this life of Spain-away-from-Spain in the borderlands was very romantic, idyllic, very beautiful.[5]

In reality, McWilliams urgently argues, life in the missions was not so rosy: the Indian neophytes were coerced into giving up their traditional ways and serving their Spanish masters, receiving in return disease and permanent bondage.

Helen Hunt Jackson's *Ramona* first popularized the pastoral vision of the California missions in 1884. The novel, which relates a tragic love story about a pair of Indians at the twilight of Californio culture, spawned an annual Ramona pageant that began in 1923 and continues to this day. Even more ambitious and popular in its time was the *Mission Play,* authored by *Los Angeles Times* journalist John Steven McGroarty and underwritten by railway mogul Henry E. Huntington. The play about the rise and fall of Franciscan missions in Alta California opened to great fanfare in a theater built especially for its performance near Mission San Gabriel in 1912. Other pageants and theaters, such as the Padua Hills Theater in Claremont, also offered romanticized portrayals of Spanish and Mexican life through combinations of dance, music, and storytelling.[6]

The city's oligarchy, led by Harry Chandler of the *Los Angeles Times,* picked up on the popular sentiment aroused by these reenactments of California's Spanish past and launched a campaign to construct a permanent site for the celebration of the "Mission Myth." At the same time that Mexicans were being forcibly sent back to Mexico and pushed out of downtown Los Angeles to make room for new development, the city's oligarchy successfully transformed the Los Angeles Plaza, the center of social and religious life for first-generation Mexican Angelenos, into a tourist destination. On the "restored" Olvera Street, now denuded of contemporary Mexican American culture, the Mission Myth was (and still is) reenacted daily for visitors in search of exotic colors and flavors.[7]

The Mission Myth provided the ideal image of a Mediterranean paradise for the Chamber of Commerce and the Los Angeles oligarchy to project to the rest of the world. As McWilliams points out, the myth delineated everybody's place to the supreme satisfaction of the Los Angeles boosters—the noble, beautiful, and pious were Spanish in origin, whereas the unsavory elements in the present were Mexican.[8] It perpetuated the prevailing belief during the European colonial period that Caucasians were meant to rule the heathens and primitives in a paternalistic social structure, beneficial for all.

Music was vital in the Mission Myth, imbuing the culture with the requisite grace and romance. A 1914 guidebook detailed an imaginary scene of a Californian-Mediterranean idyll, which featured music prominently:

> The days of the Spaniards and Mexicans seemed, reversing the old saw, to consist of no work and all play, that the men appeared to be always decking their half-wild *alazans* for a barbecue, the women plucking roses for a *baile*. . . . Santa Barbara was especially famous for its fandangos. "It was always easy," writes a gallant, a lieutenant of New York Volunteers, "to get up a ball in five minutes by cajoling in a guitar or harp player." Easy, too, to enlist merry hands and feet for a sheep-shearing or vintage revel, and banner-bearers for the church procession which was sure to be sealed with a dance.[9]

According to romantic tales of the old mission, music permeated every aspect of life, endowing everyday events with magic and gaiety.

Charles Lummis, recruited in 1885 by the ultimate Los Angeles booster, Harrison Gray Otis of the *Los Angeles Times,* expended considerable effort in tracking down the music from the olden days.[10] Although Lummis went into the field intending to preserve and help sustain the old way of life, his belief system was closely aligned with those of the Los Angeles oligarchy, and his ethnographic projects were motivated by the ideology of boosterism. Lummis's introduction to the volume of Mexican songs that he collected and transcribed, subtitled "Flowers of Our Lost Romance," overflows with the sentimentality and nostalgia of the Mission Myth:

> In old California, "Before the Gringo Came"—the California of the Franciscan Missions and the vast Ranchos—they lived the happiest, the humanest, the most beautiful life that Caucasians have ever lived anywhere under the sun. . . . There were Songs of the Soil, and songs of poets and of troubadours, in this far, lone, beautiful, happy land; and songs that came over from Mother Spain and up from Step-mother Mexico. But everybody sang; and a great many made their own songs, or verses to other songs. Not being musical critics, they felt music, and arrived at it; and the Folksong of Spanish America is a treasure of inexhaustible beauty and extent.[11]

The songs Lummis collected reflect his affinity for the romantic—songs such as "La Noche 'sta Serena (So Fair and Still the Night Is)," "Chata Cara de

Bule (Bells of the Rosário)," "La Primavera (Springtime)," and "Es el Amor Mariposa (Butterfly Love)" (Lummis's spellings). In "El Capotin," a serenade from the collection, a man avows his love for a woman, accompanied by the tin-tin-tin of the rain. Even when the text is at its most dramatic ("Do not kill me . . . / With a pistol or a knife! / Kill me, rather, with thine eyes, love, / With those red lips take my life"), the music sustains a charming atmosphere befitting an afternoon *baile* (see example 5.1). With this collection, Lummis attempted to recreate the romantic ambience of a bygone world, populated by chivalrous troubadours serenading their objects of love.

In contrast to the picturesque pastoral quality of the songs from Lummis's collection, the music of the Mexican immigrants recorded in the first decades of the twentieth century reveals a heightened social and political awareness within the growing Mexican American community.[12] The *corrido*, a traditional ballad from Mexico, sung to the accompaniment of a guitar, was a mainstay in social gatherings and established music as an important medium for airing personal and communal grievances and raising the political consciousness of Mexican migrants.[13] The songs from Guillermo Hernández's collection of transcriptions from early Chicano phonographs, *Canciones de la Raza: Songs of the Chicano Experience,* deal with contemporary issues, such as "Registro de 1918" and "Inundación of California." The song "Ramón Delgado," for example, narrates a story that was stirring up the Mexican American community during this time: "The year nineteen hundred and twenty-three that just past, in the town of Hondo, Ramón Delgado was killed. / That town of Hondo is getting a bad reputation; there they kill Mexicans just because they feel like it."[14]

In "Radios y Chicanos" from Hernández's collection, the singer expresses bewilderment over the messages that address him over the airwaves:

> That's how it is! It's hard to believe
> that those city people advertise melons
> instead of playing songs.

He concludes:

> That's how it is! It's hard to believe
> how we're treated like dummies
> by those city people around here.[15]

The music of "Radios y Chicanos" shares a few musical traits with the songs sampled in Lummis's collection, for example, its harmonization in thirds, chromatic inflection, prevalence of repeated notes, and lilting dance meter (see example 5.2). The text, however, stands in stark contrast to the sentimental

El Capotin
(The Rain Song)

Recorded and Translated by
CHARLES F. LUMMIS

Transcribed and Harmonized by
ARTHUR FARWELL

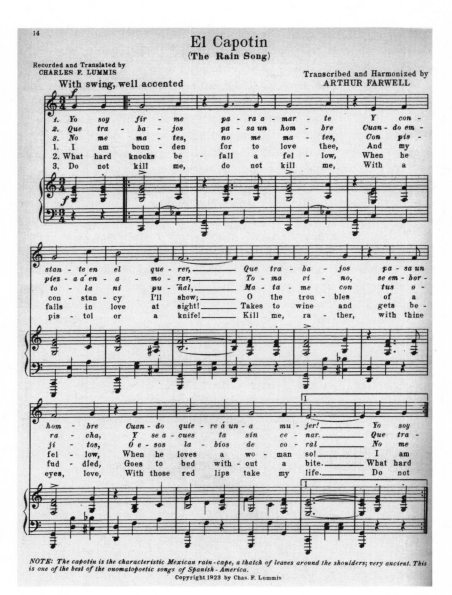

NOTE: *The capotin is the characteristic Mexican rain-cape, a thatch of leaves around the shoulders; very ancient. This is one of the best of the onomatopoetic songs of Spanish-America.*

Copyright 1923 by Chas. F. Lummis

Example 5.1. "El Capotin"

Example 5.1. Continued

ballads of yesteryear. The lyrics of Lummis's Spanish songs are limited to expressions of sentimental love, and even when the singer claims to be in pain, as in "El Capotin," the songs resort to conventions of the troubadour tradition that genericize any real emotion. The *corrido,* on the other hand, dwells on the details that flesh out the immigrant's misery with excruciating realism. Rather than employ poetic symbolism, such as the rain in "El Capotin," the *corrido* singer repeats verbatim the commercials broadcast on his radio. The words of hackneyed advertising jingles remind him that he is a victim of incomprehension, barraged by the messages of an inequitable capitalist system grinding him down.

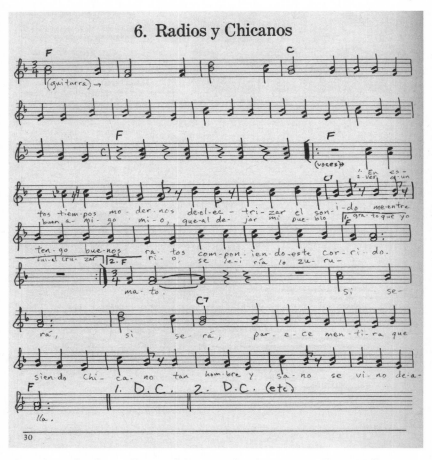

Example 5.2. "Radios y Chicanos." (Reprinted with permission from Guillermo E. Hernández)

Pedro González, one of the most popular radio personalities from the era and a one-time lead singer of Los Madrugadores, aired politically charged messages and songs on his radio shows. In 1934, Los Angeles district attorney Buron Fitts, considering González to be a potentially dangerous political agitator, put the popular deejay away in jail for six years on trumped-up charges of rape.[16] Not long after Lummis issued his collection of the romantic ballads of yesteryear, celebrating the culture of Old California, the music of contemporary Mexican Americans, challenging the status quo, was silenced by a power structure that could thrive only with the continued availability of cheap and compliant labor.

Mexican American Political Activism and the Chicano Nationalist Movement

Even the most stable cultural identities undergo transformation and adaptation in immigration. Mexican American identity, an amalgam of two multiracial and ambiguous nationalities, was a tenuous concept from the start. The challenges of identity formation were all the greater for Mexican immigrants settling down in a rapidly growing and highly unstable Los Angeles of the second and third decades of the twentieth century. In the beginning, Mexican Americans were defined ethnically by what they were not: segregated from Anglo Los Angeles, they settled in barrios in the central and east side of the city, along with blacks, Asians, and ethnic whites such as Jews and Russians. As Mexican Americans negotiated their position with the Anglo power structure and interacted with other Angelenos of color, a new collective identity began to emerge.

By 1950, the Mexican American population in California had surged in size and continued to grow throughout the next decades.[17] The Mexican American leadership made limited progress in improving the community's welfare in the 1950s, an era dominated by the conservative ethos of Senator Joseph McCarthy and President Dwight D. Eisenhower. This generation of political leadership was more interested in accommodation and assimilation than in effecting substantive changes in race relations. With the liberalization of the national political arena in the 1960s, however, new objectives and agendas became possible. The black nationalist movement provided a model of revolutionary action and rhetoric. The Watts rebellion of 1965 drew widespread attention to the worsening problems afflicting minority communities, such as police brutality, discrimination in housing and hiring practices, and the increasing blight and segregation of the inner city brought about by urban renewal programs and white flight into the suburbs. Although the riots were primarily a black/white conflict, Mexican Americans, subjected to many of the same inequitable socioeconomic public policies, followed the actions of their African American neighbors with great interest.[18]

A new generation of Mexican Americans coming of age in the 1960s embraced political radicalism and militancy. After their firsthand observation of the Cuban Revolution, students at San Jose State College associated with the Progressive Labor Party issued the first radical Mexican American student manifesto, which declared: "As sons of Mexican manual laborers in California, we have traveled to Revolutionary Cuba . . . to emphasize the historical and cultural unanimity of all Latin American peoples, north and south of the border."[19] The 1964 manifesto anticipated many aspects of the coming Chicano movement with its orientation toward youths of working-class backgrounds, rhetoric of anti-U.S. imperialism, and celebration of a pan-Latin identity. A 1965 decision of the National Farm Workers Association to join the striking Filipino grape pickers brought national media attention to labor leader César Chávez and the struggles of Mexican American agricultural workers.

By the late 1960s, a mass movement was afoot. On March 3, 1968, over one thousand students walked out of Abraham Lincoln High School, a predominantly Mexican American school in East Los Angeles, to protest racist school policies and to demand the hiring of Mexican American teachers and administrators and the expansion of the curriculum to include classes on Mexican American history and culture. Members of university student organizations pitched in, holding picket signs that read "Chicano Power!," "Viva La Raza!," and "Viva La Revolución!" Several more thousand students walked out of five other barrio high schools that day, bringing the Los Angeles city school system to a halt. A few months later, Mexican American graduating seniors and audience members attending the commencement ceremony at San Jose State College walked out, instigating a demonstration involving two hundred people. In October 1968, Mexican American students carried out a sit-in at the office of the University of California president. A month later, Mexican American students participated in a strike with other minority groups at San Francisco State College in a rainbow coalition that resulted in the formation of the Third World Liberation Front. In 1969, the various Mexican American student organizations at California and Texas universities consolidated to form the united El Movimento Estudientil Chicano de Aztlán (MEChA).[20]

In the meantime, the Brown Berets, a paramilitary nonstudent organization made up of mostly street youth, were combating police brutality and working to rid the community of drug use. On August 29, 1970, the Brown Berets and student activists participated in a Mexican American demonstration against the Vietnam War held in Laguna Park in East Los Angeles. The protest, which drew more than twenty thousand people, turned bloody when the Los Angeles police officers and the Los Angeles County Sheriff deputies started to attack the predominantly Latino crowd. Hundreds were injured, more than two hundred were arrested, and three Mexican Americans were killed. Thousands of protesters took to the streets, burning stores and cars on Whittier Boulevard, the main strip of East Los Angeles.[21]

Through the numerous student-led protests and organizational meetings of the 1960s, a coherent Chicano ideology and identity began to take shape. The National Chicano Youth Liberation Conference in 1969, hosted by Gonzáles's Crusade for Justice, urged young Chicanos to escape *gabacho* (white, Anglo-Saxon Protestant) colonization by embracing their Mexican roots and by rejecting the assimilationist ideology propagated by the melting pot myth. Its message of cultural nationalism was articulated in "El Plan Espiritual de Aztlán": "Our culture unites and educates the family of *La Raza* towards liberation with one heart and one mind. We must insure that our writers, poets, musicians and artists produce literature and art that is appealing to our people and relates to our revolutionary culture. Our cultural values of life, family and home will serve as powerful weapon to defeat the *gringo* dollar value system and encourage the process of love and brotherhood."[22]

Another conference a few months later held at the University of California campus in Santa Barbara produced the manifesto "El Plan de Santa Barbara" that further advanced many of the positions consolidated in the preceding months of turmoil. It asserted:

> The self-determination of our community is now the only acceptable mandate for social and political action; it is the essence of Chicano commitment. Culturally, the word *Chicano*, in the past a pejorative and class-bound adjective, has now become the root idea of a new cultural identity for our people. It also reveals a growing solidarity and the development of a common social praxis. The widespread use of the term *Chicano* today signals a rebirth of pride and confidence. *Chicanismo* simply embodies an ancient truth: that man is never closer to his true self as when he is close to his community.[23]

The Chicano movement advocated the construction of *La Raza Nueva* through cultural activities celebrating traditional Mexican roots and the creation of new poetry, theater, art, and music.

Youth, Style, Music, and the Chicano Subculture

In his landmark study of postwar working-class musical subcultures in Britain, *Subculture: The Meaning of Style,* Dick Hebdige links oppositional politics with the mundane objects and signs that constitute the surface of daily life. Citing the structuralist, semiotic theories of Roland Barthes, Hebdige "reads" the various sartorial and musical elements, the bodily mutations and rituals of pre-punk and punk subcultures, as signs of resistance: "The challenge to hegemony which subcultures represent is not issued directly by them. Rather it is expressed obliquely, in style. The objections are lodged, the contradictions displayed (and, as we shall see, 'magically resolved') at the profoundly super-ficial level of appearances: that is, at the level of signs." In his view, subcultural style, by defying hegemonic norms, brings into question the appearance of consensus and cohesion surrounding mainstream culture.[24]

Even before political agendas became explicit in the mid-1960s, the Mexican American youth subculture had exhibited signs of resistance. Historians chronicle the Chicano movement as a series of political meetings and protests, overt displays of political engagement among Mexican American youths. But the fashioning of a specifically "Chicano" identity, one designed to counter the dominant group's definition of "Mexican American," proceeded on the streets, at dance halls, and on college campuses, and this evolving self-conception in turn made possible the political demands for self-determinism and cultural nationalism. Hebdigean signs of youth revolt had been emergent for some time; it was only with the launch of the Chicano movement that the signs coalesced to form the basis of *La Raza Nueva*.

The zoot-suit pachuco style was the earliest manifestation of a major youth subculture in the barrios. The language and dress adopted by the pachuco youths of the 1940s gave outward expression to their sense of cultural volatil-ity and syncretism. These youths spoke Spanglish, a slang mixture of English and Spanish inflected by caló, a Spanish dialect descended from the Gyp-sies in Spain. They came to be identified by their chosen uniform, the zoot suit—a long shoulder-padded jacket worn with draped trousers tapered at the ankles—styled for the "hep" practitioners of the jitterbug. The zoot suit functioned as a form of cultural expression, a means of underscoring the minority youths' alienation and hostility to dominant society. Given the War Production Board's 1942 act that rationed how much fabric could be used per outfit, the zoot suit was recognized as a symbol of profligacy and the gross neglect of patriotic duty. The white servicemen who attacked the pachuco and black zoot-suiters sported tidy U.S. government–issued uni-forms that visually signified the binary opposition, clearly delineated in the press, between the white youths who valiantly served their country and the degenerate youths of color who flaunted their delinquency. The riots provided the servicemen a stage for the public spectacle of humiliating and neutering the racial other, as they literally stripped their victims of their zoot suits. Stuart Cosgrove suggests that although the riots were not "political" in the strictest sense, "for many participants they were an entry into the language of politics, an inarticulate rejection of the 'straight world' and its organization," and echoes Hebdige in suggesting, "It is in everyday rituals that resistance can find natural and unconscious expression."[25]

Those of the 1960s generation displayed several important differences from their predecessors. Thanks to the economic boom, teens had money at their disposal, making the pursuit of leisure activities and consumer goods a central focus of their free time. The music industry catered its production to the preferences of the new youth market. Rock, played by the young for the young, became the music of an entire generation, signifying the generational divide more resoundingly than any other aspect of the youth culture. Between 1964 and 1968, the eastside barrios of Los Angeles produced an unprecedented number of bands, playing music that provided the context in which Mexican American youths began to see themselves as a political entity. From 1968 into the early 1970s, Chicano rock was harnessed as an instrument of ideological propaganda, helping to complete the transformation of Mexican American youths into politically mobilized Chicanos.

Rejecting the culture of their parents, Mexican American youths embraced rock wholeheartedly, but their experience of rock was mediated by their exposure to black culture and did not necessarily reflect white, mainstream tastes. Because Los Angeles was segregated by color—with whites on the west side and everyone else crowded into the east—interaction between the different minority groups was inevitable. The unique mix of East Los Angeles culture was captured as early as 1927 in this description of the Club Latino on Main Street in the Plaza, the focal point of first-generation Mexican American social life: "The female employees were mostly immigrant Mexicans or Mexican Americans, although Anglo American, Italian, Filipino, Chinese, and Japanese women also were available. The band, however, was made up of black musicians and played only American pieces. Mexican immigrant men, dressed in working-class garb, danced 'Mexican style' to the American songs."[26] Children of Mexican and Asian immigrants attended the same schools near Central Avenue that produced many of the great jazz and R&B musicians of the era, and their musical tastes were influenced by their African American neighbors.[27]

Throughout the postwar era, Mexican American youths constituted a significant portion of the audiences at R&B concerts in the greater Los Angeles area. The *cholos* and members of "low-riding" car clubs, in particular, embraced R&B as their cruising music.[28] Black artists popular with the Mexican American crowd, most notably Chuck Higgins, Big Jay McNeely, and Richard Berry, played at the Orpheum, the United Artist and Paramount theaters, Angelus Hall, and the El Monte Legion Stadium.[29] In his brief history of Chicano rock, Ruben Guevara describes a typical weekend dance at the Legion that was made up of crowds that were 90 percent Chicano and 10 percent Anglo and that featured wild dancing styles called the Pachuco Hop, Hully Gully, and Corrido Rock. The concerts invariably ended with gangsters parading around in their primered cars in the parking lot and the police descending upon them and breaking up the remaining crowds.[30]

Under the influence of R&B and doo-wop, Mexican Americans started to create their own version of rock and roll. At a time when black artists often played with Mexican American artists and for Mexican American audiences, musical influences flowed multidirectionally. Chuck Higgins's tribute to his Mexican American fans, "Pachuko Hop" of 1952, was in turn answered by Li'l Bobby Rey's Masked Phantom Band number "Corrido Rock." The Rainbow Gardens' house band, The Mixtures, was led by Mexican and African American musicians and also included in its lineup Puerto Rican, Caucasian, and Indian players.[31] Ritchie Valens, the first Mexican American to attain national recognition, sang covers and wrote original music that shows the influence of R&B, country, blues, rock and roll, and traditional Mexican music. His first group, called the Silhouettes, was a multiracial band that included Mexican, African, Italian, and Japanese Americans.[32] Richard Berry, of "Louie, Louie" fame, once performed with a Latin R&B band from Los Angeles called the Rhythm Rockers. In 1970, El Chicano recorded jazz composer Gerald Wilson's "Viva Tirado," written in homage to the Mexican matador José Ramón Tirado. More recently, Kid Frost, in the 1990 single "La Raza," rapped in Spanglish over Wilson's "Viva Tirado," paying tribute to both Wilson and El Chicano.[33]

During the peak of eastside rock, the Romancers, the Blendells, Cannibal and the Headhunters, the Premiers, and Thee Midniters performed for dances at the Big Union, the Little Union, the Paramount Ballroom, and local high schools and played traditional Mexican music at weddings and other community festivities. At the height of their popularity, between 1964 and 1968, Thee Midniters played as many as four concerts a night. Record Inn owner Mike Carcano recalled, "I had Thee Midniters in the store once, to sign autographs, and all of Whittier Boulevard was jammed bumper to bumper."[34] The postwar era had seen the formation of many independent recording studios in Los Angeles, such as Imperial and Specialty, which became important R&B labels. At the peak of eastside rock, talent scouts and entrepreneurs like Bob Keane, Bill Cárdenas, and Eddie Davis began their own labels, Del-Fi, Rampart, and Whittier Records, to record the new sounds of the barrio. In 1966, Eddie Davis, with Rudy Benavides, produced *Golden Treasures—Volume One: West Coast East Side Review,* a compilation of popular hits played by the East Los Angeles bands, and issued volume 2 in 1969.[35]

According to George Lipsitz, the song "Land of a Thousand Dances" works as a potent metaphor symbolizing the significant role rock played in breaking down barriers of race, class, and ethnicity and in integrating new voices into the cultural mainstream.[36] Anthony Macías too credits R&B and rock and roll with the creation of multiethnic public spaces in which urban civility could be practiced and intercultural affinities forged. But Macías cautions against the temptation of overstating the counter-hegemonic potential of such multiculturalist configurations, pointing out that Mexican Americans and African Americans were often competing for the same limited economic opportunities and resources during this time and that Mexican Americans' love for black music did not necessarily translate into feelings of amity or respect for African Americans outside of the dance hall.[37]

I would argue for the potency of eastside rock as counter-hegemonic expression precisely because of its very monocultural orientation as a product of the East Los Angeles barrio. Rhythm and blues entered the barrio through the mediation of white deejays and black musicians, but eastside rock was music performed by and for Los Angeles Chicanos. Although a few tunes from East Los Angeles did achieve modest national success (Cannibal and the Headhunters' "Land of a Thousand Dances" became a top 30 hit; Thee Midniters' cover of the same song reached number 67 and the Premiers' "Farmer John" number 19 on the national charts), eastside rock's inability to duplicate its tremendous popularity in the barrios on the national stage had much to do with its specific cultural and commercial origin. The record producers who had little access to national distribution networks made certain to stock the local shelves with recordings of eastside bands. Barrio youths could buy their albums and even meet the musicians in person at the local music stores, the Record Rack and the Record Inn. Tony Valdez, who worked at the Record Rack, remembered how the ritual of buying the latest 45 changed when the group lived down the street: "Here were people you could go and see on a Friday night, here were people you could touch and talk to. Buying that record was some tangible piece of your relationship to them."[38]

The very situatedness of eastside rock in the East Los Angeles barrios is apparent in the series of songs written as tributes to Chicano life on Whittier Boulevard. Thee Midniters first released a hit called "Whittier Boulevard" that spawned a number of imitations. Godfrey Kerr, a popular deejay, recorded a song called "Down Whittier Boulevard";[39] Thee Impalas recorded the instrumental "Oh Yeah Whittier," followed shortly by the vocal number "Come On Up Whittier" about cruising down the boulevard, taking in the sights of the barrio.

In the music before the late 1960s, the lyrics are for the most part apolitical and typical of rock songs—about love or partying—and many of the hits were covers or instrumental numbers. The instrumentation is also typical of R&B and rock, making use of guitar, drums, bass, and horns, with other instruments, like vibes, associated with Latin sounds, rare until after 1967. It is not politically oriented lyrics nor Latinate harmonies that helped create a sense of Chicano identity and group solidarity. Rather, as Keith Negus proposes, "it is the social interactions, relations and mediations that occur around and across the music as it is created" that cast eastside rock as Chicano rock.[40]

As Mexican American youths danced in synchronized motion to the bouncy rhythm produced by members of their community from the same age group and similar economic backgrounds, a collective identity, independent of their parents' or Anglo definitions of them, became possible. When the Blendells exhorted the audience to clap their hands or Cannibal and the Headhunters sang "Na na na na na" from their perennially popular hit "Land of a Thousand Dances" and urged dancers to move their feet, it was the group solidarity—the give and take between the musicians and the audience—that brought about a sense of common identity rather than any explicit referencing of their Mexican roots. This self-enclosed musical subculture gave the Chicano generation its first taste of independence from Anglo and African American musicians and recordings, even if its sounds reflected the mixed heritage of Mexican American culture. The dance hall provided the space in which a political entity—the Chicano generation—came into being. Dancing to Chicano rock constituted the social praxis, the ritual, through which the collective identity of Chicano youths could be regularly iterated and other elements of Chicano style practiced.

Fashion and other forms of cultural expression from the streets informed the evolving style of the Chicano generation. The Brown Berets recruited heavily from street youth gangs, many of whom had previously been incarcerated by the penal system. Even for the great majority of the Chicano youths unassociated with gangs, street culture provided codes of conduct and comportment considered appropriate for revolutionary action. The National Chicano Youth Liberation Conference in 1969 concluded that in order to break free of *gabacho* colonization, Chicano students needed revolutionary role models and that street youths and ex-convicts would serve as these models. Conference speakers announced that "henceforth most crimes committed by Mexican Americans were to be interpreted as 'revolutionary acts.' The language and dress of the street youth, the *vatos locos,* would be emulated. *Carnalismo* (the brotherhood code of Mexican American youth gangs) would mold the lives of students and become a central concept in the proposed nationalist ideology."[41]

The *cholo* style that emerged on the streets in the 1960s carried on the pachuco tradition, updated for a new age. *Cholo* youths paid meticulous attention to their outfits, most often composed of neatly pressed khaki pants, a plaid Pendleton shirt (a long-sleeve dress shirt), deck shoes, and a watch cap or bandanna.[42] Khaki pants and its common substitute, the "county" jeans, both reference the dominant culture in ironic ways: the khaki is a holdover from the military fatigue worn by Mexican American soldiers in the Korean War and the jeans a remnant from doing time in detention centers. Like today's hip-hop fans who imitate the falling-down pants of inmates not allowed belts by penal dress codes, *cholos* appropriated sartorial symbols from the dominant culture and inverted their signification. Their dress, along with gestures, language, walking style, and music, asserted their Chicano identity and announced their deviance from societal norms. Portrayed by the police and mainstream media as delinquent and criminal solely because of their ethnicity, Chicano revolutionaries embraced the *cholo* image of street smarts and subversive power.

The movement spawned new cultural expressions and forms as new publications and forums created venues not only for political debates but also for the self-conscious fashioning of a new Chicano cultural identity. Luis Valdez's El Teatro Campesino began as a theatrical adjunct to the farmworkers' struggle, grappling with many of the central social and political questions of the day. As it broke away from the labor cause, the Teatro abandoned its formerly overt revolutionary content to experiment with new styles, developing the *corrido,* for example, as the basis of dramatic form.[43] Many publications, such as *El Malcriado,* which also grew out of the farmworkers' struggle, and *El Grito del Norte,* which originated in New Mexico, also featured *corridos* written in the vernacular and occupied with the concerns of daily life. Rodolfo "Corky" Gonzáles, who had quit the Democratic Party to form Crusade for Justice, wrote and distributed an epic poem, *I Am Joaquín,* in 1967, which encapsulated the desires of many young Chicanos to break free of the Anglo value system.[44] *Con Safos,* a magazine begun in the East Los Angeles barrios, celebrated not only the *cholo* lifestyle but also its aesthetic code, captured in fashion, poetry, photography, drawings, and graffiti. In the inaugural issue, it explained that the title signified "a gesture of defiance, and an overt rejection of the cold and indifferent *gabacho* imposition."[45] What ties together the diverse cultural production of the time, according to Tomás Ybarra-Frausto, is the "conscious and pronounced effort towards closing the gap between the artistic and social worlds," that is, a new signifying practice of *chicanismo.*[46]

Eastside rock was central to the street culture from which Chicanos drew many of the components of the new identity. Luis Rodríguez describes the eastside bands as "heroes and heroines of lowrider car clubs, street gangs, and high school teens."[47] The dance-hall lifestyle rejected outright the mainstream Anglo value system revolving around work and professional advancement. With the various aspects of the Chicano identity assigned to concrete symbols of street culture, Chicano rock, in the late 1960s, became self-consciously political, emphasizing its difference from mainstream rock and incorporating *chicanismo* references. Thee Midniters released "Chicano Power" on La Raza Records and "The Ballad of Cesar Chavez" on the Whittier label in 1968. Mark and the Escorts performed songs dealing with Chicano politics and culture, such as "Pre-Columbian Dream" and "I'm Brown." Spanish- or Indian-named groups, such as Tierra, Yaqui, and El Chicano, formed in the late 1960s and early 1970s, overlay their R&B and rock sounds with Latin jazz and salsa rhythms, signaling their identification with pan-Latinism, and quoted traditional Mexican folk melodies.[48]

In an interview with Steven Loza, Jesse Velo of the punk band Los Illegals described growing up in a eastside project and noted the stylistic diversity of musical influences in Los Angeles: "And the music bouncing off the walls—everything from Marvin Gaye to Los Camperos, and everything . . . it just forced it to be what it is. And besides, L.A. is nothing but, it's like a big bowl of *menudo* with everything else in it. So we have no choice but to just absorb each other's rhythms and patterns."[49] Even as Chicano music helped construct a separatist and autonomous cultural space, it absorbed the multiethnic, multiracial sounds of Los Angeles.

A 1998 compilation of Chicano music of the last three decades, *The Chicano Alliance,* shows just how diverse and hybrid Mexican American musical culture is, with songs derived from salsa, funk, R&B, rock, disco, Latin jazz, rap, and other styles, in English and Spanish or a combination thereof, and ranging from the politically impassioned to the conventionally romantic. Lipsitz considers the "inter-referentiality, inter-textuality, juxtaposition of multiple realities, and bifocality" of Chicano Angeleno music one of the reasons for its significance to the community but suggests that the music reaches outside of the community as well: "Its very identity as a part of mass popular culture, its uneasy dialogue between the Anglo and Chicano worlds, and its complicated system of codings and references express a desire to reach out to others to form a historical bloc capable of posing a counter-hegemony to the domination of today."[50] Rafael Pérez-Torres, in considering recent Chicano music, also emphasizes the eclecticism of musical influences and brings up another political implication of practicing "mestizaje": "Unlike the typically binary notions of identity within a U.S. racial paradigm (choose black or white), a focus on mestizaje allows for other forms of self-identification, other types of cultural creation, other means of social struggle."[51]

Hybridity and syncretism are perhaps the only viable cultural strategy for a community undergoing constant change, but such a strategy also precludes the maintenance of a single unified vision. The Chicano movement suffered a precipitous decline in the 1970s because of internal divisions and ideological differences within its ranks. Commonality of purpose became increasingly untenable as the Los Angeles barrios grew to absorb immigrants from other parts of Latin America, creating new competing Latin identities. Younger Chicano artists like Kid Frost and Zack de la Rocha of Rage against the Machine continue to play with multiple linguistic and musical signifiers in hip-hop/rock hybrids that attest to the fluidity and porosity of the Chicano identity, but their music belongs to a subculture that is at once bigger (in that they reach the mainstream) and smaller (in that they no longer represent an entire generation) than the East Los Angeles barrios. A musical practice that reflected the dynamism of contemporary life, as opposed to an imagined and static past, proved ultimately unable to speak for an entire community over an extended period.

The civil rights movement brought race and ethnicity to the forefront of cultural practices. It politicized many aspects of Chicano identity that had been inherent in Mexican American life long before 1968. From within the interlacing mesh of rallies, meetings, essays, poetry, paintings, and other cultural expressions that constituted the Chicano movement, music acquired and accumulated new meanings. The network of dance halls, student organizations, recording labels, and stores provided the circulation of Mexican American rock and created a site for the construction of a Chicano youth identity that was intimately tied to the East Los Angeles barrios and could stand independent of the Anglo mainstream. The convergence of music, youth, race, and politics of the late 1960s was potent, if short-lived, and is probably unlikely to recur to the same degree in the ever-more complex and fragmented cultural terrain of Los Angeles.

6. After *Sa-i-ku*

Korean American Hip-Hop
since the Rodney King Uprising

The fragmentation of Los Angeles society into myriad splinters was made visible to the rest of the world in April 1992, as incessantly looped newsreels put on ignominious display the rioting, burning, and pillaging of South Central and Koreatown. Angelenos commemorated the tenth anniversary of the 1992 riots with multicultural events that symbolized the promises from all fronts to work toward racial and ethnic harmony. In one staged event, three violinists, one black, one Latino, and one Korean American, played Pachelbel's Canon in D in a lot in front of a liquor store at the corner of Florence and Normandie avenues, what was ten years ago the epicenter of the riots. A listener commented, "It was so beautiful. . . . The music brought a sense of unity that I haven't seen in a while." Another asked rhetorically: "What better way to bring people together than through music?"

But the performance of multiculturalism left some Angelenos unmoved. Even as the strains of Pachelbel's canon mollified a few onlookers, others, like neighborhood resident Howard Mack, expressed doubt that the last ten years have brought about any improvement in interracial relations or the fruition of plans to redevelop the blighted area: "This is [just] Hollywood. . . . Nothing has changed. . . . Why don't you come here at 6 o'clock, when the sun goes down, and see reality?"[1]

Not only do such performances mask the lack of real progress in countering the economic and political disempowerment of the area, but it also seems to me that programming old European music for this occasion misses the point. Contrary to its claim to universality, European classical music does not speak for or to the majority of this polyglot population. Rather, the future of race relations rests on the shoulders of the hip-hop generation, on those who have grown up taking for granted their fragmented and multihued environment and have devised new idioms with which to communicate across social and spatial boundaries.

Even as debates rage on about the positive/negative contributions of hip-hop to American culture, there is a general consensus about its origin in black expressive culture and its potential for engaging in political discourse. Writers on hip-hop point to the confluence of technology, commercialization, and the expressive articulation of black identity as the foundation of a significant oppositional practice.[2] As hip-hop's influence spreads, not only within the United States and to other Afrodiasporic communities but also to nonblack and even non-English-speaking cultures, questions inevitably arise: How does hip-hop translate, in terms of language, music, and meaning, into other cultures? Can hip-hop be harnessed to express political and social aspirations that go against the grain of African American experiences, that may even stand in direct opposition to black identity and politics? Is hip-hop by nonblacks an authentic cultural expression, or does such borrowing always involve cultural theft?

In considering intercultural practices, earlier studies on hip-hop have focused mostly on the question of white appropriation, exploitation, and consumption of black musical forms, remaining firmly wedded to the binary framework of black versus white that informs most histories and analyses of American popular music.[3] Yet the intertwined trajectories of popular music and race relations in the United States are propelled increasingly by those who are neither black nor white. Because of the political meanings frequently read into hip-hop, it is an especially illuminating site of interaction for the two racially and socially distinct groups—Koreans and African Americans— who took center stage in the biggest civil uprising in the United States at the end of the twentieth century.

Koreans and African Americans in Los Angeles

The 1992 acquittal of the police officers charged with the brutal beating of Rodney King sparked a wave of interethnic violence throughout Los Angeles. In African American communities, anger against the police and the judicial system was transferred and redirected against local, predominantly Korean store owners, inciting arson and mass looting of neighborhood businesses. Korean businesses incurred losses of approximately $460 million, more than half of the city's total property damages.[4]

The first day of rioting, April 29, christened in Korean as *sa-i-ku,* marked a turning point in the lives of Korean immigrants. Watching helplessly as

their livelihoods went up in smoke, Korean Americans were forced to confront painful realities concerning their place in American society and their
relationships with other racial and ethnic groups. National media outlets, like
Time magazine, persisted in imposing outmoded black/white interpretations
on the post-trial events and barely mentioned Koreans in their coverage of
the riots.[5] Local coverage in Los Angeles, on the other hand, mischaracterized
the conflict by reductively casting it as a black versus Korean battle for turf.
Newspapers and evening news shows glossed over the participation of Latinos and made little mention of the role of whites—in particular the notable
absence of the police and other city officials—in the incidents of arson and
the looting of South Central businesses. News reports showed angry black
mobs breaking store windows and carrying away televisions and stereos and
vigilante Koreans sporting firearms and crying in anguish in a strange tongue.
Critics and scholars have since argued that the reality was in fact much more
complicated and nuanced than was apparent in the media coverage of the
event and that the 1992 L.A. riots were the first "multicultural," "multiethnic,"
or "multiracial" urban riots in American history.[6]

The burning and looting of South Central stores represents the culmination of a general breakdown in race relations, not only between blacks and
Koreans but between the many different ethnic and racial groups that occupy L.A.'s complex sociopolitical and cultural terrain. By the early 1990s,
plant closings had affected the economic welfare of nonwhite populations in
the city disproportionately, with the unemployment rate of undereducated
Asian males growing to be almost twice that of their white counterparts
and of black males three times that of whites.[7] South Central, a traditionally
black neighborhood, was almost half Latino by this time, and the nonwhite
disenfranchised residents here competed with one another for the limited
employment, housing, and social welfare allotments available to the city's socioeconomic margins. With the black male unemployment rate at 50 percent
in some parts of this neighborhood, it was a matter of course that scapegoats
would be made to shoulder some of the blame for its blighted condition.[8]

Since the lifting of the exclusionary quota system for Asian immigration
in 1965, Koreans had been moving to the United States in steadily increasing numbers. Between 1985 and 1987, the peak years of Korean immigration,
over 35,000 South Koreans were arriving annually in the United States. Many
of them headed for Los Angeles, which contains the largest Korean community outside of Korea.[9] Although a high percentage of post-1965 Korean
immigrants were from the educated middle class, they often had to give up
their professions in the United States because of linguistic shortcomings and
hiring discrimination in the host country. Newly immigrated Koreans, with

limited capital to invest in businesses, were able to take over the liquor stores and swap-meet booths in South Central only because whites and middle-class blacks wanted out of this impoverished neighborhood. As entrepreneurs in urban ghettos, Korean immigrants served the role of "middleman minority," subject to the hostility of both the dominant culture (white) and the subordinate group (black).[10]

Even though Korean stores provided retail services to an area that had been largely abandoned by national supermarket chains and retail outlets, many South Central residents saw Korean store owners as yet another oppressive group leaching wealth out of a black neighborhood. Both Koreans and African Americans had absorbed too well the racial stereotypes promulgated by the mainstream media, portraying Asians as unfeeling and overachieving model minorities and blacks as dangerous criminals. Increased contact seemed to help little in ameliorating those negative impressions of one another. Only thirteen days after the King beating, Korean store owner Soon Ja Du, whose son had been repeatedly harassed by black Crips gang members and whose store had been held up more than thirty times, shot and killed the teenaged Latasha Harlins during a heated argument over a bottle of orange juice. Many African Americans saw her light sentencing as further proof of racial favoritism and injustice. Even before the Rodney King verdict was reached, black activist Danny Bakewell was agitating to launch large-scale action against Korean businesses in South Central, already the targets of frequent firebombs and boycotts. Korean and African American community leaders were attempting to reach some kind of rapprochement in a series of town hall meetings with little enthusiasm on either side.[11]

The acquittal of the Rodney King police officers was the match that set off the massive conflagration of spring 1992. But the tinder had been gathering for some time, and prophetic voices had been warning of the dangers ahead. Mike Davis's *City of Quartz*, first printed in 1990, presciently described Los Angeles as the site of a future dystopia. Davis portrayed a city divided between a predominantly white moneyed class and a darkening and expanding underclass by the aggressive application of spatial surveillance and policing and the erection of fortresses around affluent neighborhoods. Long before the tape of the King beating had first aired on television, Davis was noting the disconnect between intellectual ruminations on the nature of the postmodern city and the cataclysmic social changes actually visible in Los Angeles. He suggested that filmmakers, working with fictional material, were confronting the realities of postindustrial L.A. with more integrity and honesty than the city's power brokers or the intelligentsia: "Images of carceral inner cities (*Escape from New York, Running Man*), high-tech police death squads (*Blade Runner*), sentient buildings (*Die Hard*), urban bantustans (*They Live!*), Vietnam-like street wars (*Colors*), and so on, only extrapolate from actually existing trends."[12] The late 1980s also ushered in a spate of hip-hop films that addressed the social problems of inner cities head-on. One of the first of this genre, Spike Lee's *Do the Right Thing*, and the song inspired by that film, Ice Cube's "Black Korea," anticipated the disaster of spring 1992 with chilling foresight.

Death Certificate

For his 1989 film *Do the Right Thing*, Spike Lee created an urban microcosm within a Brooklyn city block, populated by the archetypal racial characters of late-twentieth-century American metropolises. In the film, Mookie is an underemployed black youth, working at a dead-end job delivering pizza. Sal, his Italian-American boss, has run the neighborhood pizzeria for over two decades and has intimate relationships with his black customers, some more positive than others. The community elders, Da Mayor and Mother Sister, watch over the domain and entreat the residents to maintain interracial harmony through accommodation, while younger rebels like Buggin' Out agitate for direct action to change the status quo. A new business on the block, a convenience shop run by a Korean immigrant couple, provides the consumer goods that bring pleasure to the daily lives of the residents, but the foreignness of the store owners stirs up resentment among some of the neighbors. The different characters show various levels of sympathy and antipathy for the racial others who share their space.

Lee orchestrated the events leading up to the climactic scene of the riot in such a way that the racially motivated explosion seems inevitable, much like the Rodney King uprising does in retrospect. The three black nationalists—Buggin' Out, the physically intimidating Radio Raheem, and the stuttering Smiley—march into the pizzeria just as Sal is preparing to close down for the day and demand that African Americans be given representation on his wall of celebrity pictures. Sal angrily insists that Raheem shut off his blaring music, Public Enemy's confrontational "Fight the Power," and, meeting resistance, demolishes Raheem's boom box with a bat. Raheem lunges at Sal's throat, and the melee that ensues brings the police to the scene. The police officers are white, and from earlier scenes, we know that the worst of them are outright bigoted and hateful and the most sympathetic of them are fearful of the black residents who outnumber and could easily overpower them. In attempting to render Raheem docile, one of the officers chokes him with too much zeal and kills him. Witnesses to this act of police brutality are stunned and stand immobilized until Mookie sets the riot in motion by taking the first step toward the destruction of Sal's business.

As in the Los Angeles uprising, it is not the police—responsible for the actual murder—who become the target of black anger but instead the business owner who happens to be in the wrong place with the wrong skin color. As those in the crowd turn to the convenience store as their next target, the Korean store owner yells out in his broken English, "I no white, I black; you and me same!" Even as a newcomer to the United States, the Korean immigrant recognizes the reductive framework of the black and white racial paradigm and knows he must identify with one side or the other. By throwing his lot in with blacks, in this instance, the Korean store owner is delivered from violence.

Rapper Ice Cube references the Spike Lee film in "Black Korea," a pithy song that captured and further inflamed the mutual animosity and distrust felt by Korean business owners and their black customers in Los Angeles. The song hails from the album *Death Certificate,* which reached number 2 on the Billboard charts and sold 1.5 million copies in 1991 despite, or perhaps because of, the controversy inspired by the album's confrontational lyrics. As one of the progenitors of West Coast rap, Ice Cube was no stranger to controversy. The multiracial, multiethnic South Central club scene of the early 1980s had, by the end of the decade, been pushed aside by the new "gangsta" style taking over the streets, popularized by Ice Cube and Eazy E's violence-promoting, police-hating, unapologetic rap supergroup NWA (Niggaz with Attitude).[13] On his solo album *Death Certificate,* Ice Cube brought to bear all of the frustrations of a young black male living in a downward-spiraling South Central, singling out and attacking specific enemies with his racially incendiary lyrics.

The opening of "Black Korea," the most controversial track on the album, replays the dialogue between the Korean store owners and Radio Raheem from the Spike Lee film. By framing the song with audio clips from *Do the Right Thing,* Ice Cube situates his political diatribe within the interracial dynamics of the film. This scene enacts with painful clarity the racial tension between blacks and Koreans: the sales transaction is fraught with friction as the Korean store owner, with his limited knowledge of English, tries to understand what Raheem wants and becomes defensive in response to the black youth's growing anger and frustration. Like a parrot who is exposed only to obscenities, the Korean store owner repeats the phrase "Mother fuck you" several times in the scene, and the rap song uses this line as a background refrain.

By choosing this particular scene, Ice Cube is able to piggyback his rap on Public Enemy's forceful "Fight the Power" attached to the person of Radio Raheem. The salience of "Fight the Power" to Spike Lee's message is established by its prominent use in the opening title sequence and by its association with Raheem, a pivotal character who embodies both the hope and disillusionment of contemporary African Americans. The song's combative stance brings Raheem into two racial confrontations: the first, a competition of volume against the salsa music of his Latino neighbors; and the second, against Sal, who is physically disturbed by the aggressive sounds coming out of the boom box. Raheem wins the first; the second leads to his death. Further, the meeting between Raheem and the Korean store owners transpires because he needs batteries in order to continue his sonic assault on the neighborhood.[14] The lyrics of the song "speak" for the largely taciturn Raheem:

> We got to fight the powers that be
> To revolutionize make a change
> What we need is awareness
> Power to the people, no delay.[15]

Ironically, it is the silencing of his music and his untimely death that finally arouses his people to act.

"Black Korea" borrows the sounds—a fast-paced, aggressive rhythm track overlaid with horns and electric guitar screeches—of the Public Enemy anthem, but whereas the earlier song is about opposing the hegemonic forces of white America, the Ice Cube song foregrounds the racial strife between blacks and Koreans. In the time-honored tradition of black oral practices, Ice Cube "signifies" upon "Fight the Power"; "Black Korea" is a "repetition *with a difference;* the same and yet not the same."[16] Conflating different Asian stereotypes, Ice Cube directs the black nationalist message against Koreans and makes threats that anticipate the violence of the near future:

> Don't follow me up and down your crazy little market,
> or your little chop suey ass will be the target of a nationwide boycott. . . .
> Pay respect to the black fist,
> or we'll burn your store right down to a crisp.
> And then we'll see ya
> 'cause you can't turn the ghetto into Black Korea.

The difference between the two songs points to the two divergent endings. In Spike Lee's film, the Korean store is spared in the riot; in Ice Cube's song, it is the specified target of violence, the future site of a racial conflagration.

Jeff Chang's essay on "Black Korea" recounts the political and economic fallout from the song. Korean American community leaders and grocers met with some success in their boycotts of *Death Certificate* and the St. Ides malt liquor that Ice Cube endorsed. But while white critics in mainstream music magazines and newspapers complained about the racist rhetoric of the album and black writers defended Ice Cube's angry tirade, Korean American responses to the controversy were relegated to the ethnic press, receiving coverage in *Asian Week* and the Los Angeles–based *Korea Times* and ignored on the larger cultural stage. The mainstream media focused mainly on themes of censorship and rebellion and reframed the issue around a white/black racial axis.[17] Within the parameters of this song and its reception, Ice Cube, on the one hand, overemphasized the role Koreans played in contributing to the economic impoverishment of South Central and other inner-city black neighborhoods, while the mainstream media, on the other hand, discounted the complicating involvement of other racial groups and clung to a reductive and outmoded model of race relations.

Post *Sa-i-ku* Korean Rap

The "Black Korea" controversy and other incidents that foreground the place of Asians in American society do so by placing Asians in a negative position in relation to the subject, by defining Asians by what they are not—neither black nor white. As the often unacknowledged shadow presence obscured by America's paradigmatic black and white racial schema, Asian Americans have forged varying racial identities under the radar of mainstream media. In this ongoing negotiation of racial identification, music has served Asian American youths as a vehicle of self-expression as well as a marker of ethnic affiliation.

In the production and consumption of hip-hop, Korean Americans exhibit the tensions and contradictions attendant in "becoming Asian American," that is, between a racial identification with other nonwhites and an ethnonational affiliation to the diasporic Korean community, and between the desire to assimilate into mainstream America and to retain ethnic distinctiveness.[18] But even as the Korean American identity embraces a fluid and diverse set of variables—from geographic location and class to gender and sexuality—certain commonalities in the experiences of Korean Americans emerge. One such commonality is the Rodney King riots, a watershed experience for the entire community, and another, for those under a certain age, is the immersion in American popular culture.

Two models of understanding immigration and race in the United States are available for consideration: one is the ethnic American model, patterned after European immigrant processes of assimilation, and the second, the racial minority model, gleaned from the experiences of African Americans and other "colonized minorities." The process of ethnicization for Asian Americans draws upon both models. Members of an Asian ethnic group form a self-conscious, rather than superimposed, sense of belonging to a distinct group that is neither fully assimilated nor fully racialized.[19] Two theories about Asian American hip-hop relate to these models. Writing on examples of interaction and exchange between African and Asian diasporic communities, Ellie Hisama underscores the potential of hip-hop to nurture practices of polyculturalism, which revises and updates the assimilation model by acknowledging "the simultaneous existence of different cultural lineages in a single person."[20] Deborah Wong, on the other hand, suggests that in the case of hip-hop—an oppositional practice with origins in African American culture—Asian Americans move self-consciously toward "Blackness" and unequivocally away from "Whiteness."[21]

In Korean American hip-hop, one finds both the movement toward color described by Wong, conforming to the racial minority model, and evidence of polyculturalism highlighted by Hisama, which owes more to the ethnic American model. As communication and transportation technologies continue to evolve, transnational and diasporic identities are also exerting a stronger pull on young ethnic Americans.[22] With the Korean diaspora now extending around the globe, events that take place in Los Angeles make their impact felt on the worldwide Korean transnational community. Hip-hop is similarly no longer contained within the boundaries of one place, increasingly becoming the vehicle of cultural nationalist messages throughout the world. Korean rap since 1992 mirrors and expresses many of the tensions operative in the Rodney King uprising, the racial politics of hip-hop, and the coming of age of 1.5 and second-generation Korean Americans.

The story of rapper James Chang, a.k.a. Jamez, exemplifies the complexity of becoming Korean American through hip-hop. Jamez was born in the Bronx to Korean immigrant parents, grew up in Los Angeles "in denial of his ethnicity," and then began an exploration of his ethnic roots as a young adult. With few Korean Americans in the public limelight, Jamez had earlier looked to African American cultural heroes for cues on how to survive as a minority in a white-dominated society, making the move to Blackness and away from Whiteness. At the age of fifteen, he wrote his first song, titled "Black Man Singing in a White Man's World," a song that served, in his words, as "a metaphor for the alienation that I, as a young Asian kid, felt but could never elegantly express." A visit to Korea introduced him to *pansori,* a traditional Korean music that emphasizes storytelling, and spurred him on a search for Korean folk culture, largely buried under Western commercial exports. He reminisced, "For me, this retrieval symbolized my search for an identity. In the past I had always tried to be someone else (Black, White, Latino, etc.) because I never felt comfortable speaking in Korean. I spoke other people's experiences, listened to other people's dialects. Learning Korean music was like learning my native tongue, albeit musically."[23]

College provided formative experiences for Jamez as well as for other Korean Americans; 1.5 and second-generation Korean Americans have absorbed all too well the lesson that education is their strongest protection against the professional downward mobility their parents have often encountered as immigrants and enter elite colleges in disproportionately high numbers.[24] Away from home and family for the first time, many Korean Americans end up participating in Korean cultural organizations on campus and becoming members of distinctly Korean American social networks. Programs in ethnic studies and Asian American studies, which have proliferated on many university campuses since the 1980s, introduce theoretical and historical frameworks that help Korean Americans understand their personal experiences in the context of larger historical forces.[25] As an ethnic studies major at Bard College, Jamez learned not only about Asian American history but also about the history of injustice and racism that plagued many other communities in this country's checkered past. Continuing to feel a sense of affinity with other minority groups, he recalls, "I got hip to Asian Americanness when I started reading the histories of Chinese and Filipino laborers in the United States. The indignities these people suffered reminded me of the hardships of African and Native Americans."[26] These lessons inform his music and poetry, which make up his self-proclaimed movement, the "Azian/Pacific Renaissance."

After his political awakening as an Asian and Korean American, Jamez began to experiment in fusing Korean *pansori,* Indian, and Chinese music with hip-hop, creating a polycultural musical scaffolding that supports his socially progressive texts. In 1998, Jamez released his debut album, *Z-Bonics,* produced by his own label, F.O.B. (Fresh Off the Boat). A single from the album *F.O.B.* plays with the rapper's polymorphous identity—a composite of Korean and African American influences, stereotypes of Asian Americans and subversions thereof—both musically and lyrically. The song opens with a woman singing in vocalise in a traditional Korean style, with a nasal-sounding tone produced by pushing the voice through the throat, accompanied by *poongmul* drumming. Jamez enters with a more assertive rhythm track and defiantly confronts, refutes, and tries on various labels:

Tales from da Jaemygyopo [Korean American] Nation
Second Gen
Seoul-ta-Babylon my R.I.B.S.

> Rotten Banana Syndrome
> Got me thinking, "I'm a niggaman instead of zipperhead."

The Korean singer provides a soothing counterpoint to Jamez's more forceful rap delivery, and her feminine, textless voice acts as a binary opposite to that of the male, most likely white, announcer who concludes the song. A PA system amplifies the male speaker's message, endowing his pronouncement with the guise of official sanction. The anonymous male begins a few times and then finally completes his message at the end of the song: "Immigrants and refugees: we don't want your children. This wall is being put up to protect." Perhaps the Korean woman is meant to stand in for Jamez's mother, who is powerless to fight against the official culture's racist policies. According to the rap, she does not fully understand her son's perspectives as a second-generation Korean American ("my mom's castigate / she just can't relate") and can only pray (and sing wordlessly?) for his well-being. Jamez, on the other hand, fully exploits the power of his words and music, speaking in what he calls "Z-Bonics" (playing on Ebonics) to challenge hegemonic representations of Asian Americans. Jamez speaks to and for Korean audiences everywhere by deploying hip-hop and traditional folk musical elements, juxtaposing various economic, gender, linguistic, racial, and national subjects, and addressing the social concerns of immigrant communities in the United States.

The 1992 L.A. riots factor into Jamez's expressive oeuvre as well. In his poem titled "Sa-i-ku, April 29," Jamez refers to race only indirectly, choosing to focus on power relationships rather than representing the riots in polarizing terms as a Korean-black or black-white conflict:

> Committed by the city of indelible force
> Of Evangelical Sorts
> They say they treat you like a KING this time
> Whose THRONE to the ground—but nothing more
> Or so they still say, after years in court:
> "Your Blackness, we divorce."
>
> Soon after that the demonstration was had
> Some called it UPRISING
> While my people called it something worse than biases:
> Was The Season that the Fire Breathes
> And burns to the ground

He concludes with the following stanzas:

> These are the players,
> Multi-national looters (lootars)

Who can say in many languages
For profit we abandon you
Supply and we'll be damned of you
It's epidemic

Plastac-tinsel-tack
Relax, relax
That which abhors you
The INS minors you
Ethnici-piss.[27]

For Jamez, accessing blackness via hip-hop is one way of gaining critical distance from the white mainstream, to better perceive the institutional forces—the judicial system, law enforcement, multinational corporate powers, the Immigration and Naturalization Service—at work in perpetuating racism for all minorities in the United States. Just as importantly, he has pieced together for himself a polycultural identity that signals his engagement with both American politics and transnational Korean culture.

Earlier Korean American rappers like Hana Choi, formerly of Fists of Fire, Seoul Brothers (brothers Michael and Raphael Park), and Theo Chung have also grappled with issues of race and ethnicity in their music. Choi, who immigrated from Korea to New York City at age eleven, recalls her discovery of rap: "I was influenced by Public Enemy and it was a perfect form for expressing anger. I wanted to stir shit up." The Parks immigrated as toddlers to the Seattle area and together with deejay David Ford, who is half African American and half Korean, have performed throughout the Northwest. Raphael Park was also inspired by Public Enemy and read *The Autobiography of Malcolm X* in his pursuit of racial and political awareness.[28]

One of the consequences of the L.A. riots was the deepening of the rift between Korean Americans and other Asian Americans as many non-Korean Asian Americans openly disassociated themselves from Koreans. As younger Korean Americans nurtured their sense of ethnic consciousness and became politically active following the riots, they often had to acknowledge the sometimes vast separation between the different groups within Asian America. Asked about his relationships with other Asian Americans, Jeff, whose parents' store had been attacked during the riots, answered, "It's a mistake to think there's any real bond going on there. We speak different languages, have different perspectives. I was in college during the riots. I remember reading right after the riots about how the Chinese and Japanese communities in L.A. were just unfazed. I mean, it didn't concern them—it was a Korean problem."[29] Seoul Brothers' rap "I Got Your Back" expresses their feeling of abandonment by other Asian American students at the University of Washington when they failed to show their support during the brothers' trial involving a police harassment case:

> Yellow brothers and sisters I see
> Are fakin' perpetrating like Barbie and Ken
> Then, pointin' their fingers at fellas like me
> Saying yo, he's an F.O.B.

Although Korean Americans have voiced their disappointment with other Asian Americans, they are often lumped together with other Asian ethnic groups by the American mainstream and face the same problems that beset other Asian Americans. This is certainly true in hip-hop, a musical genre that is purportedly open to all but in reality is vulnerable to the larger racial tensions operative in society. Seoul Brothers, for example, tried to sell their music in the early 1990s, but record producers were not interested in Asian American rappers. Raphael Park angrily recalls a conversation with the president of Nasty Mix records: "Motherfucker, he wanted to have us jump out of some Chinese takeout boxes. He wanted us to totally sell out, do some Jerry Lewis ridiculous type stuff."[30] In 1996, the Chinese American rap trio Mountain Brothers won a national Sprite-sponsored singing concert and soon after signed a deal with Ruffhouse Records, a major hip-hop label. The relationship with the label deteriorated shortly after the production of their first album. One executive, who liked their music, bluntly explained, "There's only one problem. You're Asian." Another "wanted to use their ethnic backgrounds as a marketing vehicle and suggested they perform onstage wearing karate outfits and wielding gongs."[31]

More recently, Chinese American rapper Jin has achieved a level of fame that has thus far eluded Asian Americans, having been featured on BET's "Freestyle Friday" and on MTV and appearing beside Ludacris in the 2003 summer blockbuster 2 Fast 2 Furious. In an article in the New York Times, he confidently asserted his stance on ethnicity and rap: "I am proudly Chinese. . . . I'll embrace it but never exploit it. During a show, I might say, 'so where my Asians at?' But I'll never go out there with a sword, you know."[32] Even with his success, the specter of long-standing stereotypes lingers. Perceptions of Asian American males as emasculated, nerdy "model minority" types run counter to the dominant masculinist images of hip-hop culture.[33]

A few Korean American hip-hop artists have bypassed the American music industry altogether, achieving fame first in Korea and then developing a transnational fan base. Almost unknown in the United States, Uptown 3000, the duo of Carlos Galvin and Steve Kim, called the "pioneers of Asian hip-hip," have released seven albums that have sold over 6 million copies in Asia. Their hybrid hip-hop moves seamlessly back and forth between English, Korean, and Spanish.[34] The self-proclaimed "pioneers of *jinjja* [real] hip-hop," Drunken Tiger, made up of Korean Americans from Los Angeles and New York as well as non–Korean Americans, are also polycultural in orientation. Their bilingual rap combines reggae, Euro-techno, West Coast hip-hop, and the sentimental love ballads that accompany Korean soap operas. Although most of their songs are about partying or romance and are not overtly political in the vein of Jamez's music, the Drunken Tiger rappers do highlight their racial identity and make explicit their affinity to black culture. In "Party People," for example, they rhyme: "I got souls of blackness. . . . My people feel the flavor from the chi before they enter Oriental my essential in my Buddhist temple. . . . I'm into being like #1 Korean I represent the soul and every yellow human being."

Hearkening from Los Angeles, New York, Atlanta, and Seoul, Uptown 3000 and Drunken Tiger see themselves as international, rather than Korean, artists. DJ Shine (Lim Bung-Wook) of Drunken Tiger explains: "I mean we weren't really a Korean group. . . . In the beginning we were more of an international group, and me and J we just went [to Korea] for a vacation and shit, and we just kind of stumbled upon it, it's like we tripped over and kind of fell in a hole; we were like, 'We should get out' but it was like kind of late, and then we started doing one thing we started doing another thing, it was just like, 'Uh, how did we get here?'"[35] These second-generation Korean American artists find little success as Asians in the United States but are valued in Korea for their American-ness, for their proximity to the original source of hip-hop. One segment of the Korean public adores them for their American hipness while another vilifies them for conducting themselves in unacceptable Western ways (Drunken Tiger's DJ Shine won the group much notoriety when he was convicted of narcotics possession during his stay in Korea). Some of the same debates surrounding hip-hop's corrupting influence on the youth are replayed in Asia, with distinctive Korean inflections. In the American context, they are seen as too nerdy and square; in the Korean, as delinquent and dangerous.[36]

Even if Korean rap is largely a fledgling and unacknowledged enterprise within the United States, hip-hop can play an integral role in the racial formation of Korean Americans. Subcultural theories, advanced by Stuart Hall and Dick Hebdige, among others, stressing the significance of consumption in the construction of identity have had enormous impact in cultural studies.[37] More recently, scholars working in Asian American music have also turned to consumption as a fertile area of inquiry, mindful of the ways in which musicking, to borrow Christopher Small's term, locates meaning in all activities related to music, including listening and reacting to music.[38]

How have Korean American listeners responded to the changing racial landscape of the post-1992 era? At least within the Asian American community, there seems to be an increased awareness of the contribution Asian American hip-hop artists are making in defining an Asian American identity. Writers like Deborah Wong, Ellie Hisama, Jeff Chang, and Oliver Wang, the hip-hop artists themselves, and their fans have published numerous articles on the new phenomenon of Asian American hip-hop in scholarly journals, ethnic and alternative presses, and the newly proliferating Web sites on Asian American music.[39] On Jamez's Web site, many fans write of their enthusiasm for and identification with his Korean-styled hip-hop and the explicit celebration of his Asian American identity.[40]

Following the posting of a story on Drunken Tiger on the popular Web site *hiphopmusic.com,* a lengthy forum on Korean hip-hop ensued, with comments that show both the diversity and commonalities of attitudes among its fans.[41] When site moderator Jay Smooth introduced the Drunken Tiger article with his opinion that "this article overplays the discrimination angle somewhat" (April 24, 2003), several Koreans and other Asians wrote in to recount their experiences of racism in hip-hop. A Korean rapper working in Southern California laments (I have retained all of the original spellings, wordings, and punctuation): "As an MC every battle ive battle someone makes fun of my ethnicity(I hate it when they call me chinese), so we got to try 2 times harder" (gods will, January 16, 2004), echoing an earlier post, "prejudice towards Asians in US exists and it might be bigger than most of the people may believe" (DJ Musasahi, April 24, 2003). Another rapper, self-identified as half black, half Asian, also bemoans the anti-Asian sentiments in the hip-hop community in particular, and the United States more generally, but points out that there is a bigger market outside of this country: "Asians will never make it big with hiphop in the US. But that doesn't matter, becuz the US is only ONE country. Theres like over 50 countries azns can be successful in, in asia. So who gives a darn about this stupid stereotyping racist country?! NOT ME!!" (AznFreestylist, May 3, 2003). Many others also claim membership in a transnational Korean community and point with pride to the greater success Korean musicians are finding throughout Asia. Expressions like "AZN PRYDE" (DamienV, September 10, 2003), "Korean pride" (Korean QT, September 21, 2003), and "SUPPORT YO OWN PEOPLE!" (FOBHATER, October 16, 2003) appear often along with fan tributes—by Asians, Asian Americans, and non-Asians—to Korean hip-hop artists.

The forum is not without its detractors, however. Besides the few isolated comments that are outright racist and chauvinistic, there are several provocative comments that raise questions about the possibility of transcending cultural differences and about the validity of stylistic mimicry. One poster brings up the socioeconomic differences between the black originators of hip-hop and Korean rappers: "Korean kids rapping are nothing more than a JOKE>>_. as a Korean, myself,,,I can say this because_what the Fuck do they know about Hip hop culture_they have no street Cred_They rap about things they know nothing about_most of them are upper middle class spoiled Poor little rich kids_Driving around in their 'Beamers' and Benzes that their mommies and daddies bought them" (Chosen, April 14, 2004). Another poster also alludes to economics, finding a rapper's geo-social background more important than race: "I don't think Asians will rise up in hip hop. They don't have any street credibility. I'm not sure about what Eminem's life was like but based on what I saw in the 8 mile thats why he could get propz. Like the dude from a private school couldn't cuz he's not really from the hood y'kno? I heard Jin is from the suburbs. Thats not credibility" (Andy, November 12, 2003).

Still, others discount altogether the notion that music is attached to any specific race or ethnicity. A self-identified Korean contends, "We are all messengers. Music belongs to no one. We only relay what is being communicated to us. Plain and simple. A Korean making music does not mean it's Korean music. A white person making music does not mean it's white music, and etc." (jk, July 18, 2003). Another remarks, "hip hop got no color or race_its an expression, an art form_since when does music have a face, if u got skills, thats all it takes_since when is hip hop reserved for blacks and eminem? hip hop itself is bigger than any color or race_" but later acknowledges the polycultural and racial origins of hip-hop: "hip hop has through time expanded through fusing with a lot of artforms. you think those strings came from the streets? you think those synth riffs came from the ghetto? . . . racism is ignorance, and i would hope and pray that one of the few art forms that was created by a minority in the face of oppression would be the first ones to accept a minority expressing themselves" (hangookblazzed, April 1, 2004). The *hiphopmusic.com* forum shows Korean American hip-hop practitioners and fans covering the entire gamut from the expression of Korean transnational solidarity to celebration of American-ness, from the movement toward blackness to the embrace of the genre's polycultural aesthetics.

Authentic Korean American Hip-Hop?

The clash of stereotypes and dominant hip-hop mythologies brings us back to my earlier question: Can Korean Americans make authentic hip-hop statements? Lately, the notion of cultural authenticity has attracted much critical attention from scholars. The fluidity and mobility of music, in particular, belie the understanding of authentic cultural artifacts as fixed, static, and clearly contained. Further, authenticity discourses emerged within a colonialist context and worked to perpetuate unequal power relations, with the West identifying nonwestern cultures as authentic (read primitive and backwards), in danger of encroachment and extinction at the hands of their Western colonizers. Even within a single country such as the United States, certain communities—mostly rural, working-class, and ethnic—are thought to be in possession of more authentic cultures than others. Although the "authentic" label is generally used in a positive sense, it betrays the condescension of Western bourgeois subjects toward their geographic/ethnic/social other and posits on the other's culture an essentialized and non-changing nature in opposition to the dynamism of the modern West.[42]

African American music makes yet other kinds of claims to authenticity. Because music, so integral to African American culture, has in the past been another site of white exploitation of blacks, several notable African Americans have staked a defensive stance, taking (re)possession of their music as an authentic expression of blackness. According to the influential black nationalist writer Amiri Baraka, music is authentic when it captures the true social conditions and experiences of its creators. Without using the actual word "authentic," Baraka insists on the specificity of a socioeconomic and racial context for the blues and jazz that must elude white musicians, no matter their skill: "The music is the result of the attitude, the stance. Just as Negroes made blues and other people did not because of the Negro's peculiar way of looking at the world."[43] Like the blues, hip-hop emerged out of economically depressed and politically disenfranchised black communities. By Baraka's measure, then, Korean Americans, many of whom are from middle-class backgrounds, could never produce authentic hip-hop.

As much as Baraka instilled racial pride and gave due acknowledgment to significant African American musicians of the past, his inability to recognize nonblack participation as an essential element of the African American musical legacy remains a blind spot in his important work as a music and cultural critic. Hip-hop, as many have shown, grew out of a convergence of various cultures, even as African Americans were the dominant creative force in its gestation. Even Baraka's blues was born not in isolation but in the merging of African and European folk musics on American soil. The inevitably polycultural and hybrid nature of music thereby renders questions of musical authenticity moot for the colonizers and colonized alike.

Those who posted on *hiphopmusic.com*'s forum on Korean hip-hop subscribing to the view that hip-hop belongs to a specific race, nationality, or class are essentially advancing the authenticity argument and reinforcing status quo power relations. As Jeff Chang contends in his article on "Black Korea," African Americans enjoy easier access to the media even while Korean Americans wield more economic power, at least within the limited compass of South Central.[44] Someone like Jamez, educated at an elite college, can enjoy certain privileges unavailable to black inner-city youths but is unlikely to become a mainstream cultural icon in the current entertainment climate. Thus he turns to the one venue—academia—that has been relatively open and has yielded increased opportunities for Asian Americans, giving talks at Harvard instead of performing in concert arenas. Although Korean Americans are gaining ground in some professions, their representation in American popular culture is almost nil, and the best that Korean American musicians can hope for is to perform every now and then for members of their own ethnic community or to bypass the American market altogether.[45]

For Korean Americans, hip-hop has been and continues to be many things: an entryway into American mainstream culture, the locus of battles over identity, and a means of drawing and upending boundaries. Perhaps most important, hip-hop offers Korean Americans the opportunities to meet artists and fans from other communities and to create new relationships. There are a few groups that are already doing this type of intercultural work in music. In an article about the multiracial hip-hop group LA Symphony, for example, Flynn offered his take on his group's political message: "We obviously push the message of coming together with some racial reconciliation, healing 'cause we're definitely dealing with that in the world that we live in, and I think us coming from all various backgrounds whether it be African American, Latino, or White, we comin' together making music, livin' together, traveling together, kinda showing almost a new perspective of America."[46] The goal for LA Symphony, then, is to make not authentic but rather intercultural music that acknowledges both the polycultural legacy of this music and the changing demographic realities of Los Angeles and beyond.

The protection of turf has always been an important element of hip-hop, beginning with the staking of claim on specific blocks and projects in the Bronx to the battles between the East and West Coast styles and between old school and younger popular artists. Hip-hop purists who insist on its racial or socioeconomic specificity do not seem to recognize that it is the very success of this musical art that now renders it too big to be owned by any one person or community. As the Rodney King beating, trial, riot, and aftermath made clear, challenges—in the form of police, judicial, and governmental abuse and neglect—continue to exist for racial minorities of all social classes and educational backgrounds. With the transnational impact of hip-hop and the significance of this music to diasporic populations everywhere, such sociopolitical inequities take on importance and relevance far beyond L.A. city limits. Los Angeles has seen intercultural cooperation in various venues in the past;[47] hip-hop affords a potentially rich site for further creative work across racial, ethnic, and class lines at a time when intercultural understanding, in and out of California, is needed more urgently than ever.

Conclusion

Just a few years after the September 11 attacks and about a dozen years after the Rodney King uprising, Hollywood produced two films set in Los Angeles that grapple with the city's increasingly volatile race relations. In *Crash* (dir. Paul Haggis, 2004), Angelenos of various racial, ethnic, and class backgrounds collide calamitously, gaining little in the way of understanding or compassion for the other in their traumatic encounters. *Collateral* (dir. Michael Mann, 2004) is less overtly about race and difference, but perhaps for that very reason it succeeds in subverting existing racial paradigms with more nuance and subtlety. Under the glossy surface of its action movie sequences, *Collateral* tells a story about good guys and bad guys that reverses the conventional generic formula pitting white American heroes against villains of another color, nation, or creed. Vincent (Tom Cruise) is a white terrorist descending upon Los Angeles to assassinate witnesses for the prosecution of a big crime boss. Max (Jamie Foxx), as Vincent's hired cabbie, navigates the urban landscape with superb skill, with knowledge of the various pockets of L.A. nightlife to which Vincent is not privy as an alien in the city. Music underscores the cultural diversity of life in Los Angeles. In Max's first scene, we hear snatches of salsa, R&B, and other kinds of ethnically marked music as he drives in and out of various neighborhoods. During the course of one eventful night, Max and Vincent together visit a black-owned jazz club, a discotheque in Koreatown, and a Latin salsa club. The music is familiar yet distinct in each locale, signifying bounded yet overlapping communities, as do the Spanish spoken in an earlier scene and the Korean signs dotting the landscape.

In both films, as in the chapters of this book, images and sounds cluster around the common themes of police and spatial control, leisure and work, myths and dreams, and identity and difference. Multiculturalism is both implicit and explicit in how these themes are treated not only in these films but also in a plethora of today's books, university courses, and evening newscasts. But perhaps we don't ask often enough, "Whose multiculturalism?" Who stands to gain and who stands to lose as a result of the varying representations of cultural diversity? Are status quo power relations disrupted or perpetuated? How well do performances of multiculturalism reflect the lived experiences of a population in flux? For many, music might not be the obvious area to explore these questions. If we consider that music saturates our environment like never before and is used to sell everything from soft drinks to the U.S. Army, however, it becomes a matter of some urgency that music's imbrication in sociopolitical realities be scrutinized with closer and more critical attention.

As is evident in *Collateral,* music that is variously marked as black, Asian, Latin, and white can be heard throughout Los Angeles, as well as on radio dials across the country. Even as the black/white racial paradigm continues to frame political debates in this country, California is pointing the way to a new future, its culture exemplifying the Latinization and Asiafication of America in this new post-NAFTA, post-Vietnam century. Its musical life provides a glimpse of both the challenges and opportunities availed by an increasingly pluralistic society. At its best, its heterogeneous population engenders intercultural dialogues that result in new creative collaboration and artistic production; at its worst, it implodes under the pressures of racism, as happened in 1965 and 1992.

Just as California's sociopolitical terrain will become more complex with the demographic changes under way, its musical culture too will encompass ever more numerous subcultures, countercultures, and hybrids. Taste publics are becoming increasingly fractured and balkanized in California's metropolitan centers. Local music scenes in San Francisco, Los Angeles, Sacramento, and San Diego are vibrant, with nightclubs, radio stations, concert series, and universities presenting locally and nationally renowned artists. At the same time, the Internet and easier air travel provide listeners with access to music from around the world, allowing them to reach beyond the limited offering of the big recording companies. For many Californians today, polycultural and transnational identities trump an allegiance to the more narrowly defined American identity of yesteryear. And Californians, attuned to the latest technological trends and to international movements of people and ideas, will continue to lead other Americans in new practices of musical production and consumption, shaped by both the peculiarities of local California scenes and larger global trends.

I undertook the writing of this book to try to understand how race and ethnicity have shaped different musical subcultures in California over the course of the last century. By juxtaposing within one book different time periods, communities, and musical genres, I hope to have demonstrated that debates surrounding race and culture are fluid, contingent on the specificities of a given historical moment and geographic location. At times, California culture reflects or leads the trends of the nation, and at other times, it stands apart, distinctive and exceptional. Even within a single moment in time, the people of California espouse extreme progressive and reactionary opinions on matters of race and immigration. It is this very dynamism that makes California such a rewarding subject of historical study and that suggests for the region many possible and fascinating futures.

The case studies that make up this book do not, by any means, exhaust the possible topics on the convergence of music, race, and ethnicity in California. Other scholars will no doubt pick up where I left off to sort through the region's rich trove of music and related materials that await further examination. These future studies will help us to better comprehend not only the culture of this region but also, as an extension, the social relations of the United States at large, which is gradually coming to resemble that of California's. It is through the knowledge of our pluralistic environment that we, like *Collateral*'s Max, can hope to quell interracial conflict and violence and ultimately achieve self-understanding and realization.

Notes

Introduction

1. See Maria L. La Ganga and Shawn Hubler, "California Grows to 33.9 Million, Reflecting Increased Diversity," and Robin Fields, "A Deepening Diversity, but a Growing Divide," *Los Angeles Times,* March 30, 2001.

2. Recent literature that analyzes the more complex demographic makeup of California includes Tomás Almaguer, *Racial Fault Lines: The Historical Origins of White Supremacy in California;* W. A. U. Clark, *The California Cauldron: Immigration and the Fortunes of Local Communities;* and Howard DeWitt, *The Fragmented Dream: Multicultural California.* For books more specifically about Los Angeles, see Roger Waldinger and Mehdi Bozorgmehr, eds., *Ethnic Los Angeles;* and Roger Keil, *Los Angeles: Globalization, Urbanization and Social Struggles.*

3. Michael Omi and Howard Winant, *Racial Formation in the United States: From the 1960s to the 1990s,* 55–56.

4. See, for example, Richard Crawford, *America's Musical Life: A History;* John Rockwell, *All American Music;* Gilbert Chase, *America's Music: From the Pilgrims to the Present;* and H. Wiley Hitchcock, *Music in the United States: A Historical Introduction.*

5. John Rockwell, "A Life Tuned to the Sound of California," *New York Times,* February 9, 2003.

6. There have been several notable books written about California music in recent years. Some of the few books that have begun to look in depth at the music of specific groups in the region are: Ronald Riddle, *Flying Dragons, Flowing Streams: Music in the Life of San Francisco's Chinese;* Ted Gioia, *West Coast Jazz: Modern Jazz in California, 1945–1960;* Steven Loza, *Barrio Rhythm: Mexican American Music in Los Angeles;* Jacqueline DjeDje and Eddie Meadows, eds., *California Soul: Music of African Americans in the West;* Gerald Haslam, *Workin' Man Blues: Country Music in California;* Barney Hoskyns, *Waiting for the Sun: Strange Days, Weird Scenes, and the Sound of Los Angeles;* Brian Cross, *It's Not About a Salary—: Rap, Race, and Resistance in Los Angeles.* The last ten years have also seen the publication of important biographical and analytical studies

of California composers and their music: Heidi Von Gunden, *The Music of Lou Harrison;* Leta E. Miller and Fredric Lieberman, *Lou Harrison: Composing a World;* Bob Gilmore, *Harry Partch: A Biography;* Michael Hicks, *Henry Cowell, Bohemian;* and David Nicholls, ed., *The Cambridge Companion to John Cage.*

7. Stephanie Chavez and Jose Cardenas, "Using the Arts to Celebrate L.A.'s Cultures," *Los Angeles Times,* October 7, 2001.

8. Lisa Lowe, *Immigrant Acts: On Asian American Cultural Politics,* 89.

9. The literature in this area is growing. See, for example, Ronald Radano and Philip V. Bohlman, eds., *Music and the Racial Imagination;* Yayoi Uno Everett and Frederick Lau, eds., *Locating East Asia in Western Art Music;* Georgina Born and David Hesmondhalgh, eds., *Western Music and Its Others: Difference, Representation, and Appropriation in Music;* Timothy D. Taylor, *Global Pop: World Music, World Markets;* Jonathan Bellman, ed., *The Exotic in Western Music.*

10. Radano and Bohlman, "Introduction," in *Music and the Racial Imagination,* 8–9.

Chapter 1: The Early History of California Cultural and Musical Life

1. For more background on the history of Spanish occupation of California, see Carey McWilliams, *North from Mexico: The Spanish-Speaking Peoples of the United States;* and Douglas Monroy, *Thrown among Strangers: The Making of Mexican Culture in Frontier California.*

2. David Lavender, *California: Land of New Beginnings,* 165.

3. For a comparison with other U.S. cities during this era, see table 5 in Robert M. Fogelson, *The Fragmented Metropolis: Los Angeles, 1850–1930,* 79.

4. See Kevin Starr, *Americans and the California Dream: 1850–1915,* 365–414.

5. Roger Waldinger and Mehdi Bozorgmehr, "The Making of a Multicultural Metropolis," in *Ethnic Los Angeles,* 8.

6. Kevin Starr, *Endangered Dreams: The Great Depression in California,* 224–27.

7. See Ronald Takaki, *Strangers from a Different Shore: A History of Asian Americans,* 21–78.

8. For a thorough discussion of the struggles between the white majority and ethnic minorities in California's early history, see Roger Daniels and Spencer C. Olin Jr., eds., *Racism in California: A Reader in the History of Oppression;* and Sucheng Chan and Spencer C. Olin, eds., *Major Problems in California History: Documents and Essays.*

9. Oscar Lewis, *Bay Window Bohemia: An Account of the Brilliant Artistic World of Gaslit San Francisco,* 65.

10. William Issel and Robert W. Cherny, *San Francisco, 1865–1932: Politics, Power, and Urban Development,* 16.

11. In 1924, San Francisco citizens voted to support Propositions 28 and 29, which laid the financial responsibility of the Palace of the Legion of Honor and the De Young Memorial Museum on the city government. In 1926, voters authorized the city to accept the deed on the Palace of Fine Arts, originally built for the Panama Pacific International Exposition of 1915, and to spend $100,000 in the rehabilitation of the building. Issel and Cherny, *San Francisco, 1865–1932,* 112–14.

12. Lewis, *Bay Window Bohemia,* 70. See also George Pettitt, *A History of Berkeley.*

13. See Derrick R. Cartwright, "Chronology."

14. Los Angeles's power players controlled the press, transit, water, and politics, all in the name of real estate speculation. See Kevin Starr, *Inventing the Dream: California through the Progressive Era,* 72; and Robert Gottlieb and Irene Wolt, *Thinking Big: The Story of the* Los Angeles Times, *Its Publishers and Their Influence on Southern California,* 144.

15. By 1939, the year of *Gone with the Wind, Ninotchka, Wuthering Heights,* and *The Wizard of Oz,* movie making was the nation's eleventh-largest industry, with an output of some four hundred new movies every year. More than fifty million Americans went to the theater every week, earning the movie industry an annual gross of nearly $700 million. See Otto Friedrich, *City of Nets: A Portrait of Hollywood in the 1940s,* xi.

16. See Cartwright, "Chronology"; and Peter Plagens, *Sunshine Muse: Contemporary Art on the West Coast.*

17. Kevin Starr cites numbers indicative of the immense scope of urban expansion during one five-year period: "New construction at once met the needs of this self-tripling population and maintained its momentum. Only 6000 new building permits were issued in Los Angeles in the war year 1918. The annual figure jumped to 13,000 in 1919. But by 1921 it had climbed to 37,000; by 1922 to 47,000. In 1923, the peak year of the boom, an astonishing 62,548 building permits for some $200 million in building projects were being issued." *Material Dreams: Southern California through the 1920s,* 69.

18. Reyner Banham, *Los Angeles: The Architecture of Four Ecologies,* 124. For more on architecture in California, see Esther McCoy, *Five California Architects.*

19. See Carolyn Peter, "California Welcomes the World: International Expositions, 1894–1940, and the Selling of a State."

20. Quoted in Robert W. Rydell, *All the World's a Fair: Visions of Empire at American International Expositions, 1876–1916,* 211.

21. See Lawrence W. Levine, *Highbrow/Lowbrow: The Emergence of Cultural Hierarchy in America,* 171–242.

22. John Dizikes, *Opera in America: A Cultural History,* 109–19; George Martin, *Verdi at the Golden Gate: Opera and San Francisco in the Gold Rush Years.*

23. J. C. Freund, *Musical America,* March 5, 1910.

24. The list of visiting artists includes Schumann-Heink, contralto; Jascha Heifetz, violinist; Jacques Thibaud, violinist; Riccardo Stracciari, baritone; Percy Grainger, pianist; Galli-Curci, soprano; Eugene Ysaye and Mischa Elman in a joint recital; John McCormack, tenor; Benno Moiseiwitsch, pianist; the London String Quartet; Joseph Lhevinne, pianist; and Serge Prokofieff [*sic*], pianist. Writer's Program, California, *An Anthology of Music Criticism,* 444–45.

25. Alfred Metzger, *Pacific Coast Musical Review,* December 2, 1912.

26. Redfern Mason, *San Francisco Examiner,* April 13, 1930.

27. For more on the San Francisco Symphony, see David Schneider, *The San Francisco Symphony: Music, Maestros, and Musicians.* For more on musical life in the San Francisco Bay Area, see Jose Rodriguez, ed., *Music and Dance in California,* 289–92; Writer's Program, California, *Anthology of Music Criticism;* and Michael Saffle, "Promoting the Local Product: Reflections on the California Musical Press, 1874–1914," 167–96.

28. Some of the other ensembles from this time include Stamm's Orchestra, the first professional musical organization in Southern California, which performed between 1893 and 1895, and the Women's Symphony Orchestra, founded in 1893. The *Los Angeles Times* covered musical events as part of its general effort to raise cultural standards of the city, and a periodical, *Pacific Coast Musician,* was published there from 1911 to 1941. The School of Music at the University of Southern California opened its doors in 1892, and UCLA began conferring music degrees in 1939. See Howard Swan, *Music in the Southwest, 1825–1950,* 156–85; Robert Stevenson, "Music in Southern California: A Tale of Two Cities"; and Pauline Alderman, *We Build a School of Music: The Commissioned History of Music at the University of Southern California.*

29. Caroline Estes Smith, *The Philharmonic Orchestra of Los Angeles, "The First Decade," 1919–1929,* 56–57. The book quotes extensively from newspaper reviews of the concert, 57–61.

30. See Catherine Parsons Smith's "Symphony and Opera in Progressive-Era Los Angeles," and "'Popular Prices Will Prevail': Setting the Social Role of European-Based Concert Music." Kenneth Marcus argues that the sacralization process was accompanied by opposing desacralizing and democratizing forces in *Musical Metropolis: Los Angeles and the Creation of a Music Culture, 1880–1940.*

31. The Bowl property was purchased by popular subscription and then given to the County of Los Angeles for use by all citizens of the Southland. See Bruno David Ussher, "A History of the Hollywood Bowl," 29; Swan, *Music in the Southwest,* 244; Rodriguez, *Music and Dance in California,* 262–69; and Marcus, *Musical Metropolis,* 65–86.

32. Swan, *Music in the Southwest,* 272.

33. Among the many essays Adorno penned criticizing the culture industry, the best known is the book co-authored with Max Horkheimer, *Dialektik der Aufklärung: philosophische Fragmente.*

34. Quoted in Peter Yates, *Evenings on the Roof, 1939–1954,* transcript of oral history conducted in 1967 by Adelaide G. Tusler, collection 300/94, Department of Special Collections, Charles E. Young Research Library, University of California, Los Angeles, 46.

35. For more on Schoenberg and Stravinsky's exile in Los Angeles, see Reinhold Brinkmann and Christoph Wolff, eds., *Driven into Paradise: The Musical Migration from Nazi Germany to the United States.*

36. Evenings on the Roof was taken over administratively by the Music Guild in 1945 and with the departure of Peter Yates in 1954 assumed the new name of Monday Evening Concerts. See Dorothy Crawford, *Evenings On and Off the Roof: Pioneering Concerts in Los Angeles, 1939–1971.* The series continues to present adventurous programs in Zipper Concert Hall at the Colburn School in downtown Los Angeles.

37. For complete listing of repertoire and personnel of chamber music concerts in Los Angeles during this period, see Brian S. Walls, "Chamber Music in Los Angeles, 1922–1954: A History of Concert Series, Ensembles and Repertoire."

38. See Cyrilla Barr, *Elizabeth Sprague Coolidge: American Patron of Music.*

39. Redfern Mason, *San Francisco Examiner,* February 15, 1931.

40. In Los Angeles, private teachers advertising in the city directories increased in number from 5 in 1881–82 to 808 in 1916. In the first half of the twentieth century, San Francisco produced a number of prodigies who went on to pursue successful concert

careers, including Yehudi Menuhin, Isaac Stern, Ruggiero Ricci, and Leon Fleisher. Los Angeles cultivated the talents of Leonard Slatkin, Michael Tilson Thomas, André Previn, and Adele Marcus Stevenson. To learn more about local talents in San Francisco, see History of Music Project, *Fifty Local Prodigies.*

41. Since 1852, when the Tong Hook Tong Company (also chronicled as Hong Took Tong by contemporary newspapers), a Chinese performance troupe of 123 members, disembarked in the Bay for its run at the American Theatre, nonwestern musics had coexisted alongside the dominant strand of European concert music in California. For more on Asian music in California, see Mina Yang, "Orientalism and the Music of Asian Immigrant Communities in California, 1924–1945"; Riddle, *Flying Dragons, Flowing Streams;* Wei Hua Zhang, "The Musical Activities of Chinese American Community in San Francisco Bay Area"; and George Yoshida, *Reminiscing in Swingtime: Japanese Americans in American Popular Music, 1925–1960.*

42. See Martin R. Kalfatovic, *The New Deal Fine Arts Projects: A Bibliography, 1933–1992;* and Stephen Fry, *California's Musical Wealth: Sources for the Study of Music in California,* 2–3. The *Baton,* a newsletter produced by the Los Angeles chapter of the FMP, reported on the musical events of the region from 1936 to 1937.

43. Ernst Bacon, "Musical Needs," *Argonaut,* January 7, 1935.

44. Marjory Fisher, *San Francisco News,* February 14, 1935.

45. Alexander Fried, *San Francisco Examiner,* March 18, 1935.

46. Alfred Frankenstein, "San Francisco Rejuvenated," *Modern Music* 18, no. 3 (1941): 185.

47. Rodriguez, *Music and Dance in California,* 35.

48. Isabel Morse Jones, "Music of Two Decades Enjoyed at Playhouse," *Los Angeles Times,* March 3, 1942.

49. Alfred Frankenstein, "A General Survey of Music in San Francisco," *San Francisco Chronicle,* April 9, 1939.

Chapter 2: *The Transpacific Gaze*

1. For examples of orientalism in Western art music and operas from this era, see Derek B. Scott, "Orientalism and Musical Style"; Ralph P. Locke, "Constructing the Oriental 'Other': Saint-Saëns's *Samson et Dalila*"; and Susan McClary, *Georges Bizet: Carmen.* For in-depth discussions of orientalism in various musical genres, see Born and Hesmondhalgh, *Western Music and Its Others;* and Bellman, *The Exotic in Western Music.*

2. For a more detailed discussion of Redding and Eichheim's works and of orientalism in California in general, see Yang, "Orientalism and the Music of Asian Immigrant Communities."

3. David Nicholls also recognizes this shift in emphasis. See "Transethnicism and the American Experimental Tradition."

4. Said was interested specifically in orientalist practices invoking the Middle East, but his theories have come to be applied to any orientalist practice that references Asia. Edward W. Said, *Orientalism.*

5. J. J. Clarke, *Oriental Enlightenment: The Encounter between Asian and Western Thought,* 27.

6. John Edmunds, interview with Henry Cowell, c. 1959, Oral History, American Music, Yale University, New Haven, Conn., 15. Partch quoted in Peter Garland, *Americas: Essays on American Music and Culture, 1973–80*, 61. Vincent Plush, interview with Lou Harrison, 1983, Oral History, American Music, Yale University. Quotations from the oral histories of Cowell and Harrison are reprinted by permission of The David and Sylvia Teitelbaum Fund, as successors to Henry and Sidney Cowell. Thomas S. Hines, "Then Not Yet 'Cage': The Los Angeles Years, 1912–38," 65.

7. See Nan Alamilla Boyd, *Wide-Open Town: A History of Queer San Francisco to 1965*. The promotion of sex and race tourism was not without its critics. The very characteristics that the Chamber of Commerce marketed as distinctively San Franciscan were often attacked as sources of public health and moral menace. In addition, Chinatown, with its severe gender imbalance, provided models of "queer domesticity," living arrangements that departed significantly from normative heterosexual family structures, which was seen as a welcome alternative to some but as anathema to the majority. See Nayan Shah, *Contagious Divides: Epidemics and Race in San Francisco's Chinatown*.

8. See Robert W. Rydell, John E. Findling, and Kimberly D. Pelle, *Fair America: World's Fairs in the United States*, 97. The Californian expositions inherited the legacy of exhibiting exoticism that originated with the European fairs but with the emphasis shifted to the Pacific.

9. See Golden Gate International Exposition, *Official Guide Book 1940;* and Richard Reinhardt, *Treasure Island: San Francisco's Exposition Years*, 55.

10. For more on the interconnection between the expo and the growing gay subculture in San Francisco, see Boyd, *Wide-Open Town*, 54, 79–81. For more on Harrison's visit to the expo, see Miller and Lieberman, *Lou Harrison*, 20.

11. Nadine Hubbs, *The Queer Composition of America's Sound: Gay Modernists, American Music, and National Identity*, 170.

12. I am borrowing here from Carol Oja's chapter title, "The Transatlantic Gaze of Aaron Copland," in *Making Music Modern: New York in the 1920s*, 237–51.

13. Philip Brett was one of the first scholars to theorize queer musicality. See his influential essay "Musicality, Essentialism, and the Closet." Before his untimely death in 2002, Brett was working on this very topic of the Californian experimentalists and orientalism. Unfortunately, I was unable to hear the preliminary version of the paper read at the Annual National Meeting of the American Musicological Association (Columbus, Ohio, 2002), and it was never published.

14. Hicks, *Henry Cowell, Bohemian*.

15. For more on Cowell's first New York visit, see ibid., 75–82. For a discussion of Ornstein and of *A la Chinoise*, see Oja, *Making Music Modern*, 11–24. For a comprehensive discussion of Cowell's tone clusters, see Michael Hicks, "Cowell's Clusters."

16. However, Cowell's wife later claimed that the composer made Asian references in manuscripts as early as 1912. In a letter from Sidney Cowell to KPFK regarding an Evenings on the Roof broadcast, dated July 11, 1962, in Peter Yates Papers, housed in the University of California, San Diego Library Special Collections (MSS 14, box 3, folio 45).

17. Dane Rudhyar, "The Relativity of Our Musical Conceptions," 117.

18. Dane Rudhyar, "Oriental Influence in American Music," 185.

19. For more on Cowell in Halcyon, see Steven Johnson, "Henry Cowell, John Varian,

and Halcyon." The quote is from John Varian, foreword to *Tirawa* (San Diego: Troubadour Press, 1930), cited in Johnson, "Henry Cowell," 16. Not incidentally, Cowell had his first significant homosexual relationship in 1922 in Halcyon, and the temple's authority figures proved to be less permissive than might have been expected. See Hicks, *Henry Cowell, Bohemian,* 127.

20. Henry Cowell, "Music of the Hemispheres," *Modern Music* 6, no. 3 (1929): 14.

21. For Cowell's account of his gamelan studies in Berlin, see Ada Hanifin, "Henry Cowell, Composer, Talks on Primitive Music and Modern Composers," *San Francisco Examiner,* June 11, 1933.

22. See Rita Mead, *Henry Cowell's New Music, 1925–1936: The Society, the Music Editions, and the Recordings.* An overview of their correspondences shows that Cowell, Cage, and Harrison arranged concerts for and heard numerous performances of one particular Japanese American shakuhachi player, Kitaro Nyohyo Tamada. See Yates Papers (MSS 14). Thanks to Leta Miller for informing me of Tamada's first name, abbreviated in most documents as "K."

23. John Cage remarked on this very point: "Henry Cowell . . . was not attached . . . to what seemed to so many to be the important question: Whether to follow Schoenberg or Stravinsky." In Cage, "History of Experimental Music in the United States," in *Silence,* 71.

24. Cowell, taking his cue from Varèse, dedicated *Ostinato Pianissimo* to Nicolas Slonimsky, who had conducted the premiere of *Ionisation*. Nicolas Slonimsky, *Music since 1900,* 355.

25. Hitchcock suggests that Cowell may have been especially preoccupied with rhythm during the time he was working on this piece, since he had spent the summer of 1934 teaching music for dancers at Stanford University and Mills College. H. Wiley Hitchcock, "Henry Cowell's *Ostinato Pianissimo*." Leta Miller further examines the influence of modern dance on Cowell's music in "Henry Cowell and Modern Dance: The Genesis of Elastic Form."

26. Susan McClary, *Feminine Endings,* 68–69.

27. See Oja, *Making Music Modern,* 32–44.

28. Henry Cowell, "Drums along the Pacific," *Modern Music* 18, no. 1 (1940): 46–47.

29. Alfred Frankenstein, "A Program of Percussion," *San Francisco Chronicle,* July 28, 1939.

30. Unfortunately for Cowell, his arrest took place at a time when moralists across the nation were waging a crusade against sex offenders and the reactionary governor Frank Merriam was putting into practice his tough-on-crime policies. See Michael Hicks, "The Imprisonment of Henry Cowell."

31. Scholars had formerly believed Ives resumed cordial relations with Cowell only after he left prison and married Sidney Robertson, but a recent article refutes this simplified account of the Ives and Cowell relationship and reveals a more ambivalent response to Cowell's imprisonment on the part of Ives. See Leta E. Miller and Rob Collins, "The Cowell-Ives Relationship: A New Look at Cowell's Prison Years." For more on Ives's homo- and gynophobia, see Hubbs, *Queer Composition,* 74–79; and Judith Tick, "Charles Ives and Gender Ideology."

32. For more on his early life and career, see Hines, "Then Not Yet 'Cage.'"

33. For more biographical background, see Miller and Lieberman, *Lou Harrison.* For more about his studies with Cowell, see Lou Harrison, "Learning from Henry."

34. The design is based on mathematical calculations. According to Leta Miller, Cage divided "the two hundred measures into fourteen sections of fourteen (with a four-measure coda), each section subdivided into units of 4 + 3 + 2 + 5. Harrison decided on twenty-one units of nine and one-half measures, adding the extra half-measure at the end." See "The Art of Noise: John Cage, Lou Harrison, and the West Coast Percussion Ensemble," 242; see also Leta E. Miller, "Cage's Collaborations," 154–55; and David Carey, "*Double Music:* A Historio-Analytic Study."

35. John Cage, "A Composer's Confessions," in *John Cage: Writer: Previously Uncollected Pieces,* ed. Richard Kostelanetz, 38.

36. In the program notes for "Lou Harrison: 40 Years of Music, a 60th Birthday Tribute, May 14, 1977," in the Betty Freeman Papers, housed in the University of California, San Diego Library Special Collections (MSS 227, box 5, folio 9).

37. John Cage, "The East in the West," *Modern Music* 23, no. 2 (1946): 113.

38. Cage invented this method of playing the piano while searching for a way to produce percussion effects for Sylvia Fort's dance, evocative of her African heritage. In lieu of an actual percussion piece, he wrote *Bacchanale* (1938), his first work for the prepared piano. *Amores* was performed in Cage's historic concert at New York's Museum of Modern Art in 1943.

39. From interview with Winston Leyland, in Peter Garland, *Lou Harrison Reader,* 71.

40. Ibid., 72.

41. Miller and Lieberman, *Lou Harrison,* 191.

42. "Program Notes," program for the world premiere of *Young Caesar: An Opera for Puppets ("X-Rated")* (Pasadena: California Institute of Technology, 1971) in the Yates Papers (MSS 14, box 7, folio 1). See also Harrison's description of this work in Leyland's interview in Garland, *Lou Harrison Reader,* 79; Miller and Lieberman, *Lou Harrison,* 199.

43. Miller and Lieberman, *Lou Harrison,* 191; Leyland interview in Garland, *Lou Harrison Reader,* 84.

44. Jonathan D. Katz, "John Cage's Queer Silence; or, How to Avoid Making Matters Worse." Caroline Jones also makes an interesting connection between Cage's homosexuality and suppression of ego in "Finishing School: John Cage and the Abstract Expressionist Ego."

45. A presentation at a symposium, John Cage, "The Changing Audience for the Changing Arts" (1966), reprinted in Richard Kostelanetz, ed., *John Cage: An Anthology,* 77.

46. David W. Patterson, "Cage and Asia: History and Sources," 59. Hines and Nicholls also argue that European and American modernism had a much bigger impact on Cage's music than Asian music or philosophy during his formative years. Hines, "Then Not Yet 'Cage'"; Nicholls, "Transethnicism and the American Experimental Tradition."

47. John Corbett, "Experimental Oriental," 173.

48. Interview with Leyland in Garland, *Lou Harrison Reader,* 82.

49. Katz, "John Cage's Queer Silence," 61.

50. For more extensive biographical background, see Gilmore, *Harry Partch;* and Philip Blackburn, ed., *Enclosure 3: Harry Partch,* a scrapbook of articles about Partch and his correspondence and photos.

51. See, for example, Cowell's mixed review of Harry Partch's book, *Genesis of a Music*, in *Saturday Review*, November 26, 1949, reprinted in Blackburn, *Enclosure 3*, 122; and John Cage's letters to Peter Yates mentioning Partch's work in less than kindly terms, Yates Papers (MSS 14 box 3, folio 1), in particular, letters dated August 4, 1953, and May 23, 1966. Vicious aspersions against Cowell, Cage, and other notable American artists are found throughout the Partch documents in Blackburn.

52. Harry Partch, *Genesis of a Music*, 12.

53. Harry Partch, "Note before lecture 'The Ancient Magic,'" April 24, 1959, reprinted in Blackburn, *Enclosure 3*, 276.

54. Blackburn, *Enclosure 3*, 459.

55. Harry Partch, "Lecture at Sheraton Palace Hotel, San Francisco," June 20, 1963, reprinted in ibid., 317.

56. Liner notes, Harry Partch, *Enclosure 2* (St. Paul: INNOVA Recordings, Minnesota Composers Forum, 1995), 15–16.

57. Letter to Alwyn Nikolais, February 19, 1957, reprinted in Blackburn, *Enclosure 3*, 238.

58. See, for example, Gail Bederman, *Manliness and Civilization: A Cultural History of Gender and Race in the United States, 1880–1917*; Eve Kosofsky Sedgwick, *Epistemology of the Closet*; and Siobhan B. Somerville, *Queering the Color Line*.

59. From an article written by his longtime student Ben Johnston, "The Corporealism of Harry Partch"; interview with Stephen Pouliot, June 17, 1972, quoted in Blackburn, *Enclosure 3*, 54.

60. See W. Anthony Sheppard, *Revealing Masks: Exotic Influences and Ritualized Performance in Modernist Music Theater*, 180–203. For a detailed musical analysis of *Delusion*, see Paul Earls, "Harry Partch: Verses in Preparation for *Delusion of the Fury*."

61. Partch, *Genesis of a Music*, 351.

62. See Philip Brett, "Eros and Orientalism in Britten's Operas." Partch may have been more directly influenced by Yeats's enthusiasm for the Japanese tradition, since Partch met the poet and set his *King Oedipus* to music. See Sheppard, *Revealing Masks*, 72–95, 126–54.

63. From a letter to Peter Reed from Harry Partch, December 8, 1954, quoted in Gilmore, *Harry Partch*, 223.

64. Harry Partch, "Proposal for Studies in the Creative Arts," reprinted in Blackburn, *Enclosure 3*, 316.

65. Edmunds, interview with Cowell, 15.

66. Lou Harrison, *Music Primer*, 129.

67. Toshie Kakinuma and Mamoru Fujieda, "I Am One of Mr. Ives' Legal Heirs: An Interview with Lou Harrison," 56.

68. Quoted in Peter Burt, *The Music of Tōru Takemitsu*, 110.

Chapter 3: A Thin Blue Line down Central Avenue

1. Fogelson, *The Fragmented Metropolis*, 70.

2. Keith Collins, *Black Los Angeles: The Maturing of the Ghetto, 1940–1950*, 41.

3. For more about racial strife in Los Angeles in the 1940s and before, see B. Gordon Wheeler, *Black California: The History of African-Americans in the Golden State*; Almaguer,

Racial Fault Lines; Kevin Starr, *Embattled Dreams: California in War and Peace, 1940–1950;* and Daniels and Olin, *Racism in California.*

4. See Bette Yarbrough Cox, *Central Avenue—Its Rise and Fall, 1890–c. 1955: Including the Musical Renaissance of Black Los Angeles;* Clora Bryant et al., *Central Avenue Sounds: Jazz in Los Angeles;* Tom Reed, *The Black Music History of Los Angeles: Its Roots;* and DjeDje and Meadows, *California Soul.*

5. See, for example, Yoshida, *Reminiscing in Swingtime;* Anthony F. Macías, "From Pachuco Boogie to Latin Jazz: Mexican Americans, Popular Music, and Urban Culture in Los Angeles, 1940–1965"; and Loza, *Barrio Rhythm.*

6. Art Pepper and Laurie Pepper, *Straight Life: The Story of Art Pepper,* 41–42.

7. Ernie Andrews, *Central Avenue Sounds,* transcript of oral history conducted in 1989 and 1990 by Steven L. Isoardi, collection 300/397, Department of Special Collections, Charles E. Young Research Library, University of California, 71.

8. Art Farmer, *Central Avenue Sounds,* transcript of oral history conducted in 1991 by Steven L. Isoardi, collection 300/440, 57–58.

9. Clora Bryant, *Central Avenue Sounds,* transcript of oral history conducted in 1990 by Steven L. Isoardi, collection 300/415, 252.

10. Hampton Hawes and Don Asher, *Raise Up off Me: A Portrait of Hampton Hawes,* 29. Fictional accounts also offer vivid pictures of the Central Avenue music scene. Noir writers, in particular, have held a strange fascination for both the glamorous and nightmarish aspects of Central Avenue. Chester Himes featured Central Avenue prominently in his 1945 novel *If He Hollers Let Him Go,* and more recent neo-noir writers Walter Mosley and James Ellroy have portrayed this neighborhood in their nostalgic, if somewhat dark and cynical, evocations of postwar Los Angeles.

11. For more comprehensive discussions of the Los Angeles Police Department and Chief Parker, see Joe Domanick, *To Protect and to Serve: The LAPD's Century of War in the City of Dreams;* and Gerald Woods, *The Police in Los Angeles: Reform and Professionalization.*

12. William H. Parker, *Parker on Police,* 8.

13. Ibid., 101.

14. William H. Parker, *Police Chief William H. Parker Speaks,* 9.

15. See Edward J. Escobar, *Race, Police, and the Making of a Political Identity: Mexican Americans and the Los Angeles Police Department, 1900–1945,* 105.

16. The strained relations between the police and the South Central community are evident upon perusal of the headlines from the *California Eagle.* The following are sample headlines from around the time of Parker's appointment as chief in August 1950: "Hit Newton Police for Delayed Answer to Near Fatal Call" (December 1, 1949), "Police Bullets Fell Man" (March 30, 1950), "Committee Report Hits Police Discrimination in Los Angeles" (April 6, 1950), "Bail Bondsman Unconscious 6 Hours After Police Beating" (April 20, 1950), "Indignation on Shooting of Mentally Ill Youth by Police" (May 4, 1950), "Police Intimidation Fails to Halt Anti-Minstrel Pickets" (May 11, 1950), "Patrolmen Brutally Assault War Vet on Public Highway" (June 1, 1950), "Beverly Hills Police Beat Him, Broke Hand, Man Claims" (July 14, 1950), "Negro, Not Man, Policeman Tells Citizen" (August 11, 1950), "Police Kick Youth, Call Him Black S.O.B." (August 18, 1950).

17. "Jimmy Witherspoon Beaten," *California Eagle,* January 24, 1952.

18. Parker, *Parker on Police,* 162.

19. "Grand Jury Probe of Police Brutality," *California Eagle,* March 20, 1952.

20. Andrews, Central Avenue Sounds, 71.

21. David Bryant, *Central Avenue Sounds,* transcript of oral history conducted in 1993 by Steven L. Isoardi, collection 300/458, 63.

22. Judith Butler, "Endangered/Endangering: Schematic Racism and White Paranoia," *Reading Rodney King/ Reading Urban Uprising,* 18.

23. Farmer, *Central Avenue Sounds,* 84.

24. C. Bryant, Central Avenue Sounds, 251, 103.

25. "Be-bop Be-bopped," *Time,* March 25, 1946. Gibson was a white pianist who achieved notoriety by mimicking black slang and musical styles for the entertainment of white audiences. Gaillard was an entertainer who was, on the one hand, dismissed by Gillespie as one of the "'Toms' and musical nothings" that spoiled his time in California and, on the other, celebrated by hip-hoppers as a progenitor of vocal virtuosity. See Scott DeVeaux, *The Birth of Bebop: A Social and Musical History,* 397–98.

26. "Boppers 'Rowdy.' Shrine Joins Philharmonic Aud. in Banning Concerts," *Variety,* February 2, 1949.

27. "Hate Flare Is Directed at Jews and Negroes," *California Eagle,* October 6, 1949.

28. See Ralph Eastman, "Central Avenue Blues: The Making of Los Angeles Rhythm and Blues, 1942–47."

29. Cecil McNeely, *Central Avenue,* transcript of oral history conducted in 1989 by Steven L. Isoardi, collection 300/392, 10–11.

30. Johnny Otis is of Greek ancestry but grew up in an African American community in Northern California and considers himself an "honorary Negro." He has been deeply involved as a musician, talent scout, and minister in L.A.'s black community for decades. See his account of the Central Avenue musical culture, *Upside Your Head! Rhythm and Blues on Central Avenue* (quotes are from 60–61), and his autobiography, *Listen to the Lambs.*

El Monte's American Legion Stadium experienced less intense police scrutiny than music venues within Los Angeles city borders and eventually became an important performance venue for R&B and, later, rock and roll bands. See Matt Garcia's description of the music culture in El Monte in *A World of Its Own: Race, Labor, and Citrus in the Making of Greater Los Angeles, 1900–1970,* 198–214.

31. Los Angeles is the famous site of Charlie Parker's 1945–46 drug and alcohol binge, which led to his lockup at Camarillo. Heroin's availability in the city was limited at this time, and Parker had to make do with combinations of morphine and alcohol, laced with heroin when he could get it. Parker's example may have further exacerbated the drug abuse problem within the jazz circle, as younger musicians sought to imitate everything their idol did, good and bad.

32. Los Angeles Police Department, *Annual Report* (Los Angeles: LAPD, 1952), 27.

33. Farmer, *Central Avenue Sounds,* 57–58, 106–7.

34. Miles Davis with Quincy Troupe, *Miles, the Autobiography,* 163.

35. Horace Tapscott, *Central Avenue Sounds,* transcript of oral history conducted in 1993 by Steven L. Isoardi, collection 300/484, 108.

36. Farmer, *Central Avenue Sounds,* 103–4.

37. C. Bryant, *Central Avenue Sounds,* 103, 251.

38. Frank Morgan, *Central Avenue Sounds,* transcript of oral history conducted in 1992 and 1993 by Steven L. Isoardi, collection 300/474, 35.

39. Marshall Royal, *Central Avenue Sounds,* transcript of oral history conducted in 1993 by Steven L. Isoardi, collection 300/463, 95.

40. Tapscott, Central Avenue Sounds, 175.

41. Gertrude Gipson, "Candid Comments," *California Eagle,* December 8, 1949.

42. Ibid., August 25, 1950.

43. "People and Places," *California Eagle,* May 17, 1951.

44. Ibid., July 26, 1951.

45. Lillian Cumber, "Hollywood Scratch Pad," *Los Angeles Tribune,* January 16, 1953.

46. "People and Places," *California Eagle,* December 18, 1952.

47. Los Angeles Police Department, *Annual Report* (Los Angeles: LAPD, 1950), 17.

48. *Los Angeles Daily Journal,* September 9, 1960.

49. Domanick, *To Protect and to Serve,* 108.

50. Dick West, "Chief Parker Collapses, Dies at Award Banquet," *Los Angeles Times,* July 17, 1966.

51. Paul Houston, "Police Chief Parker Widely Mourned; Tributes Pour In," ibid., July 18, 1966.

52. Collins, *Black Los Angeles,* 24.

53. Walter J. Raine, *Los Angeles Riot Study: The Perception of Police Brutality in Southern California, Los Angeles,* 14, 28.

54. Art Berman, "Scores of Fires Rage Unchecked; Damage Exceeds $10 Million," *Los Angeles Times,* August 14, 1965.

55. Not incidentally, Darryl Gates, the chief of the LAPD at the time of the Rodney King beating, was a protégé of Chief Parker, serving as his chauffeur and bodyguard in the 1950s.

56. Mike Davis, *City of Quartz: Excavating the Future in Los Angeles,* 223–322; Michel Foucault, *Discipline and Punish: The Birth of the Prisons.*

57. Davis, City of Quartz, 250, 277.

58. Charles Emge, "Jazz Moves Underground in L.A. and Is Prospering," *Down Beat* (August 13, 1952): 8.

59. Nesuhi Ertegun, "Modern Jazz," *Record Changer* (Summer 1954): 19.

60. Teddy Charles, "The West Coast Cats Wig and Wail," *Metronome* (December 1953): 17.

61. Dave Dexter, "Smogtown: The Los Angeles Story," *Billboard* (December 27, 1969): 118.

62. Gioia, *West Coast Jazz,* 201. See also Robert Gordon, *Jazz West Coast: The Los Angeles Jazz Scene of the 1950s.*

63. Davis and Troupe, *Miles,* 156. Davis did meet Baker during one of his Lighthouse gigs and conceded that he was a "nice enough guy, cool and a good player." According to Davis, Baker was embarrassed to have won the *Down Beat* poll and seemed to tacitly acknowledge that race played into the outcome (167).

64. Quoted in Otis, *Upside Your Head!,* 4.

65. There has, however, been a resurgence of interest in Central Avenue's past and a

reassessment of its significance in recent years. The documentary *Ernie Andrews Blues for Central Avenue* (dir. Lois Shelton, New York: Rhapsody Films, 1988) was well received, the Fountain Theater in Hollywood premiered Stephen Sachs's play *Central Avenue* in 2001 to critical acclaim, and *Trumpestically Clora Bryant,* a documentary directed by Zeinabu irene Davis, premiered in 2004 at the Los Angeles Pan African Film and Arts Festival. Some notable recent publications on the subject are Cox, *Central Avenue—Its Rise and Fall;* Bryant et al., *Central Avenue Sounds;* Reed, *Black Music History of Los Angeles;* and Michael B. Bakan, "Way Out on Central: Jazz in the African-American Community of Los Angeles before 1930," and Ralph Eastman, "'Pitchin' Up a Boogie': African-American Musicians, Nightlife, and Music Venues in Los Angeles, 1930–1945," in *California Soul,* ed. DjeDje and Meadows, 23–103. Other books dealing more generally with music on the West Coast also include important sections on the Central Avenue music scene—for example, Gioia, *West Coast Jazz;* Hoskyns, *Waiting for the Sun;* and Cross, *It's Not About a Salary—.* This music is available on two recently issued compilations: *The West Coast Jazz Box: An Anthology of California Jazz* (Contemporary 1998); and *Central Avenue Sounds: Jazz in Los Angeles (1921–1956)* (Rhino 1999).

Chapter 4: Noir Entanglements

1. Lary May, *Screening Out the Past: The Birth of Mass Culture and the Motion Picture Industry,* 167–99.

2. See Lary May, *The Big Tomorrow: Hollywood and the Politics of the American Way;* and Lewis A. Erenberg, *Swingin' the Dream: Big Band Jazz and the Rebirth of American Culture.*

3. For a comprehensive description of postwar Los Angeles, see Kevin Starr, *Embattled Dreams.*

4. Davis, *City of Quartz,* 18. The first chapter of this book is devoted to exploring the tensions between the cultures of boosterism and criticism and is aptly titled "Sunshine or *Noir?*" (15–97).

5. See May, *The Big Tomorrow,* 175–256; Dana Polan, *Power and Paranoia: History, Narrative, and the American Cinema, 1940–1950;* Frank Krutnik, *In a Lonely Street: Film Noir, Genre, Masculinity;* E. Ann Kaplan, ed., *Women in Film Noir;* Alain Silver and James Ursini, *Film Noir Reader,* both the first and second editions; and Steven Cohan, *Masked Men: Masculinity and the Movies in the Fifties.* Applying theories of gender and performance as developed by Judith Butler and other cultural theorists, Cohan attempts to explain how film noir approached the formidable project of reconstructing and representing masculinity against the backdrop of shifting gender and familial relations of the postwar years. The various essays in *Women in Film Noir* further grapple with the problematics of gender roles in this genre. The French film critic Nino Frank used the label "film noir" to designate a new genre of films in his 1946 essay "A New Kind of Police Drama: The Criminal Adventure." Reprinted in Alain Silver and James Ursini, *Film Noir Reader 2,* 15–20.

6. For discussions of race, ethnicity, and the American cinema, see Thomas Cripps, *Making Movies Black: The Hollywood Message Movie from World War II to the Civil Rights Era;* Lester D. Friedman, ed., *Unspeakable Images: Ethnicity and the American Cinema;* and Daniel Bernardi, ed., *Classic Hollywood, Classic Whiteness.*

7. Black music, at least before the merger of the black and white musicians' unions 767 and 47 in 1953, was almost always played by white studio musicians. For more on black music and films, see Krin Gabbard, *Jammin' at the Margins: Jazz and the American Cinema;* Ella Shohat and Robert Stam, *Unthinking Eurocentrism: Multiculturalism and the Media,* 226–30; and Arthur Knight, "*Jammin' the Blues,* or the Sight of Jazz, 1944." Michael Rogin points out that even though African Americans were largely absent in early cinema, blackface performances were commonplace, and that it was through such racial impersonations that "ethnic" Americans, such as Jews, became "white." See Rogin, *Blackface, White Noise: Jewish Immigrants in the Hollywood Melting Pot.* Carol J. Clover makes an interesting case for the inadequate attribution and even erasure of African American musicians and dancers in one of the most beloved musicals of all times, *Singin' in the Rain,* in "Dancin' in the Rain."

8. Caryl Flinn, *Strains of Utopia: Gender, Nostalgia, and Hollywood Film Music,* 17, 5.

9. Robert Porfirio, "Dark Jazz: Music in the *Film Noir.*" David Butler also describes this scene from *Phantom Lady,* as well as the jazz scene in *D.O.A.,* in *Jazz Noir: Listening to Music from* Phantom Lady *to* The Last Seduction, 61–71.

10. For Flinn's more extensive analysis of the use of music in *Detour,* see *Strains of Utopia,* 123–32.

11. For a vivid portrayal of life in Hollywood, including the social scene on Central Avenue, see Otto Friedrich, *City of Nets: A Portrait of Hollywood in the 1940s;* and Jim Heimann, *Out with the Stars: Hollywood Nightlife in the Golden Era.*

Richard Widmark, in preparing to play the antihero of *Kiss of Death* (1947), made a point of visiting the swing joints on Fifty-second Street and Greenwich Village. Although these are New York rather than Los Angeles locations, the association of black music with sex and violence is in line with my discussion. From Philip Scheur, "Interview with Richard Widmark on the Set of *Kiss of Death,*" *Los Angeles Times,* unknown date in 1947, quoted in May, *The Big Tomorrow,* 221.

12. Claudia Gorbman, *Unheard Melodies: Narrative Film Music,* 2–3. For further discussion of how music and sound are used to structure the way in which the audience sees film images, see also Michel Chion's *Audio-Vision: Sound on Screen.*

13. David Fine, "Beginning in the Thirties: The Los Angeles Fiction of James M. Cain and Horace McCoy," 44.

14. Eric Lott, "The Whiteness of Film Noir," 84–85. James Naremore surveys, without offering conclusive critical insights, usages of Asian, Latin, and African American elements in *More Than Night: Film Noir in Its Contexts,* 220–53. Manthia Diawara also observes that "a film is *noir* if it puts into play light and dark in order to exhibit a people who become 'Black' because of their low moral behavior" but, rather than pursuing the line of argument adopted by Lott, goes on to discuss how black writers and directors have appropriated noir conventions for very different ends. See Diawara, "*Noir* by Noirs: Towards a New Realism in Black Cinema."

15. Lott, "Whiteness of Film Noir," 85–86.

16. Ibid., 85. E. Ann Kaplan argues in her analysis of *Cat People* and *The Lady from Shanghai* that the white femme fatale in film noir often aligns herself with or has access to the otherness of alien races and ethnicities, thereby throwing doubt on her moral purity and whiteness. Kaplan, "The 'Dark Continent' of Film Noir: Race, Displacement and Metaphor in Tourneur's *Cat People* (1942) and Welles' *The Lady from Shanghai* (1948)."

17. See Billy Wilder, *Double Indemnity,* 103.

18. Miklós Rósza, *Double Life,* 142.

19. Chion, *Audio-Vision,* 8.

20. Paramount was the same studio that had produced *Double Indemnity.* "Tangerine" headlined best-selling records by Jimmy Dorsey, Vaughn Monroe, Orrin Tucker, and Hal McIntyre in 1942. Roger D. Kinkle, *The Complete Encyclopedia of Popular Music and Jazz, 1900–1950.*

21. *The Johnny Mercer Songbook* (Hialeah, Fla.: Columbia Pictures Publications, 1981), 190–92. The song was originally published by Famous Music, a musical subsidiary of Paramount Studios. Lyrics are reprinted with permission from the Hal Leonard Corporation.

22. Naremore points to other Latin elements in *Double Indemnity*—Phyllis's perfume bought in Enseneda and Neff's final destination, Mexico, in his flight from the law—that hold out "the elusive, ironic promise of a warmth and color that will countervail the dark mise-en-scène and the taut, restricted coolness of the average noir protagonist." Naremore, *More Than Night,* 230.

Hollywood's conflation of different ethnic groups into a larger category of the "other" to the white mainstream is not unlike the political and social policies of postwar Los Angeles that in effect segregated the white and nonwhite populations.

23. As Krin Gabbard reminds us in a survey of the films of Kay Kyser, the once popular but now forgotten white bandleader, jazz was conceived of much more broadly before the 1950s, before an art discourse about jazz emerged as an adjunct to the bebop revolution. The music of Count Basie, Benny Goodman, Duke Ellington, the Dorseys, and Glenn Miller were all considered to be jazz by mainstream audiences, and "[a]lthough black jazz artists did find their way onto film throughout the 1930s and 1940s, Americans at the movies were much more likely to see white musicians holding the saxophones and drumsticks and snapping their fingers with hip insouciance." Gabbard, *Jammin' at the Margins,* 20.

24. Ronald Radano explores the linkage between rhythm, sex, and African American bodies in "Hot Fantasies: American Modernism and the Idea of Black Rhythm."

25. Janey Place surveys the various women in film noirs who represent the two poles of female archetypes in "Women in Film Noir." Her description of how the redeemer type is often presented matches the Hollywood Bowl scene in key details: "In order to offer this alternative to the nightmare landscape of film noir, she herself must not be a part of it. She is then linked to the pastoral environment of open spaces, light, and safety characterised by even, flat, high-key lighting" (60–61).

This opposition between the good and evil feminine archetypes can be contained within one woman. The musical examples discussed here, the Schubert symphony development section and "Tangerine," are used again in another film noir starring Barbara Stanwyck, *Sorry, Wrong Number* (1948). Stanwyck plays an invalid woman, awaiting the return of her husband. She becomes agitated when she overhears a phone conversation between two men plotting murder. She turns on the radio to distract herself from her growing unease at her husband's absence, but the Schubert symphony only exacerbates her agitation. Later in the film, a flashback shows her in a car with the man who will later become her husband. As the car radio plays "Tangerine," Stanwyck's character seduces Henry Stevenson (Burt Lancaster), her friend's beau, by dangling her father's riches as reward for marrying her. In the first instance, the Schubert accompanies the emotional turmoil of a woman the viewer still considers a sympathetic wife, perhaps a victim of neglect; in the second, "Tangerine" reveals her to be what she really is—a duplicitous seductress out to steal another woman's man. It can hardly be coincidental that the exact same parts of the same musical works accompany a character played by Barbara Stanwyck in a movie also produced by Paramount.

26. Naremore argues that the original ending of the film, showing Neff's death in the gas chamber, would have better registered the critical perspective of Wilder, Cain, and the film's screenwriter, Raymond Chandler. See Naremore, *More Than Night*, 81–95.

27. James M. Cain, *The Postman Always Rings Twice*, 5.

28. Ibid., 12. This description of the Greek American is a good example of the construct-edness of race. This passage could just as easily be a description of an African American or Mexican man, but because writing about miscegenation was taboo, racial otherness is projected onto a Greek, considered an ethnic outsider at one time in American history.

29. Ibid., 31.

30. Barbara Stanwyck in *Double Indemnity* and Rita Hayworth in *The Lady from Shang-hai*, two of the most notorious femmes fatales in film noir, both sported blonde hair (not their natural hue) and appeared in their first scenes in white costume. On his insistence on outfitting Stanwyck in a blonde wig, Billy Wilder explained, "I wanted her to look as sleazy as possible." Blonde women conjure up stereotypes of excessive sexuality, but the way in which these women are captured in black and white also plays up the whiteness of their hair, which in effect serves as a halo, endowing the characters with an angelic aura. They are rendered visually white in the beginning and only later accrue accessories of blackness, symbolizing their moral degeneration or our gradual comprehension of their innate evil. Wilder's quote is taken from Friedrich, *City of Nets*, 165.

31. Cain, *Postman*, 7.

32. Anahid Kassabian, *Hearing Film: Tracking Identifications in Contemporary Hollywood Film Music*, 84.

33. Kinkle, *Complete Encyclopedia*.

34. Peter Bogdanovich, *Fritz Lang in America*, 84.

35. E. Ann Kaplan, "The Place of Women in Fritz Lang's *The Blue Gardenia*."

36. Note the interesting similarity of the "Blue Gardenia" to a real L.A. murder case involving a color and a flower, the "Black Dahlia" case of 1947.

37. Janet Bergstrom, "The Mystery of *The Blue Gardenia*," 106–7.

38. Gabbard, *Jammin' at the Margins*, 239–55.

39. See Daniel Mark Epstein, *Nat King Cole*, 206.

40. Ibid., 178–82.

41. Ibid., 252–62. See also Brian Ward, *Just My Soul Responding: Rhythm and Blues, Black Consciousness, and Race Relations*, 130–34.

42. I am borrowing Gabbard's phrase describing the song, although he reaches conclu-sions different from mine in his analysis of the song as it is used in the extradiegetic score. See Gabbard, *Jammin' at the Margins*, 248.

43. For more on film noir and the politics of dissension, see May, *The Big Tomorrow*, 215–56; and Naremore, *More Than Night*, 96–135.

44. Hanns Eisler, *Composing for the Films*, 114. Adorno collaborated with Eisler in the writ-ing of this book but removed his name from the cover out of fear of political reprisals.

Chapter 5: From the Mission Myth to Chicano Nationalism

1. George J. Sánchez, *Becoming Mexican American: Ethnicity, Culture and Identity in Chicano Los Angeles, 1900–1945,* 9.

2. For in-depth historical studies of the Mexicans in California, see Richard Griswold del Castillo, *The Los Angeles Barrio, 1850–1890: A Social History;* Douglas Monroy, *Rebirth: Mexican Los Angeles from the Great Migration to the Great Depression;* and Rodolfo F. Acuña, *Occupied America: A History of Chicanos.*

3. For a thorough analysis of the events and discourses surrounding the Sleepy Lagoon case and the Zoot Suit riots, see Mauricio Mazón, *The Zoot-Suit Riots: The Psychology of Symbolic Annihilation.*

4. See Escobar, *Race, Police, and the Making of a Political Identity.*

5. McWilliams, *North from Mexico,* 43.

6. For a description of the music performed in these pageants, see Marcus, *Musical Metropolis,* 87–118. For a more in-depth critique of these productions, see Garcia, *A World of Its Own,* 121–56.

7. See W. W. Robinson, *Los Angeles from the Days of the Pueblo: A Brief History and a Guide to the Plaza Area;* and William D. Estrada, "Los Angeles' Old Plaza and Olvera Street: Imagined and Contested Space."

8. McWilliams, *North from Mexico,* 45. Garcia expands on this thesis in his examination of citrus workers in *A World of Its Own.*

9. Ruth Kedzie Wood, *The Tourist's California,* 69.

10. During a highly productive career, the writer contributed to the *Times;* edited *Land of Sunshine* (later renamed *Out West*), which began as a publication subsidized by the Chamber of Commerce; served as the city librarian of Los Angeles; founded the Southwest Museum and cofounded the Landmarks Club, which restored Franciscan missions; and traveled extensively throughout the Southwest, collecting artifacts and folklore of the indigenous people and the bygone Spanish era. See Frances E. Watkins, "'He Said It with Music': Spanish-California Folk Songs Recorded by Charles F. Lummis"; Michael Heisley, "Lummis and Mexican-American Folklore"; John Koegel, "Mexican-American Music in Nineteenth-Century Southern California: The Lummis Wax Cylinder Collection at the Southwest Museum, Los Angeles"; and Arthur Farwell, *"Wanderjahre of a Revolutionist" and Other Essays on American Music,* 104–10.

11. Charles F. Lummis, *Spanish Songs of Old California,* 3. Arthur Farwell helped transcribe these fourteen songs. Eleanor Hague, a pioneer in the study of Latin American music, transcribed nine more songs in 1933 for *The Masterkey* and eight other songs that are archived in the Southwest Museum Library in manuscript form. She also collected Spanish Californian songs, five of which were harmonized and transcribed for piano and voice by Gertrude Ross; see her *Early Spanish-Californian Folk-Songs* (New York: J. Fischer & Bro., 1922). For more about Hague, see Robert Stevenson, "Eleanor Hague (1875–1954), Pioneer Latin Americanist." Also see Helen H. Roberts, *Form in Primitive Music: An Analytical and Comparative Study of the Melodic Form of Some Ancient Southern California Indian Songs.*

12. The quick dissemination of new musical styles made possible by radio broadcast stimulated the development of a thriving popular music scene, with music written for immediate and mass consumption and distributed by the large mainstream recording

companies, such as Decca, Vocalion, Columbia, and Victor. See Richard K. Spottswood, *Ethnic Music on Records: A Discography of Ethnic Recordings Produced in the United States, 1893 to 1942*, vol. 4.

13. For a brief overview of Mexican American music in California in the first part of the twentieth century, see Manuel H. Peña's "Notes towards an Interpretive History of California-Mexican Music" and *The Mexican American Orquesta Music: Music, Culture, and the Dialectic of Conflict*, 166–202.

14. Transcribed and translated in Guillermo Hernández, *Canciones de la Raza: Songs of the Chicano Experience*, 18.

15. Hernández, *Canciones de la Raza*, 32.

16. See Loza, *Barrio Rhythm*, 33–34. See also Sánchez, *Becoming Mexican American*, 183–84, and a video of a telecast documentary on the life of Pedro J. González, *Ballad of an Unsung Hero* (San Diego: Cinewest/KPBS, 1983).

17. In 1950, the number of Mexican Americans in Los Angeles was 156,356; by 1960, the number had reached 291,959, showing an 87 percent growth in the ten-year period. Ernesto Chávez, *"¡Mi Raza Primero!" (My People First!): Nationalism, Identity, and Insurgency in the Chicano Movement in Los Angeles, 1966–1978*, 10.

18. For details on Mexican American and Anglo-American relations in Los Angeles, as played out in the political, judiciary, and economic realms, see Rodolfo F. Acuña, *A Community under Siege: A Chronicle of Chicanos East of the Los Angeles River, 1945–1975*.

19. Quoted in Carlos Muñoz Jr., *Youth, Identity, Power: The Chicano Movement*, 52.

20. See ibid., 64. Aztlán is the mythic place of origin of the Aztec people, claimed to be the formerly Mexican southwestern region of the United States, including California. The acronym MEChA means match or matchstick and symbolizes the fire that fuels the movement.

21. For more on the Brown Berets, the Chicano Moratorium, and other Los Angeles–based activist groups and events, see Chávez, *"¡Mi Raza Primero!"*

22. "Documents of the Chicano Struggle," *International Socialist Review* 31 (June 1970): 44.

23. Muñoz, *Youth, Identity, Power*, 191–92 (entire *Plan* reprinted in appendix of this book, 191–202).

24. Dick Hebdige, *Subculture: The Meaning of Style*, 17–18.

25. Stuart Cosgrove, "The Zoot-Suit and Style Warfare," 89. See also James Diego Vigil, *Barrio Gangs: Street Life and Identity in Southern California*.

26. From "Observaciones–Los Salones de Baile," *Observations of Luis Felipe Racinos*, 1927, quoted in Sánchez, *Becoming Mexican American*, 172.

27. See, for example, Yoshida's account of music in the Japanese American community, *Reminiscing in Swingtime*.

28. See Macías, "From Pachuco Boogie to Latin Jazz," 197.

29. See David Reyes and Tom Waldman, *Land of a Thousand Dances: Chicano Rock 'n' Roll from Southern California*, 11–18; Steven Loza, "Identity, Nationalism, and Aesthetics among Chicano/Mexicano Musicians in Los Angeles," 52–53; and Garcia, *A World of Its Own*, 189–222.

30. Ruben Guevara, "The View from the Sixth Street Bridge: The History of Chicano Rock."

31. Garcia, *A World of Its Own,* 202.

32. Anthony Macías, *"Rock con Raza, Raza con Jazz:* Latinos/as and Post–World War II Popular American Music."

33. See Loza, *Barrio Rhythm,* 102.

34. Quoted in Reyes and Waldman, *Land of a Thousand Dances,* 90.

35. A reissue of the two volumes, containing the top barrio hits from 1963 to 1968, was released under the title *East Side Revue.* For a comprehensive list of Chicano performers during this time, see Ruben Molina, *The Old Barrio Guide to Low Rider Music, 1950–1975.*

36. George Lipsitz, "Land of a Thousand Dances: Youth, Minorities, and the Rise of Rock and Roll."

37. Macías, "From Pachuco Boogie to Latin Jazz," 223.

38. Quoted in Reyes and Waldman, *Land of a Thousand Dances,* xviii.

39. Godfrey Kerr was actually an Irish immigrant who deejayed for the R&B station KTYM. He was friends with many of the Mexican American musicians on the scene and spoke out on behalf of Chicano activists. See Reyes and Waldman, *Land of a Thousand Dances,* 51–53.

40. Keith Negus, *Popular Music in Theory: An Introduction,* 122.

41. Muñoz, *Youth, Identity, Power,* 76.

42. Vigil, *Barrio Gangs,* 40.

43. See Tomás Ybarra-Frausto, "The Chicano Movement and the Emergence of a Chicano Poetic Consciousness."

44. See Rodolfo Gonzales, *I Am Joaquin: An Epic Poem,* 1.

45. *Con Safos* 1 (Winter 1971): 62.

46. Ybarra-Frausto, "Chicano Movement," 105. For more on the various periodicals and other media outlets of the Chicano Movement, see Francisco J. Lewels Jr., *The Uses of the Media by the Chicano Movement: A Study in Minority Access.*

47. Luis Rodríguez, "Eastside Sound," *Q-VO* 2 (1980): 27.

48. See articles on this music written by Mark Guerrero compiled on his Web site: www.markguerrero.net.

49. Loza, *Barrio Rhythm,* 224.

50. George Lipsitz, "Cruising around the Historical Bloc-Postmodernism and Popular Music in East Los Angeles," 173.

51. Rafael Pérez-Torres, "Mestizaje in the Mix: Chicano Identity, Cultural Politics, and Postmodern Music," 209.

Chapter 6: *After* Sa-i-ku

1. K. Connie Kang and Kenneth Reich, "L.A. Reflects, Looks to City's Future," *Los Angeles Times,* April 30, 2002.

2. In her widely acclaimed book *Black Noise,* Tricia Rose situates hip-hop firmly within the circuit of Afrodiasporic cultures, tracing its sounds, methods, aesthetics, and lyrical content to black oral traditions and the political and economic conditions specific to an underprivileged social group in America's postindustrial urban enclaves. George Lipsitz sees in hip-hop's move out of the ghetto the means of connecting and thus strengthen-

ing the position of Afrodiasporic communities everywhere by taking their place within the larger Black Atlantic. See Tricia Rose, *Black Noise: Rap Music and Black Culture in Contemporary America;* and George Lipsitz, *Dangerous Crossroads: Popular Music, Postmodernism and the Poetics of Place,* 25–48. Other recent books have also covered this ground: see Jeff Chang, *Can't Stop, Won't Stop: A History of the Hip-Hop Generation;* and Cheryl Keyes, *Rap Music and Street Consciousness.*

3. See, for example, Rose, *Black Noise,* 4–9. A collection of essays about hip-hop outside of the United States, *Global Noise,* addresses some of my concerns, looking at the intersection of Afrodiasporic styles and local and indigenous musical practices in Europe, Asia, Australia, and Canada. But since the relationship of non-English rap to American politics is tenuous at best, these essays shed only limited light on how the questions I raise inflect the interracial and intercultural meanings of hip-hop in California. See Tony Mitchell, ed., *Global Noise: Rap and Hip-Hop outside the USA.*

4. *Korea Times,* July 4, 1992. According to the California Senate Office of Research, Korean-owned businesses claimed up to $400 million in losses out of the total $470 million in damages incurred by businesses in South Central, Koreatown, and nearby areas during the 1992 L.A. riots. Senate Office of Research, *The South-Central Los Angeles and Koreatown Riots.*

5. The May 11, 1992, issue of *Time* was devoted entirely to the L.A. riots. The articles cite one poll after another that asked black and white respondents to gauge their reactions to the events preceding and following the riots. Apart from two paragraphs tucked away in a story titled "L.A. Lawless: The Violence Sparked by the King Verdict Reveals Racial Divisions That Have Plagued the City for Years," Koreans are not mentioned at all, and their opinions and reactions appear nowhere in the *Time* coverage.

6. See Nancy Abelmann and John Lie, *Blue Dreams: Korean Americans and the Los Angeles Riots* (Cambridge, Mass.: Harvard University Press, 1995), 7 fn. 11. In addition to Abelmann and Lie's comprehensive study, see Edward T. Chang and Jeannette Diaz-Veizades, *Ethnic Peace in the American City: Building Community in Los Angeles and Beyond;* Robert Gooding-Williams, ed., *Reading Rodney King, Reading Urban Uprising;* Don Hazen, ed., *Inside the L.A. Riots: What Really Happened and Why It Will Happen Again;* Mark Baldassare, ed., *The Los Angeles Riots: Lessons for the Urban Future;* Kwang Chung Kim, ed., *Koreans in the Hood: Conflict with African Americans;* Karin Aguilar-San Juan, ed., *The State of Asian America: Activism and Resistance in the 1990s;* and *Amerasia Journal* 19, no. 2 (1993), a volume devoted entirely to the L.A. riots.

7. Lawrence D. Bobo, et al., eds., *Prismatic Metropolis: Inequality in Los Angeles,* 222.

8. James Johnson, Cloyzelle K. Jones, Walter Farrell, and Melvin Oliver, "The Los Angeles Rebellion, 1992: A Preliminary Assessment from Ground Zero," 6.

9. The increasing numbers made Korea the third largest sender nation, following Mexico and the Philippines, for U.S. immigration. See Herbert R. Barringer, Robert W. Gardner, and Michael Y. Levin, *Asians and Pacific Islanders in the United States,* 4. The number of Koreans in Los Angeles County reached 186,350 by 2000. See Table DP-1, "Profile of General Demographic Characteristics: 2000," *Census 2000,* www.census.gov.

10. For more on Koreans as middleman minorities, see Pyong Gap Min, *Caught in the Middle: Korean Communities in New York and Los Angeles.* Although Korean immigrants are more likely to be entrepreneurs than any other Asian immigrant groups in Los Angeles,

the Korean Angeleno community shows tremendous economic disparities. The prevailing belief that Korean business owners were taking money out of black neighborhoods obscured some very real economic problems that beset Korean immigrants. See Paul Ong, Kye Young Park, and Yasmin Tong, "The Korean-Black Conflict and the State."

11. See Chang and Diaz-Veizades, *Ethnic Peace in the American City*, 105–28; and Elaine H. Kim, "Between Black and White: An Interview with Bong Hwan Kim."

12. Davis, *City of Quartz*, 223.

13. See Jeff Chang, *Can't Stop*, 299–329.

14. I am borrowing Victoria Johnson's phrase "sonic assault" from her characterization of "Fight the Power." Victoria E. Johnson, "Polyphony and Cultural Expression: Interpreting Musical Traditions in *Do the Right Thing*." See also Guthrie P. Ramsey Jr.'s chapter on soundtracks in hip-hop films, which includes a discussion of *Do the Right Thing*, in his *Race Music: Black Cultures from Bebop to Hip-Hop*, 163–89.

15. Public Enemy, "Fight the Power," from *Do the Right Thing* soundtrack (Motown, B00005MK88, 1989).

16. Definition of "Signifyin(g)" in Russell A. Potter, *Spectacular Vernaculars: Hip-Hop and the Politics of Postmodernism*, 27. Potter's emphasis.

17. Jeff Chang, "Race, Class, Conflict and Empowerment: On Ice Cube's 'Black Korea.'"

18. I borrow the phrase from Nazli Kibria's *Becoming Asian American*, which examines the individual experiences of "ethnicization"—the process whereby the meaning and significance of an Asian American identity emerge—of 1.5 and second-generation Korean Americans. Nazli Kibria, *Becoming Asian American: Second-Generation Chinese and Korean American Identities*.

19. See ibid., 5.

20. Ellie M. Hisama, "Afro-Asian Crosscurrents in Contemporary Hip Hop." Historians and cultural critics have, in recent years, turned increasingly to the idea of polyculturalism. See Robin D. G. Kelley, *Freedom Dreams: The Black Radical Imagination;* and Vijay Prashad, *Everybody Was Kung Fu Fighting: Afro-Asian Connections and the Myth of Cultural Purity*.

21. Deborah Wong, "The Asian American Body in Performance," 88.

22. For more on culture and diasporic communities, see Jana Evans Braziel and Anita Mannur, eds., *Theorizing Diaspora: A Reader*. Scholars have recently begun to explore transnational musical cultures. See, for example, Sunaina Maira, *Desis in the House: Indian American Youth Culture in New York City*.

23. James Chang, "Jamez Chang: Hip-Hop and Rap Artist," 356.

24. Although the numbers are somewhat outdated at this point, Cheng and Yang's article breaks down the realities behind the model minority myth and provides statistics on Asian matriculation at various levels of education, particularly in California. See Lucie Cheng and Philip Q. Yang, "Asians: The 'Model Minority' Deconstructed."

25. See Kibria, *Becoming Asian American*, 102–30.

26. James Chang, "Jamez Chang," 356.

27. Ibid., 360.

28. The Parks were not ignorant of the tension between African American and Korean communities, however: Michael wrote one of the few articles defending the Korean American position during the "Black Korea" controversy in an English edition of *Korea*

Times. Michael Park, "Ice Cube Stereotypes All Asians, Not Just Koreans," *Korea Times* (Los Angeles ed.), January 20, 1992.

29. Kibria, *Becoming Asian American,* 123.

30. The quote from Hana Choi and Raphael Park and the lyrics from Seoul Brothers' rap are excerpted from Judy Tseng, "Asian American Rap: Expression through Alternate Forms," available online at http://modelminority.com/modules.php?name=News&file=article&sid=128.

31. See Daisy Nguyen, "The Color of Rap: It's a Tough Climb for Asian American Hip-Hop Artists," available online at http://www.columbia.edu/itc/journalism/gissler/anthology/Rappers-Nguyen.html; and Deborah Wong, *Speak It Louder: Asian Americans Making Music,* 233–56.

32. See Erin Chan, "Slim Shady, Watch It: Asian Rapper's Got It," *New York Times,* August 12, 2003.

33. The "model minority" myth was first established by a 1966 *U.S. News and World Report* article that held up Chinese Americans, diligent and studious, as exemplary ethnic minorities. Published at the height of the civil rights movement, the article used the example of Asian Americans to chastise other minority groups struggling for equal opportunities. More recently, a 1987 article by David Brand in *Time* magazine, "The New Whiz Kids" (August 31), perpetuated many of the stereotypes delineated in the earlier article.

34. See the interview of Uptown 3000 in the PBS documentary film *Los Angeles Now* (dir. Phillip Rodriguez, 2004).

35. Rickey Kim, "In the Studio with Drunken Tiger," *Evil Monito* 1, no. 2 (2001), www .evilmonito.com.

36. For a brief overview of the hip-hop scene in Korea, see Sarah Morelli, "'Who Is Dancing Hero?' Rap, Hip-Hop, and Dance in Korean Popular Culture."

37. See Stuart Hall and Tony Jefferson, eds., *Resistance through Rituals: Youth Subcultures in Post-War Britain;* and Hebdige, *Subculture.*

38. See, for example, Deborah Wong, "Finding an Asian American Audience: The Problem of Listening"; and Joseph Lam, "Embracing 'Asian American Music' as an Heuristic Device." See also Christopher Small, *Musicking: The Meanings of Performing and Listening.*

39. Web sites, such as ImaginAsian Entertainment's iaLink ("the Ultimate Guide to Asian America") at www.iatv.tv, provide up-to-date information on Asian and Asian American musicians.

40. See www.jamez.iama.com.

41. The forum began with moderator Jay Smooth's posting of an article from the *Korea Herald,* "Tigers Roar, Who's Listening?" (April 25, 2003), and ran until November 1, 2004.

42. For an excellent summary of the critical literature on cultural authenticity, see John Connell and Chris Gibson, *Sound Tracks: Popular Music, Identity and Place,* 19–44.

43. Amiri Baraka, "Jazz and the White Critic," 185.

44. Jeff Chang, "Race, Class, Conflict and Empowerment."

45. The number of such opportunities is growing. Kollaboration in Los Angeles's Koreatown, for example, has presented Korean American artists annually since 1999 and

has launched similar enterprises in other major cities in the United States. A recent *New York Times* article on the Korean pop sensation Rain took note of his upcoming concert in New York City and reported on the eager anticipation of his Korean American fans. See Deborah Sontag, "The Ambassador," *New York Times,* January 29, 2006.

46. Rickey Kim, "Lounging with LA Symphony," *Evil Monito* 1, no. 4 (2001).

47. See, for example, Daniel Widener, "'Perhaps the Japanese Are to Be Thanked?' Asia, Asian Americans, and the Construction of Black California."

Works Cited

Primary Sources: Newspapers, Periodicals, Interviews

Argonaut
Asian Week
Billboard
California Eagle
Con Safos
Down Beat
Evil Monito
Korea Herald
Korea Times
Los Angeles Daily Journal
Los Angeles Police Department,
    Annual Report
Los Angeles Times
Los Angeles Tribune
Metronome
Modern Music
Musical America

New York Times
Pacific Coast Musical Review
Pacific Coast Musician
Record Changer
San Francisco Chronicle
San Francisco Examiner
San Francisco News
Time
U.S. News and World Report
Variety
Department of Special Collections,
    Charles E. Young Research Library,
    University of California, Los Angeles
Interview transcripts housed at Oral
    History, American Music, Yale
    University, New Haven, Conn.

Secondary Sources

Abelmann, Nancy, and John Lie. *Blue Dreams: Korean Americans and the Los Angeles Riots*. Cambridge, Mass.: Harvard University Press, 1995.

Acuña, Rodolfo F. *A Community under Siege: A Chronicle of Chicanos East of the Los Angeles River, 1945–1975*. Los Angeles: Chicano Studies Research Center, University of California, Los Angeles, 1984.

———. *Occupied America: A History of Chicanos*, 4th ed. New York: Longman, 2000.

Adorno, Theodor W., and Max Horkheimer. *Dialektik der Aufklärung: philosophische Fragmente*. 1981. Frankfurt am Main: Suhrkamp, 1984.

Aguilar-San Juan, Karin, ed. *The State of Asian America: Activism and Resistance in the 1990s.* Boston: South End Press, 1993.

Alderman, Pauline. *We Build a School of Music: The Commissioned History of Music at the University of Southern California.* Los Angeles: Alderman Book Committee, School of Music, University of Southern California, 1989.

Almaguer, Tomás. *Racial Fault Lines: The Historical Origins of White Supremacy in California.* Berkeley: University of California Press, 1994.

Baldassare, Mark, ed. *The Los Angeles Riots: Lessons for the Urban Future.* Boulder: Westview Press, 1994.

Banham, Reyner. *Los Angeles: The Architecture of Four Ecologies.* New York: Harper and Row, 1971.

Baraka, Amiri. "Jazz and the White Critic." 1963. In *The Leroi Jones/Amiri Baraka Reader,* edited by William J. Harris, 179–185. New York: Thunder's Mouth Press 1999.

Barr, Cyrilla. *Elizabeth Sprague Coolidge: American Patron of Music.* New York: Schirmer, 1998.

Barringer, Herbert R., Robert W. Gardner, and Michael Y. Levin. *Asians and Pacific Islanders in the United States.* New York: Russell Sage Foundation, 1993.

Barron, Stephanie, Sheri Bernstein, and Ilene Susan Fort, eds. *Reading California: Art, Image, and Identity, 1900–2000.* Los Angeles and Berkeley: Los Angeles County Museum of Art and University of California Press, 2000.

Bederman, Gail. *Manliness and Civilization: A Cultural History of Gender and Race in the United States, 1880–1917.* Chicago: University of Chicago Press, 1995.

Bellman, Jonathan, ed. *The Exotic in Western Music.* Boston: Northeastern University Press, 1998.

Bergstrom, Janet. "The Mystery of *The Blue Gardenia.*" In *Shades of Noir: A Reader,* edited by Joan Copjec, 97–120. London: Verso, 1993.

Bernardi, Daniel, ed. *Classic Hollywood, Classic Whiteness.* Minneapolis: University of Minnesota Press, 2001.

Blackburn, Philip, ed. *Enclosure 3: Harry Partch.* St. Paul: American Composers Forum, 1997.

Bobo, Lawrence D., et al., eds. *Prismatic Metropolis: Inequality in Los Angeles.* New York: Russell Sage Foundation, 2000.

Bogdanovich, Peter. *Fritz Lang in America.* London: Studio Vista, 1967.

Born, Georgina, and David Hesmondhalgh, eds. *Western Music and Its Others: Difference, Representation, and Appropriation in Music.* Berkeley: University of California Press, 2000.

Boyd, Nan Alamilla. *Wide-Open Town: A History of Queer San Francisco to 1965.* Berkeley: University of California Press, 2003.

Brett, Philip. "Eros and Orientalism in Brietten's Operas." In *Queering the Pitch,* edited by Philip Brett, Elizabeth Wood, and Gary C. Thomas, 235–56. New York: Routledge, 1994.

———. "Musicality, Essentialism, and the Closet." In *Queering the Pitch,* edited by Philip Brett, Elizabeth Wood, and Gary C. Thomas, 9–26. New York: Routledge, 1994.

Brinkmann, Reinhold, and Christoph Wolff, eds. *Driven into Paradise: The Musical Migration from Nazi Germany to the United States.* Berkeley: University of California Press, 1999.

Bryant, Clora, et al. *Central Avenue Sounds: Jazz in Los Angeles.* Berkeley: University of California Press, 1998.

Burt, Peter. *The Music of Tōru Takemitsu.* Cambridge: Cambridge University Press, 2001.

Butler, David. *Jazz Noir: Listening to Music from* Phantom Lady *to* The Last Seduction. Westport, Conn.: Praeger, 2002.

Butler, Judith. "Endangered/Endangering: Schematic Racism and White Paranoia." In *Reading Rodney King/ Reading Urban Uprising,* edited by Robert Gooding-Williams, 15–22. New York: Routledge, 1993.

Cage, John. *Silence.* Middletown, Conn.: Wesleyan University Press, 1961.

Cain, James M. *The Postman Always Rings Twice.* 1934. Reprinted in *Crime Novels: American Noir of the 1930s and 40s.* New York: Literary Classics of the United States, 1997.

Carey, David. "*Double Music:* A Historio-Analytic Study." Master's thesis, University of California, San Diego, 1978.

Cartwright, Derrick R. "Chronology." In *On the Edge of America: California Modernist Art, 1900–1950,* edited by Paul J. Karlstrom, 274–85. Berkeley: University of California Press, 1996.

Chan, Sucheng, and Spencer C. Olin, eds. *Major Problems in California History: Documents and Essays.* Boston: Houghton Mifflin, 1997.

Chang, Edward T., and Jeannette Diaz-Veizades. *Ethnic Peace in the American City: Building Community in Los Angeles and Beyond.* New York: New York University Press, 1999.

Chang, James. "Jamez Chang: Hip-Hop and Rap Artist." In *Yellow Light: The Flowering of Asian American Arts,* edited by Amy Ling, 355–60. Philadelphia: Temple University Press, 1999.

Chang, Jeff. *Can't Stop, Won't Stop: A History of the Hip-Hop Generation.* New York: St. Martin's Press, 2005.

———. "Race, Class, Conflict and Empowerment: On Ice Cube's 'Black Korea.'" *Amerasia Journal* 19, no. 2 (1993): 87–107.

Chase, Gilbert. *America's Music: From the Pilgrims to the Present.* Urbana: University of Illinois Press, 1992.

Chávez, Ernesto. "*¡Mi Raza Primero!" (My People First!): Nationalism, Identity, and Insurgency in the Chicano Movement in Los Angeles, 1966–1978.* Berkeley: University of California Press, 2002.

Cheng, Lucie, and Philip Q. Yang. "Asians: The 'Model Minority' Deconstructed." In *Ethnic Los Angeles,* edited by Roger Waldinger and Mehdi Bozorgmehr, 305–44. New York: Russell Sage Foundation, 1996.

Chion, Michel. *Audio-Vision: Sound on Screen.* 1990. Edited and translated by Claudia Gorbman. New York: Columbia University Press, 1994.

Clark, W. A. U. *The California Cauldron: Immigration and the Fortunes of Local Communities.* New York: Guilford, 1998.

Clarke, J. J. *Oriental Enlightenment: The Encounter between Asian and Western Thought.* London: Routledge, 1997.

Clover, Carol J. "Dancin' in the Rain." *Critical Inquiry* 21, no. 4 (1995): 722–47.

Cohan, Steven. *Masked Men: Masculinity and the Movies in the Fifties.* Bloomington: Indiana University Press, 1997.

Collins, Keith. *Black Los Angeles: The Maturing of the Ghetto, 1940–1950.* Saratoga, Calif.: Century Twenty-One Publishers, 1980.

Connell, John, and Chris Gibson. *Sound Tracks: Popular Music, Identity and Place.* London: Routledge, 2003.

Corbett, John. "Experimental Oriental." In *Western Music and Its Others,* edited by Georgina Born and David Hesmondhalgh, 163–86. Berkeley: University of California Press, 2000.

Cosgrove, Stuart. "The Zoot-Suit and Style Warfare." *History Workshop Journal* 18 (1984): 79–91.

Crawford, Dorothy. *Evenings On and Off the Roof: Pioneering Concerts in Los Angeles, 1939–1971.* Berkeley: University of California Press, 1995.

Crawford, Richard. *America's Musical Life: A History.* New York: W. W. Norton, 2001.

Cripps, Thomas. *Making Movies Black: The Hollywood Message Movie from World War II to the Civil Rights Era.* New York: Oxford University Press, 1993.

Cross, Brian. *It's Not about a Salary—: Rap, Race, and Resistance in Los Angeles.* London: Verso, 1993.

Daniels, Roger, and Spencer C. Olin Jr., eds. *Racism in California: A Reader in the History of Oppression.* New York: Macmillan, 1972.

Davis, Mike. *City of Quartz: Excavating the Future in Los Angeles.* 1990. New York: Vintage, 1992.

Davis, Miles, with Quincy Troupe. *Miles, the Autobiography.* New York: Simon and Schuster, 1989.

DeVeaux, Scott. *The Birth of Bebop: A Social and Musical History.* Berkeley: University of California Press, 1997.

DeWitt, Howard. *The Fragmented Dream: Multicultural California.* Dubuque, Iowa: Kendall/Hunt, 1996.

Diawara, Manthia. "*Noir* by *Noirs*: Towards a New Realism in Black Cinema." *African American Review* 27, no. 4 (1993): 525–38.

Dizikes, John. *Opera in America: A Cultural History.* New Haven, Conn.: Yale University Press, 1993.

DjeDje, Jacqueline, and Eddie Meadows, eds. *California Soul: Music of African Americans in the West.* Berkeley: University of California Press, 1998.

Domanick, Joe. *To Protect and to Serve: The LAPD's Century of War in the City of Dreams.* New York: Simon and Schuster, 1994.

Earls, Paul. "Harry Partch: Verses in Preparation for *Delusion of the Fury.*" In *Harry Partch: An Anthology of Critical Perspectives,* edited by David Dunn, 79–106. Australia: Harwood Academic Publishers, 2000.

Eastman, Ralph. "Central Avenue Blues: The Making of Los Angeles Rhythm and Blues, 1942–47." *Black Music Research Journal* 9, no. 1 (1989): 19–34.

Eisler, Hanns. *Composing for the Films.* 1947. London: Athlone, 1994.

Epstein, Daniel Mark. *Nat King Cole.* New York: Farrar, Straus and Giroux, 1999.

Erenberg, Lewis A. *Swingin' the Dream: Big Band Jazz and the Rebirth of American Culture.* Chicago: University of Chicago Press, 1998.

Escobar, Edward J. *Race, Police, and the Making of a Political Identity: Mexican Americans and the Los Angeles Police Department, 1900–1945.* Berkeley: University of California Press, 1995.

Estes Smith, Caroline. *The Philharmonic Orchestra of Los Angeles, "The First Decade,"* *1919–1929*. Los Angeles: United Printing, 1939.

Estrada, William D. "Los Angeles' Old Plaza and Olvera Street: Imagined and Contested Space." *Built L.A.: Folklore and Place in Los Angeles.* Special issue, *Western Folklore* 58, no. 2 (1999): 107–29.

Evans Braziel, Jana, and Anita Mannur, eds. *Theorizing Diaspora: A Reader.* Malden, Mass.: Blackwell, 2003.

Farwell, Arthur. *"Wanderjahre of a Revolutionist" and Other Essays on American Music.* Rochester, N.Y.: University of Rochester Press, 1995.

Fine, David. "Beginning in the Thirties: The Los Angeles Fiction of James M. Cain and Horace McCoy." In *Los Angeles in Fiction,* edited by David Fine, 43–66. Albuquerque: University of New Mexico Press, 1984.

Flinn, Caryl. *Strains of Utopia: Gender, Nostalgia, and Hollywood Film Music.* Princeton, N.J.: Princeton University Press, 1992.

Fogelson, Robert M. *The Fragmented Metropolis: Los Angeles, 1850–1930.* 1967. Berkeley: University of California Press, 1993.

Foucault, Michel. *Discipline and Punish: The Birth of the Prisons.* Translated by Alan Sheridan. New York: Vintage, 1979.

Friedman, Lester D., ed. *Unspeakable Images: Ethnicity and the American Cinema.* Urbana.: University of Illinois Press, 1991.

Friedrich, Otto. *City of Nets: A Portrait of Hollywood in the 1940s.* Berkeley: University of California Press, 1997.

Fry, Stephen. *California's Musical Wealth: Sources for the Study of Music in California.* Glendale: Music Library Association, Southern California Chapter, 1988.

Gabbard, Krin. *Jammin' at the Margins: Jazz and the American Cinema.* Chicago: University of Chicago Press, 1996.

Garcia, Matt. *A World of Its Own: Race, Labor, and Citrus in the Making of Greater Los Angeles, 1900–1970.* Chapel Hill: University of North Carolina Press, 2001.

Garland, Peter. *Americas: Essays on American Music and Culture, 1973–80.* Santa Fe: Soundings Press, 1982.

———. *Lou Harrison Reader.* Santa Fe: Soundings Press, 1987.

Gilmore, Bob. *Harry Partch: a Biography.* New Haven, Conn.: Yale University Press, 1998.

Gioia, Ted. *West Coast Jazz: Modern Jazz in California, 1945–1960.* New York: Oxford University Press, 1992.

Golden Gate International Exposition. *Official Guide Book 1940.* San Francisco: San Francisco Bay Exposition, 1940.

Gonzales, Rodolfo. *I Am Joaquin: An Epic Poem.* 1967. Denver: R. Gonzales, 1991.

Gooding-Williams, Robert, ed. *Reading Rodney King, Reading Urban Uprising.* New York: Routledge, 1993.

Gorbman, Claudia. *Unheard Melodies: Narrative Film Music.* Bloomington: Indiana University Press, 1987.

Gordon, Robert. *Jazz West Coast: The Los Angeles Jazz Scene of the 1950s.* London: Quartet Books, 1986.

Gottlieb, Robert, and Irene Wolt. *Thinking Big: The Story of the* Los Angeles Times, *Its Publishers and Their Influence on Southern California.* New York: G. P. Putnam's Sons, 1977.

Griswold del Castillo, Richard. *The Los Angeles Barrio, 1850–1890: A Social History.* Berkeley: University of California Press, 1979.

Guevara, Ruben. "The View from the Sixth Street Bridge: The History of Chicano Rock." In *The First Rock and Roll Confidential Report,* edited by Dave Marsh, 118. New York: Pantheon Books, 1985.

Hall, Stuart, and Tony Jefferson, eds. *Resistance through Rituals: Youth Subcultures in Post-War Britain.* London: Routledge, 1993.

Harrison, Lou. "Learning from Henry." In *The Whole World of Music: A Henry Cowell Symposium,* edited by David Nicholls, 161–67. Amsterdam: Harwood Academic Press, 1997.

———. *Music Primer.* New York: Peters, 1971.

Haslam, Gerald. *Workin' Man Blues: Country Music in California.* Berkeley: University of California Press, 1999.

Hawes, Hampton, and Don Asher. *Raise Up off Me: A Portrait of Hampton Hawes.* New York: Da Capo Press, 1979.

Hazen, Don, ed. *Inside the L.A. Riots: What Really Happened and Why It Will Happen Again.* New York: Institute for Alternative Journalism, 1992.

Hebdige, Dick. *Subculture: The Meaning of Style.* 1979. London: Routledge, 1987.

Heimann, Jim. *Out with the Stars: Hollywood Nightlife in the Golden Era.* New York: Abbeville Press, 1985.

Heisley, Michael. "Lummis and Mexican-American Folklore." In *Charles M. Lummis: The Centennial Exhibition Commemorating His Tramp across the Continent,* edited by Daniel P. Moneta, 60–67. Los Angeles: Southwest Museum, 1985.

Hernández, Guillermo. *Canciones de la Raza: Songs of the Chicano Experience.* Berkeley: El Fuego de Aztlan, 1978.

Hicks, Michael. "Cowell's Clusters." *Musical Quarterly* 77, no. 3 (1993): 428–58.

———. *Henry Cowell, Bohemian.* Urbana: University of Illinois Press, 2002.

———. "The Imprisonment of Henry Cowell." *Journal of the American Musicological Society* 44, no. 1 (1999): 92–119.

Hines, Thomas S. "Then Not Yet 'Cage': The Los Angeles Years, 1912–38." In *John Cage: Composed in America,* edited by Marjorie Perloff and Charles Junkerman, 65–99. Chicago: University of Chicago Press, 1994.

Hisama, Ellie M. "Afro-Asian Crosscurrents in Contemporary Hip Hop," *ISAM Newsletter* 32, no. 1 (2002). Available online at http://depthome.brooklyn.cuny.edu/isam/hisama1.html.

History of Music Project. *Fifty Local Prodigies, 1906–1940.* New York: AMS Press, 1972.

Hitchcock, H. Wiley. "Henry Cowell's *Ostinato Pianissimo.*" *Musical Quarterly* 70, no. 1 (1984): 23–44.

———. *Music in the United States: A Historical Introduction.* Englewood Cliffs, N.J.: Prentice-Hall, 1974.

Hoskyns, Barney. *Waiting for the Sun: Strange Days, Weird Scenes, and the Sound of Los Angeles.* New York: St. Martin's Press, 1996.

Hubbs, Nadine. *The Queer Composition of America's Sound: Gay Modernists, American Music, and National Identity.* Berkeley: University of California Press, 2004.

Issel, William, and Robert W. Cherny. *San Francisco, 1865–1932: Politics, Power, and Urban Development.* Berkeley: University of California Press, 1986.

The Johnny Mercer Songbook. Hialeah, Fla.: Columbia Pictures Publications, 1981.

Johnson, James, Cloyzelle K. Jones, Walter Farrell, and Melvin Oliver. "The Los Angeles Rebellion, 1992: A Preliminary Assessment from Ground Zero." *UCLA Center for the Study of Urban Poverty.* Occasional Working Paper Series 2, no. 7. Los Angeles: UCLA Center for the Study of Urban Poverty, 1992.

Johnson, Steven. "Henry Cowell, John Varian, and Halcyon." *American Music* 11 (1993): 1–27.

Johnson, Victoria E. "Polyphony and Cultural Expression: Interpreting Musical Traditions in *Do the Right Thing.*" In *Spike Lee's* Do the Right Thing, edited by Mark A. Reid, 50–72. Cambridge: Cambridge University Press, 1997.

Johnston, Ben. "The Corporealism of Harry Partch." *Perspectives of New Music* 13, no. 2 (1975): 87–88.

Jones, Caroline. "Finishing School: John Cage and the Abstract Expressionist Ego." *Critical Inquiry* 19, no. 4 (1993): 628–65.

Kakinuma, Toshie, and Mamoru Fujieda. "I Am One of Mr. Ives' Legal Heirs: An Interview with Lou Harrison." *Sonus* 9, no. 2 (1989): 46–58.

Kalfatovic, Martin R. *The New Deal Fine Arts Projects: A Bibliography, 1933–1992.* Metuchen, N.J.: Scarecrow, 1994.

Kaplan, E. Ann. "The 'Dark Continent' of Film Noir: Race, Displacement and Metaphor in Tourneur's *Cat People* (1942) and Welles' *The Lady from Shanghai* (1948)." 1978. In *Women in Film Noir,* edited by E. Ann Kaplan, 183–201. London: British Film Institute, 1998.

———. "The Place of Women in Fritz Lang's *The Blue Gardenia.*" 1978. In *Women in Film Noir,* edited by E. Ann Kaplan, 81–88. London: British Film Institute, 1998.

———, ed. *Women in Film Noir.* London: British Film Institute, 1978.

Karlstrom, Paul J., ed. *On the Edge of America: California Modernist Art, 1900–1950.* Berkeley: University of California Press, 1996.

Kassabian, Anahid. *Hearing Film: Tracking Identifications in Contemporary Hollywood Film Music.* New York: Routledge, 2001.

Katz, Jonathan D. "John Cage's Queer Silence; or, How to Avoid Making Matters Worse." In *Writings through John Cage's Music, Poetry, and Art,* edited by David W. Bernstein and Christopher Hatch, 41–61. Chicago: University of Chicago Press, 2001.

Kedzie Wood, Ruth. *The Tourist's California.* New York: Dodd, Mead, 1914.

Keil, Roger. *Los Angeles: Globalization, Urbanization and Social Struggles.* Chichester, U.K.: John Wiley and Sons, 1998.

Kelley, Robin D. G. *Freedom Dreams: The Black Radical Imagination.* Boston: Beacon Press, 2002.

Keyes, Cheryl. *Rap Music and Street Consciousness.* Urbana: University of Illinois Press, 2002.

Kibria, Nazli. *Becoming Asian American: Second-Generation Chinese and Korean American Identities.* Baltimore: Johns Hopkins University Press, 2002.

Kim, Elaine H. "Between Black and White: An Interview with Bong Hwan Kim." In *The State of Asian America: Activism and Resistance in the 1990s,* edited by Karin Aguilar-San Juan, 71–100. Boston: South End Press, 1993.

Kim, Kwang Chung, ed. *Koreans in the Hood: Conflict with African Americans.* Baltimore: Johns Hopkins University Press, 1999.

Kinkle, Roger D. *The Complete Encyclopedia of Popular Music and Jazz, 1900–1950.* New Rochelle, N.Y.: Arlington House, 1974.

Knight, Arthur. *"Jammin' the Blues,* or the Sight of Jazz, 1944." In *Representing Jazz,* edited by Krin Gabbard, 11–53. Durham, N.C.: Duke University Press, 1995.

Koegel, John. "Mexican-American Music in Nineteenth-Century Southern California: The Lummis Wax Cylinder Collection at the Southwest Museum, Los Angeles." Ph.D. diss., Claremont Graduate University, 1994.

Kosofsky Sedgwick, Eve. *Epistemology of the Closet.* Berkeley: University of California Press, 1990.

Kostelanetz, Richard, ed. *John Cage: An Anthology.* New York: Da Capo Press, 1991.

———, ed. *John Cage: Writer: Previously Uncollected Pieces.* New York: Limelight Editions, 1993.

Krutnik, Frank. *In a Lonely Street: Film Noir, Genre, Masculinity.* London: Routledge, 1991.

Lam, Joseph. "Embracing 'Asian American Music' as an Heuristic Device." *Journal of Asian American Studies* 2, no. 1 (1999): 29–60.

Lavender, David. *California: Land of New Beginnings.* New York: Harper and Row, 1972.

Levine, Lawrence W. *Highbrow/Lowbrow: The Emergence of Cultural Hierarchy in America.* Cambridge, Mass.: Harvard University Press, 1988.

Lewels, Francisco J., Jr. *The Uses of the Media by the Chicano Movement: A Study in Minority Access.* New York: Praeger, 1974.

Lewis, Oscar. *Bay Window Bohemia: An Account of the Brilliant Artistic World of Gaslit San Francisco.* Garden City, N.Y.: Doubleday, 1956.

Lipsitz, George. "Cruising around the Historical Bloc—Postmodernism and Popular Music in East Los Angeles." *Cultural Critique* 5 (1986): 157–77.

———. *Dangerous Crossroads: Popular Music, Postmodernism and the Poetics of Place.* New York: Verso, 1994.

———. "Land of a Thousand Dances: Youth, Minorities, and the Rise of Rock and Roll." In *Recasting America: Culture and Politics in the Age of Cold War,* edited by Lary May, 267–84. Chicago: University of Chicago Press, 1989.

Locke, Ralph P. "Constructing the Oriental 'Other': Saint-Saëns's *Samson et Dalila.*" *Cambridge Opera Journal* 3, no. 3 (1991): 261–302.

Lott, Eric. "The Whiteness of Film Noir." In *Whiteness: A Critical Reader,* edited by Mike Hill, 81–101. New York: New York University Press, 1997.

Lowe, Lisa. *Immigrant Acts: On Asian American Cultural Politics.* Durham, N.C.: Duke University Press, 1996.

Loza, Steven. *Barrio Rhythm: Mexican American Music in Los Angeles.* Urbana: University of Illinois Press, 1993.

———. "Identity, Nationalism, and Aesthetics among Chicano/Mexicano Musicians in Los Angeles." In *Musical Aesthetics and Multiculturalism in Los Angeles: Selected Reports in Ethnomusicology X,* edited by Steven Loza, 51–58. Los Angeles: University of California, Los Angeles, Department of Ethnomusicology and Systematic Musicology, 1994.

Lummis, Charles F. *Spanish Songs of Old California.* New York: Schirmer, 1923.

Macías, Anthony F. "From Pachuco Boogie to Latin Jazz: Mexican Americans, Popular Music, and Urban Culture in Los Angeles, 1940–1965." Ph.D. diss., University of Michigan, 2001.

———. "*Rock con Raza, Raza con Jazz*: Latinos/as and Post–World War II Popular American Music." In *Musical Migrations, Volume 1: Transnationalism and Cultural Hybridity in Latin/o America,* edited by Frances R. Aparicio and Cándida F. Jáquez, 183–98. New York: Palgrave Macmillan, 2003.

Maira, Sunaina. *Desis in the House: Indian American Youth Culture in New York City.* Philadelphia: Temple University Press, 2002.

Marcus, Kenneth. *Musical Metropolis: Los Angeles and the Creation of a Music Culture, 1880–1940.* New York: Palgrave Macmillan, 2004.

Martin, George. *Verdi at the Golden Gate: Opera and San Francisco in the Gold Rush Years.* Berkeley: University of California Press, 1993.

May, Lary. *The Big Tomorrow: Hollywood and the Politics of the American Way.* Chicago: University of Chicago Press, 2000.

———. *Screening Out the Past: The Birth of Mass Culture and the Motion Picture Industry.* 1980. Chicago: University of Chicago Press, 1983.

Mazón, Mauricio. *The Zoot-Suit Riots: The Psychology of Symbolic Annihilation.* Austin: University of Texas Press, 1984.

McClary, Susan. *Feminine Endings.* 1991. Minneapolis: University of Minnesota Press, 2002.

———. *Georges Bizet:* Carmen. Cambridge: Cambridge University Press, 1992.

McCoy, Esther. *Five California Architects.* New York: Reinhold, 1960.

McWilliams, Carey. *North from Mexico: The Spanish-Speaking Peoples of the United States.* 1949. New York: Greenwood, 1990.

Mead, Rita. *Henry Cowell's New Music, 1925–1936: The Society, the Music Editions, and the Recordings.* Ann Arbor.: UMI Research Press, 1981.

Miller, Leta E. "The Art of Noise: John Cage, Lou Harrison, and the West Coast Percussion Ensemble." In *Perspectives on American Music, 1900–1950,* edited by Michael Saffle, 215–64. New York: Garland, 2000.

———. "Cage's Collaborations." In *The Cambridge Companion to John Cage,* edited by David Nicholls, 151–68. New York: Cambridge University Press, 2002.

———. "Henry Cowell and Modern Dance: The Genesis of Elastic Form." *American Music* 20, no. 1 (2002): 1–24.

Miller, Leta E., and Rob Collins. "The Cowell-Ives Relationship: A New Look at Cowell's Prison Years." *American Music* 23, no. 4 (2005): 473–92.

Miller, Leta E., and Fredric Lieberman. *Lou Harrison: Composing a World.* New York: Oxford University Press, 1998.

Min, Pyong Gap. *Caught in the Middle: Korean Communities in New York and Los Angeles.* Berkeley: University of California Press, 1996.

Mitchell, Tony, ed. *Global Noise: Rap and Hip-Hop outside the USA.* Middletown, Conn.: Wesleyan University Press, 2001.

Molina, Ruben. *The Old Barrio Guide to Low Rider Music, 1950–1975.* La Puente, Calif.: Mictlan Publishing, 2002.

Monroy, Douglas. *Rebirth: Mexican Los Angeles from the Great Migration to the Great Depression.* Berkeley: University of California Press, 1999.

———. *Thrown among Strangers: The Making of Mexican Culture in Frontier California.* Berkeley: University of California Press, 1990.

Morelli, Sarah. "'Who Is Dancing Hero?' Rap, Hip-Hop, and Dance in Korean Popular

Culture." *Global Noise: Rap and Hip-Hop outside the USA,* edited by Tony Mitchell, 248–58. Middletown, Conn.: Wesleyan University Press, 2001.

Muñoz, Carlos, Jr. *Youth, Identity, Power: The Chicano Movement.* London: Verso, 1989.

Naremore, James. *More Than Night: Film Noir in Its Contexts.* Berkeley: University of California Press, 1998.

Negus, Keith. *Popular Music in Theory: An Introduction.* Hanover, N.H.: University Press of New England, 1997.

Nicholls, David, ed. *The Cambridge Companion to John Cage.* Cambridge and New York: Cambridge University Press, 2002.

———. "Transethnicism and the American Experimental Tradition." *Musical Quarterly* 80, no. 4 (1996): 569–94.

Oja, Carol. *Making Music Modern: New York in the 1920s.* New York: Oxford University Press, 2000.

Omi, Michael, and Howard Winant. *Racial Formation in the United States: From the 1960s to the 1990s.* 2nd ed. New York: Routledge, 1994.

Ong, Paul, Kye Young Park, and Yasmin Tong. "The Korean-Black Conflict and the State." In *The New Asian Immigration in Los Angeles and Global Restructuring,* edited by Paul Ong, Edna Bonacich, and Lucie Cheng, 266–68. Philadelphia: Temple University Press, 1994.

Otis, Johnny. *Listen to the Lambs.* New York: Norton, 1968.

———. *Upside Your Head! Rhythm and Blues on Central Avenue.* Hanover, N.H.: Wesleyan University Press, 1993.

Parker, William H. *Parker on Police.* 1950. Edited by Orlando W. Wilson. Springfield, Ill: Charles C. Thomas, 1957.

———. *Police Chief William H. Parker Speaks.* Compiled by the Community Relations Conference of Southern California. Los Angeles: The Conference, 1965.

Parsons Smith, Catherine. "'Popular Prices Will Prevail': Setting the Social Role of European-Based Concert Music." In *Musical Aesthetics and Multiculturalism in Los Angeles: Selected Reports in Ethnomusicology X,* edited by Steven Loza, 207–21. Los Angeles: University of California, Los Angeles, Department of Ethnomusicology and Systematic Musicology, 1994.

———. "Symphony and Opera in Progressive-Era Los Angeles." In *Music and Culture in America, 1861–1918,* edited by Michael Saffle, 299–322. New York: Garland, 1998.

Partch, Harry. *Genesis of a Music.* 2nd ed. Madison: University of Wisconsin Press, 1974.

Patterson, David W. "Cage and Asia: History and Sources." In *The Cambridge Companion to John Cage,* edited by David Nicholls, 41–62. New York: Cambridge University Press, 2002.

Peña, Manuel H. *The Mexican American Orquesta Music: Music, Culture, and the Dialectic of Conflict.* Austin: University of Texas Press, 1999.

———. "Notes towards an Interpretive History of California-Mexican Music." In *From the Inside Out: Perspectives on Mexican and Mexican-American Folk Art,* edited by Karana Hattersly-Drayton, Joyce M. Bishop, and Tomás Ybarra-Frausto, 64–75. San Francisco: The Mexican Museum, 1989.

Pepper, Art, and Laurie Pepper. *Straight Life: The Story of Art Pepper.* New York: Da Capo Press, 1994.

Pérez-Torres, Rafael. "Mestizaje in the Mix: Chicano Identity, Cultural Politics, and Post-modern Music." In *Music and the Racial Imagination,* edited by Ronald Radano and Philip V. Bohlman, 206–30. Chicago: University of Chicago Press, 2000.

Peter, Carolyn. "California Welcomes the World: International Expositions, 1894–1940, and the Selling of a State." In *Reading California: Art, Image, and Identity, 1900–2000,* edited by Stephanie Barron, Sheri Bernstein, and Ilene Susan Fort, 69–84. Los Angeles and Berkeley: Los Angeles County Museum of Art and University of California Press, 2000.

Pettitt, George. *A History of Berkeley.* Berkeley: Alameda County Historical Society, 1976.

Place, Janey. "Women in Film Noir." 1978. In *Women in Film Noir,* edited by E. Ann Kaplan, 47–68. London: British Film Institute, 1998.

Plagens, Peter. *Sunshine Muse: Contemporary Art on the West Coast.* New York: Praeger, 1974.

Polan, Dana. *Power and Paranoia: History, Narrative, and the American Cinema, 1940–1950.* New York: Columbia University Press, 1986.

Porfirio, Robert. "Dark Jazz: Music in the *Film Noir.*" In *Film Noir Reader 2,* edited by Alain Silver and James Ursini, 181–82. New York: Limelight Editions, 1999.

Potter, Russell A. *Spectacular Vernaculars: Hip-Hop and the Politics of Postmodernism.* Albany: State University of New York Press, 1995.

Prashad, Vijay. *Everybody Was Kung Fu Fighting: Afro-Asian Connections and the Myth of Cultural Purity.* Boston: Beacon Press, 2001.

Radano, Ronald. "Hot Fantasies: American Modernism and the Idea of Black Rhythm." In *Music and the Racial Imagination,* edited by Ronald Radano and Philip V. Bohlman, 459–80. Chicago: University of Chicago Press, 2000.

Radano, Ronald, and Philip V. Bohlman, eds. *Music and the Racial Imagination.* Chicago: University of Chicago Press, 2000.

Raine, Walter J. *Los Angeles Riot Study: The Perception of Police Brutality in Southern California, Los Angeles.* Los Angeles: Institute of Government and Public Affairs, University of California, Los Angeles, 1967.

Ramsey, Guthrie P., Jr. *Race Music: Black Cultures from Bebop to Hip-Hop.* Berkeley: University of California Press, 2003.

Reed, Tom. *The Black Music History of Los Angeles: Its Roots.* Los Angeles: Black Accent on L.A. Press, 1992.

Reinhardt, Richard. *Treasure Island: San Francisco's Exposition Years.* San Francisco: Scrimshaw Press, 1973.

Reyes, David, and Tom Waldman. *Land of a Thousand Dances: Chicano Rock 'n' Roll from Southern California.* Albuquerque: University of New Mexico Press, 1998.

Riddle, Ronald. *Flying Dragons, Flowing Streams: Music in the Life of San Francisco's Chinese.* Westport, Conn.: Greenwood, 1983.

Roberts, Helen H. *Form in Primitive Music: An Analytical and Comparative Study of the Melodic Form of Some Ancient Southern California Indian Songs.* New York: W. W. Norton, 1933.

Robinson, W. W. *Los Angeles from the Days of the Pueblo: A Brief History and a Guide to the Plaza Area.* San Francisco: California Historical Society, 1981.

Rockwell, John. *All American Music.* New York: Alfred A. Knopf, 1983.

Rodriguez, José, ed. *Music and Dance in California*. Hollywood: Bureau of Musical Research, 1940.

Rodríguez, Luis. "Eastside Sound." *Q-VO* 2 (1980): 27.

Rogin, Michael. *Blackface, White Noise: Jewish Immigrants in the Hollywood Melting Pot*. Berkeley: University of California Press, 1996.

Rose, Tricia. *Black Noise: Rap Music and Black Culture in Contemporary America*. Middletown, Conn.: Wesleyan University Press, 1994.

Ross, Gertrude. *Early Spanish-Californian Folk-Songs*. New York: J. Fischer, 1922.

Rósza, Miklós. *Double Life*. New York: Wynwood Press, 1989.

Rudhyar, Dane. "Oriental Influence in American Music." 1933. *American Composers on American Music: A Symposium,* edited by Henry Cowell, 164–85. New York: Frederick Ungar, 1962.

——. "The Relativity of Our Musical Conceptions." *Musical Quarterly* 8 (1922): 108–18.

Rydell, Robert W. *All the World's a Fair: Visions of Empire at American International Expositions, 1876–1916*. Chicago: University of Chicago Press, 1984.

Rydell, Robert W., John E. Findling, and Kimberly D. Pelle. *Fair America: World's Fairs in the United States*. Washington, D.C.: Smithsonian Institution Press, 2000.

Saffle, Michael. "Promoting the Local Product: Reflections on the California Musical Press, 1874–1914." In *Music and Culture in America, 1861–1918,* edited by Michael Saffle, 167–96. New York: Garland, 1998.

Said, Edward W. *Orientalism*. New York: Vintage, 1978.

Sánchez, George J. *Becoming Mexican American: Ethnicity, Culture and Identity in Chicano Los Angeles, 1900–1945*. New York: Oxford University Press, 1993.

Schneider, David. *The San Francisco Symphony: Music, Maestros, and Musicians*. Novato, Calif.: Presidio Press, 1983.

Scott, Derek B. "Orientalism and Musical Style." *Musical Quarterly* 82, no. 2 (1998): 309–35.

Senate Office of Research. *The South-Central Los Angeles and Koreatown Riots*. Sacramento: California Senate, 1992.

Shah, Nayan. *Contagious Divides: Epidemics and Race in San Francisco's Chinatown*. Berkeley: University of California Press, 2001.

Sheppard, W. Anthony. *Revealing Masks: Exotic Influences and Ritualized Performance in Modernist Music Theater*. Berkeley: University of California Press, 2001.

Shohat, Ella, and Robert Stam. *Unthinking Eurocentrism: Multiculturalism and the Media*. London: Routledge, 1994.

Silver, Alain, and James Ursini. *Film Noir Reader*. New York: Limelight Editions, 1996.

——. *Film Noir Reader 2*. New York: Limelight Editions, 1999.

Slonimsky, Nicolas. *Music since 1900*. 5th ed. New York: Schirmer, 1994.

Small, Christopher. *Musicking: The Meanings of Performing and Listening*. Hanover, Conn.: Wesleyan University Press, 1998.

Somerville, Siobhan B. *Queering the Color Line*. Durham, N.C.: Duke University Press, 2000.

Spottswood, Richard K. *Ethnic Music on Records: A Discography of Ethnic Recordings Produced in the United States, 1893 to 1942*. Vol. 4. Urbana: University of Illinois Press, 1990.

Starr, Kevin. *Americans and the California Dream: 1850–1915.* New York: Oxford University Press, 1973.

——. *Embattled Dreams: California in War and Peace, 1940–1950.* New York: Oxford University Press, 2002.

——. *Endangered Dreams: The Great Depression in California.* New York: Oxford University Press, 1996.

——. *Inventing the Dream: California through the Progressive Era.* New York: Oxford University Press, 1985.

——. *Material Dreams: Southern California through the 1920s.* New York: Oxford University Press, 1990.

Stevenson, Robert. "Eleanor Hague (1875–1954), Pioneer Latin Americanist." In *Musical Aesthetics and Multiculturalism in Los Angeles: Selected Reports in Ethnomusicology X,* edited by Steven Loza, 129–38. Los Angeles: University of California, Los Angeles, Department of Ethnomusicology and Systematic Musicology, 1994.

——. "Music in Southern California: A Tale of Two Cities." *Inter-American Music Review* 10, no. 1 (1988): 39–112.

Swan, Howard. *Music in the Southwest, 1825–1950.* San Marino, Calif.: Huntington Library, 1952.

Takaki, Ronald. *Strangers from a Different Shore: A History of Asian Americans.* Boston: Little, Brown, 1989.

Taylor, Timothy D. *Global Pop: World Music, World Markets.* New York: Routledge, 1997.

Tick, Judith. "Charles Ives and Gender Ideology." In *Musicology and Difference: Gender and Sexuality in Music Scholarship,* edited by Ruth A. Solie, 83–106. Berkeley: University of California Press, 1993.

Uno Everett, Yayoi, and Frederick Lau, eds. *Locating East Asia in Western Art Music.* Middletown, Conn.: Wesleyan University Press, 2004.

Ussher, Bruno David. "A History of the Hollywood Bowl." In *Who's Who in Music and Dance in Southern California,* edited by Bruno David Usher, 29. Hollywood: Bureau of Musical Research, 1933.

Vigil, James Diego. *Barrio Gangs: Street Life and Identity in Southern California.* Austin: University of Texas Press, 1988.

Von Gunden, Heidi. *The Music of Lou Harrison.* Metuchen, N.J.: Scarecrow Press, 1995.

Waldinger, Roger, and Mehdi Bozorgmehr, eds. *Ethnic Los Angeles.* New York: Russell Sage Foundation, 1996.

Walls, Brian S. "Chamber Music in Los Angeles, 1922–1954: A History of Concert Series, Ensembles and Repertoire." M.A. diss., California State University, Long Beach, 1980.

Ward, Brian. *Just My Soul Responding: Rhythm and Blues, Black Consciousness, and Race Relations.* Berkeley: University of California Press, 1998.

Watkins, Frances E. "'He Said It with Music': Spanish-California Folk Songs Recorded by Charles F. Lummis." *California Folklore Quarterly* 1 (October 1942): 359–67.

Wheeler, B. Gordon. *Black California: The History of African-Americans in the Golden State.* New York: Hippocrene Books, 1993.

Widener, Daniel. "'Perhaps the Japanese Are to Be Thanked?' Asia, Asian Americans, and the Construction of Black California." *the afro-asian century.* Special issue, *positions* 11, no. 1 (2003): 135–82.

Wilder, Billy. *Double Indemnity.* Berkeley: University of California Press, 2000.

Wong, Deborah. "The Asian American Body in Performance." In *Music and the Racial Imagination,* edited by Ronald Radano and Philip V. Bohlman, 57–94. Chicago: University of Chicago Press, 2000.

———. "Finding an Asian American Audience: The Problem of Listening." *American Music* 19, no. 4 (2001): 365–84.

———. *Speak It Louder: Asian Americans Making Music.* New York: Routledge, 2004.

Woods, Gerald. *The Police in Los Angeles: Reform and Professionalization.* New York: Garland, 1993.

Writer's Program, California. *An Anthology of Music Criticism.* San Francisco: Works Progress Administration, 1939.

Yang, Mina. "Orientalism and the Music of Asian Immigrant Communities in California, 1924–1945." *American Music* 19, no. 4 (2001): 385–416.

Yarbrough Cox, Bette. *Central Avenue-Its Rise and Fall, 1890–c. 1955: Including the Musical Renaissance of Black Los Angeles.* Los Angeles: BEEM Foundation for the Advancement of Music, 1996.

Ybarra-Frausto, Tomás. "The Chicano Movement and the Emergence of a Chicano Poetic Consciousness." In *New Directions in Chicano Scholarship,* edited by Ricardo Romo and Raymund Paredes, 81–110. La Jolla, Calif.: Chicano Studies Monograph Series at the University of California, San Diego, 1978.

Yoshida, George. *Reminiscing in Swingtime: Japanese Americans in American Popular Music, 1925–1960.* San Francisco: National Japanese American Historical Society, 1997.

Zhang, Wei Hua. "The Musical Activities of Chinese American Community in San Francisco Bay Area." Ph.D. diss., University of California, Berkeley, 1994.

Discography

Central Avenue Sounds: Jazz in Los Angeles (1921–1956). Rhino R275872 (1999).

Do the Right Thing. Motown B00005MK88 (1989).

Gray, Wardell. *The Chase.* Dial D-1083–D (1947).

———. *Memorial Volume One.* Prestige 7008 (1952).

Ice Cube. *Death Certificate.* Priority Records B00008BL9W (2003).

Jamez. *Z-Bonics.* F.O.B. (1998).

Shelly Manne and His Men. *The West Coast Sound, Vol. 1.* Contemporary C3507 (1953).

Various Artists. *The Chicano Alliance.* R-Town 5699 (1998).

Various Artists. *The East Side Sound, 1959–1968.* Bacchus BA08-2 (1996).

Various Artists. *East Side Sound Vol. 2.* Bacchus 1139 (2000).

Various Artists. *The West Coast East Side Sound, Vol. 1, 2, 3 & 4.* Varese Sarabande (1999).

The West Coast Jazz Box: An Anthology of California Jazz. Contemporary 4CCD-4425–2 (1998).

Index

Page numbers in italics refer to illustrations.

MINA YANG is assistant professor of musicology at the University of Southern California. An accomplished pianist as well as a scholar, Yang focuses on popular and experimental music as well as music of the Pacific Rim.

Music in American Life

The University of Illinois Press
is a founding member of the
Association of American University Presses.

Composed in 10.5/13 Adobe Minion Pro
by Jim Proefrock
at the University of Illinois Press
Manufactured by Thomson-Shore, Inc.

University of Illinois Press
1325 South Oak Street
Champaign, IL 61820-6903
www.press.uillinois.edu